Mary, Daughter of Sion

MARY, DAUGHTER OF SION

by

Rev. Lucien Deiss, C.S.Sp.

translated by

Barbara T. Blair

THE LITURGICAL PRESS

Collegeville   Minnesota

In five languages

MARY, DAUGHTER OF SION
MARIA HIJA DE SION
MARIA TOCHTER SION
ELEMENTI FONDAMENTALI DI MARIOLOGIA
MARIE, FILLE DE SION

MARY, DAUGHTER OF SION is the authorized English translation of *Marie, Fille de Sion*, Coll. "Thèmes Bibliques", published by Desclée de Brouwer, Bruges, Belgium.

Nihil obstat: William G. Heidt, O.S.B., S.T.D., *Censor deputatus*. *Imprimatur:* ✠ George H. Speltz, D.D., Bishop of St. Cloud. June 13, 1972.

TO THE FATHER
BE GLORY
IN THE CHURCH AND IN CHRIST JESUS
DOWN THROUGH ALL THE AGES OF TIME WITHOUT END.
AMEN.
Ephesians 3:21

TRANSLATOR'S FOREWORD

I should like to mention the interest that Father Deiss has taken in the production of this English translation, and to express my warm appreciation of the opportunity afforded me, during the course of this work, to meet him in person.

In addition I wish to acknowledge my deep indebtedness to the Rev. Richard F. Kugelman, C.P., Professor of Scripture at St. John's University, Jamaica, New York, and member of the translation committee of the Confraternity of Christian Doctrine, for his valuable suggestions and checking of the entire English text.

B.T.B.

CONTENTS

INTRODUCTION

We have chosen to speak of Mary as the Daughter of Sion because we feel that this title is the richest expression of her destiny to become, in the fullness and purity of the mystery of her own person, the living embodiment of the mystery of the Church — both the Church of the Old Testament, which prepared for the coming of Christ, and the Church of the New Testament, which perpetuates the presence of Jesus in our midst under the dimensions of space and time.

Before our subject can be considered, it is necessary first to pin down the theological significance of some of the terminology that will be encountered.

In biblical language, the expression "daughter of such and such a town" denotes the rural districts or tent settlements and villages which are the dependencies of that town. Thus the "daughters" of the towns of Hesebon, Yaser, and Qenat are to be understood as meaning the villages and outlying settlements dependent on Hesebon, Yaser and Qenat.[1] In its original sense, then, the expression "Daughter of Sion" signifies a district dependency of Sion. In the words of Micah 4:8:

> And you, Tower of the Flock [Migdal-Eder],
> Hillock of the daughter of Sion,
> To you shall return the kingship of old,
> The royal rule over the house of Israel,

the daughter of Sion is "the new quarter of Jerusalem, to the north of the city of David, the gathering place of the refugees who fled the north after the disaster of Samaria — the remnant of Israel."[2]

In ancient Israel, "Sion" was shortly to lose its original topographical meaning. The author of 2 Kings 5:7 (cf. 1 Par. 11:5) will already be considering it suitable to explain to his readers that "the fortress of Sion" is "the city of David," thereby depicting, at a time when Jerusalem had undergone considerable development, the particular significance of the territory of the ancient Jebusite city taken by David. With the prophets and in the psalms, "Sion" serves as a

poetic synonym for Jerusalem.[3] Just as the capital of the kingdom
can stand as a metonym for the entire country, so can the expression
"Daughter of Sion" or "Daughter of Jerusalem" stand for the entire
nation. With this in mind, we can understand clearly the poem
of Isaias 62:11: "Say to the Daughter of Sion: Behold, your Savior
comes," as expressing that the entire people are the beneficiary
of the salvific coming of their God. Likewise, as we listen to the
cry of Lamentations (Lam. 2:13):

> To whom can I liken you? Or to whom compare you,
> Daughter of Jerusalem?
> Who will be able to save and comfort you,
> Virgin Daughter of Sion?
> Great as the sea is the wreckage of your sorrow;
> Who is coming to save you?

we hear the sobs of a whole people whom suffering has crushed
to the ground.

The "Daughter of Sion" image is beautifully suited to the bridal
theme which the prophet Osee[4] develops in a special way and
delights in suffusing with an aura of tenderness: the covenant that
unites Israel with her God is a bond of love; God chooses for himself
a people — the Daughter of Sion! — and loves it as a man chooses
and loves his bride, "from among thousands," and the Daughter
of Sion belongs to her God as a spouse to her husband.

Ezechiel 16 will develop this theme in a lengthy parable. Once
upon a time Israel was like a little girl whose parents were the
Amorrites and Hittites; at her birth she was exposed in the fields;
as she lay feebly struggling in her own blood, Yahweh passed by,
gathered her up and spreading over her the corner of his cloak
covered her nakedness and raised her up; then when she reached
puberty and the time of lovers, adorned her with jewels and clothed
her with splendor (Ez. 16). Jeremias, in "The Book of Consolation,"
describes the restoration of Israel as the renewal of the eternal
love which unites Yahweh with the "Virgin Israel":

> Israel marches towards her rest.
> From afar Yahweh appears to her:
> With an eternal love have I loved you,
> and unto you have I kept my mercy.
> Once again will I build you up, and you shall be rebuilt,
> Virgin Israel.
> Once again your tamborines shall resound to your beauty,
> And your dancing shall celebrate your joy. . . .
> For thus says Yahweh:

Shout with joy for Jacob,
Acclaim the first among the nations!
In psalms proclaim your praise:
Yahweh has saved his people,
The remnant of Israel (Jer. 31:2-4, 7).

To say that Mary is the Daughter of Sion is to affirm that she embodies the mystery of the Church under the aspect of the Old Testament expectation of Christ, which mystery has been personified in the Daughter of Sion figure, and that Mary's calling possesses the ecclesial dimensions which are prefigured in the Daughter of Sion imagery. This of course does not mean that all the Daughter of Sion images in the Old Testament will automatically have their counterpart in the New. There are certain passages that could not — or would not — have emerged into the greater light of the New Testament without having first been transfigured by the grace of the New Covenant. Often they merely bear witness to certain historical situations and as such are marked with the stamp of their own times.

On occasion they anticipate the Gospel simply by the density of their shadows, just as night heralds day or sin precedes grace. The Old Testament is in fact nothing less than a collection of edifying stories that prophesy Christ's coming. It would be even better to say that it is a sacred history, the thread of which is woven with the stories of sinners and drawn only toward salvation in Jesus Christ. Not all the features that the Word of God attributes to the Daughter of Sion can automatically be transferred to our Lady in her supernatural vocation. When Jeremias shows the Daughter of Sion trailed by a multitude of lovers, her eyes widened with paints but tearful with cries for pity, moaning in agony like a woman in labor with her firstborn and falling under the blows of her murderers (cf. Jer. 4:30-31), this oracle is only a particularly colorful description of faithless Israel and her punishment.

Like the Old Testament figures that anticipate Jesus Christ, the Marian prophecies are fulfilled on the highest spiritual level. While Christ is indeed the new David announced by the prophets, he has nothing in common with the atrocities and wars conducted by his royal ancestor or with his adventures with Bethsabee. David's sins point forward to him because he will come as their Redeemer. As they progress gradually towards the clarity of the Gospel, the biblical themes become purer and more deeply spiritual, the more strongly to highlight the newness of the Gospel. Mary is the Daughter of Sion in the greatest degree of perfection this figure can possess, just as Jesus is the Son of David in virtue of his loftier degree of divine sonship.

The Old Testament is the prophecy of the New, but the New is itself drawn toward the infinite fullness of the promised new heaven and new earth. We can say that the Daughter of Sion theme does not halt at the threshold of the New Testament where it is superseded and completed by the figure of the Church, "the pure virgin bride of Christ," the spouse all-resplendent with glory, without spot or wrinkle, but holy and immaculate (cf. 2 Cor. 11:3; Eph. 5:27). Rather, this entire theme tends toward an ultimate and decisive fulfillment at the end of time, when the angel of God will have harvested the last sheaves and gathered in the last grapes (cf. Apoc. 14:14-19), when the book of history will be closed and God finally will be "all in all" (1 Cor. 15:28).

The history of the Daughter of Sion does not stop at the end of the Old Testament or even with the story of our Lady; it continues on through the lifetime of the Church of today, in its journey toward the Parousia. We ourselves are this Church. As we study the theme of the Daughter of Sion, we are looking at our own history, as the Old Testament foretold it and as Mary lived it.

With these few introductory notes that were needed to outline the image of the Daughter of Sion, we must now go on to ask what the features of this image are that belong to the mother of Jesus; or better, how Mary "fulfills" the Daughter of Sion prophecies. The New Testament will give us the answer.

It is our hope that this study-outline will illumine more fully the ecclesial dimension of our Lady's vocation, and will show how the "Israel of God" (Gal. 6:16), continously shaped in the hands of the divine Wisdom that guided it through the various stages of its sacred history, arrives at its full flowering in the person of the Virgin Mary. In her, Israel not only attains to its spiritual perfection but shines forth in a beauty that wholly transcends the course of its development. Mary can truly be described as the living treasury of all the spiritual riches of the people of God, for the sum of all the gifts that had been bestowed upon this people finds incarnate expression, in the highest degrees of purity and perfection, in her alone:

— Mary is the Daughter of Abraham, the heiress to the ancient promises; in her, God is mindful of his mercy, even as he spoke to our fathers, to Abraham and to his posterity forever (Luke 1:54-55).

The obscure calling that Yahweh had given to Abraham nearly four thousand years ago was, in fact, in the hidden plan of God, a calling to be, one day, the father of the Son of God; in Mary, Abraham becomes the forefather of Christ (pages 1–21).

— Mary is the Daughter of David, the rose blossoming on the rough stem of Jesse; the mother of the new David who is the King, the Priest, and the Savior of the world. In Mary, the royal history of the line of David is grafted into the infinite history of the Son of God, and the seed of David will be as the sand on the shore of eternity (pages 23–48).

— Mary is equally the Daughter of Sion, whom Yahweh brings to a new birth in his love; on the day of the Annunciation she alone is the representative, in her own person, of the holy and spotless Church, arrayed in the splendor of Christ's glory (pages 49–85).

— In Mary all the poor of the Old Testament arrive at the goal of their spiritual journey and, singing the song of their deliverance, enter straight into the kingdom of Christ, the new Poor Man of Israel (pages 112–126).

— Mary is also the Woman clothed with the sun and crowned with stars, the Mother of Christ and of the rest of her offspring (pages 127–168). At the foot of the Cross, her messianic and royal motherhood is revealed as a motherhood of sorrows, with its embrace opened to receive the entire Mystical Body (pages 185–198).

This study-outline is not intended to establish the Scriptural basis of the various Mariological dogmas. Our readers should not expect to find in this book what it neither intends to provide nor is capable of providing. The deposit of Scripture is one thing; the establishing of dogmatic proof, another. Sometimes — and as is most particularly the case in Mariology — the proof of certain dogmas lies outside the scope of exegesis;[5] but it can also be true that it is in the very deposit of Scripture that the riches which the dogmatic definitions lack are to be found.[6] We must, accordingly, keep in mind that the definitions of the magisterium are intended, not to furnish an exhaustive inventory of the deposit of Scripture, but in general only to defend or supply a fuller illustration of a point of doctrine on which there is danger of error.[7]

It is this deposit of Scripture, particularly the tradition of Luke and John, that we are taking as our point of departure, resorting to theological reasoning only to the extent that it appears indispensable for a comprehensive grasp of the mystery of Mary. At first sight, the material relating to our Lady that Scripture does provide may seem to be somewhat limited, and we are bound to experience a certain uneasiness in comparing it with the prominence of the Virgin's place in contemporary theology and devotion. We are left with the impression that we confronting an edifice of exquisitely structured proportions, but erected on foundations too fragile to support its weight. To the extent, however, that we are careful to follow the lead of Scripture itself, setting the mystery of Mary within the perspective of Christ and the Church, this first impression will disappear.

The importance of Mary's position in salvation history is not measured by the number of Scriptural verses devoted to her, but by the place she occupies in relation to Christ and the Church. The discerning reserve with which the New Testament account surrounds the mystery of her life should not lead us to devote to it only a minimum of our attention, but, quite the contrary, to contemplate this mystery after the very manner of Scripture, with the same discernment and the same love.

It seems to us that it is due precisely to a neglect of Scripture, or even to an exaggeration of its contents out of due proportion (which is tantamount to neglect), that some have at times gone astray in the wilderness of their own personal "theological" elaborations, constructing a Mariology in which Luke or John would never have felt at home, letting themselves be guided more by their sentiments (the mystery of Mary is so utterly captivating!) than by the facts of Scripture. It is sometimes forgotten that all Christian praise, considered here under the aspect of homage given to Mary, must be primarily, as St. Paul has so sublimely expressed it, a praise of glory offered to the Father, "in the Church and in Christ Jesus" (Eph. 3:21). By making the Word of God our central point of reference, we can hope to rediscover this Christological and ecclesiological dimension of the mystery of Mary.

Ignorance of Scripture, said St. Jerome, is ignorance of Christ;[8] it is likewise ignorance of the Virgin, and a failure to appreciate her rightful place in our faith and our love. It is true even in Mariology that Scripture is the "lamp shining in a dark place, until the day dawns and the morning star rises in [our] hearts" (2 Peter 1:19). It is impossible, in our view, fully to grasp the richness of our Lady's vocation if we detach that vocation from the biblical context in which it is rooted; it is impossible to penetrate the secret of her life if we do not know the salvation history of the people of God.

Although we have said that we shall appeal to the theological reasoning and the faith of the Church insofar as this will be required or useful for the full understanding of the mystery of Mary, we nevertheless do not present this as a purely exegetical work. For just as we cannot ignore the data of Scripture, neither can we ignore the conclusions that twenty centuries of theological reflection have drawn from meditation on the Word. The Word can be likened to a seed that God has planted in the very heart of the Church: it germinates, develops, grows to mature height, and bears rich fruit. The most recent definitions of the magisterium, those of the Immaculate Conception and of the Assumption, are an illustration of this mysterious fruitfulness. In comparing the seed with its fruit, we can only admire the irresistible energy of the seed, the sureness with which the Spirit of truth is leading his Church toward the fullness of truth (cf. John 16:13).

These notes were originally compiled for our Mariology course at the Chevilly major seminary. But beyond this more immediate purpose, they will also be helpful to others of the faithful who are interested in a deeper exploration of the alluring — and mysterious — world of Scripture. Within its depths, and in the wonder of faith, they will find themselves face to face with Jesus, and at his side, Mary his Mother.

—Lucien Deiss, C.S.Sp.

---

[1] Num. 21:25, 32; 1 Par. 2:25.

[2] H. Cazelles, "La Fille de Sion," *Mariologie et Oecuénisme* (*Études Mariales*, Paris, 1964), p. 57.

[3] Cf. Is. 2:3 (= Michah 4:2); 4:3; 30:19; 33:20; 40:9; 41:27; Jer. 26:18; Amos 1:2; Micah 3:10, 12; Soph. 3:16; Zach. 1:14, 17; 8:3; Pss. 51:20; 76:3. Cf. D. Correa, *De significatione montis Sion in S. Scriptura* (Rome, 1954). Fohrer, art. Σιών, *Theological Dictionary of the New Testament*, Vol. 7, pp. 292ff.

[4] Osee 2:16-17; 21:22; 3:1. See also Jer. 2:2; 31:2-4; 21:22; Ez. 16, 23; Is. 54:4-6; 62:4-5. For further consultation: W. Eichrodt, *Theology of the Old Testament*, I (Philadelphia, 1961), pp. 490–504; P. Grelot, *Le couple humain dans l'Écriture*, Coll. *Lectio Divina*, 31, pp. 50–59; Stauffer, art. Γαμέω, *Theological Dictionary of the New Testament*, Vol. 1, pp. 648ff.; and J. Jeremias, art. Νύμφη, *op. cit.*, Vol. 4, pp. 1099ff.

[5] Such, for example, is the case of the Immaculate Conception and the Assumption. On these points the deposit of Scripture is hardly explicit; hence, appeal had to

be made to the deposit of faith in its entirety (Scripture, tradition, theological reflection, the faith of the Church), interpreted and set forth by the magisterium as a fresh exposition of the truth.

[6] Thus it is defined that Mary is the Mother of God, namely, that she has given birth to the Person of Christ; but it is not defined that she cooperated with her whole soul in the mystery that was accomplished in her flesh. It is clear, however, that this spiritual participation of her soul constitutes the most profound aspect of her divine maternity (see pp. 14–15).

[7] For example, the divine maternity was defined at the Council of Ephesus (431) against the Nestorian heresy, and at the Council of Chalcedon against the Monophysite heresy.

[8] *Comm. in Isaiam Prophetam, Prol.* (PL 24, 17B).

Mary, Daughter of Sion

"With Mary,
the exalted Daughter of Sion,
and after a long expectation of the promise,
the times are fulfilled
and the new economy established,
when the Son of God took a human nature from her,
that he might in the mysteries of his flesh
free man from sin."

—*The Constitution on the Church*, § 55.

Part I

MARY, DAUGHTER OF ABRAHAM

He has given help to Israel, his servant,
mindful of his mercy —
even as he spoke to our fathers —
to Abraham and to his posterity
forever.
(Luke 1:54-55)

Chapter 1

THE FATHERHOOD OF ABRAHAM
and
THE MOTHERHOOD OF MARY

A. The Fatherhood of Abraham

Yahweh said to Abram: "Leave your country, your kinsfolk and your father's house, for the land which I will show you; I will make a great nation of you. I will bless you, and make your name great, so that you shall be a blessing. I will bless them that bless you, and curse them that curse you. In you shall all the nations of the earth be blessed" (Gen. 12:1-3).

With these words begins the wondrous course of the history of Abraham, the story that is the life-story of all the faithful of the Old and the New Covenant (in him all the nations are blessed!) and whose marvels will reach to the unsurpassably sublime in Mary, the Daughter of Abraham and the Mother of Jesus:

He has given help to Israel, his servant, mindful of his mercy — Even as he spoke to our fathers — to Abraham and to his posterity forever (Luke 1:54-55).

On God's part this covenant will involve the bestowal of his spiritual blessings; the promise of possession of the "land"; the assurance of a posterity as numberless "as the stars of the heavens, as the sands on the seashore."[1]

Abraham's response will be the reply of faith: "Abram believed the Lord, who credited the act to him as justice" (Gen. 15:6). From henceforth human fruitfulness will be for Jewish piety not only the sign of fidelity to the covenant, but at the same time the guarantee of its fulfillment:

3

As your reward for heeding these decrees and observing them carefully, the Lord, your God, will keep with you the merciful covenant
which he promised on oath to your fathers. He will love and bless
and multiply you; he will bless the fruit of your womb. . . . You
will be blessed above all peoples; no man or woman among you
shall be childless . . . (Deut. 7:12-14).

In the minds of the people of the covenant, who took pride in
the title "the people of Abraham" and in their divine election, the
blessings of the spirit and the fruitfulness of the body were inextri-
cably bound together. Both the high-spirited devotion of this people,
who knew that they had been chosen from among all the nations,
and at the same time a deep and genuine piety are revealed in
this epithalamium addressed by Laban to his sister Rebecca on
the occasion of her marriage to Isaac: "May you, sister, become
a thousand times ten thousand, and may your descendants conquer
the gates of their foes" (Gen. 24:60). The sentiments expressed in
these lines are an even more forceful illustration that the truth of
personal immortality had not yet been clearly revealed; self-
perpetuation was envisioned solely in terms of the number of
children that would be born to assure one's "living on" in the future
history of the clan.

At times human fecundity appears to have been conceived in
such close association with the covenant as to be confused with
it and viewed as its essential feature. A fruitful wife was compared
to a vine; one's children, to olive plants set about the family ta-
ble — such was the portion reserved for Yahweh's faithful servants.
Psalm 127, a tender recital of these anticipated blessings, in its
simplicity affords us more than a glimpse into the deep meaning
of these hopes:

> Happy are you who fear the Lord,
>   who walk in his ways!
> Your wife shall be like a fruitful vine
>   in the recesses of your home;
> Your children like olive plants
>   around your table.
> Behold, thus is the man blessed
>   who fears the Lord.
> The Lord bless you from Sion:
>   may you see the prosperity of Jerusalem
>   all the days of your life;
> May you see your children's children (vv. 1, 3-6).

To live a long and happy life, in a Jerusalem of joy, surrounded
by one's children to the third and fourth generations — such was

the badge of holiness awarded by the Lord to those who loved him. This reward would be, in effect, a sharing in the promise made to Abraham, in the rebuilding of the new Jerusalem of the messianic age, and the assurance of victory for his clan in time of war:

> Behold, sons are a gift from the Lord;
> the fruit of the womb is a reward.
> Like arrows in the hand of a warrior
> are the sons of one's youth.
> Happy the man whose quiver
> is filled with them (Ps. 126:3-5).

On the contrary, "an unfruitful womb and dry breasts" (Osee 9:14) will appear as the sign of divine rejection.[2] Against Joachin, who had failed to continue the reforms that Josias had directed against idol-worship, the prophet Jeremias pronounced this divine judgement, which tolls like a sentence of death: "Thus says the Lord: Write this man down as one childless, who will never thrive in his lifetime! No descendant of his shall achieve a seat on the throne of David as ruler again over Juda" (Jer. 22:30).

We must especially keep in mind that Yahweh had taught his people to expect more from him than mere earthly goods. The entire life of Abraham, and later the history of Israel itself, particularly the hallowed period of the Exodus, is totally characterized by this spirituality of complete dependence. For a son of Abraham, no good is "natural" — everything is God's gift; the fruit of the womb as well as the other fruits of the Promised Land are "the inheritance of Yahweh." Indeed, this idea is expressed at the birth of the very first child: "I have given birth to a man-child with the help of the Lord," cried Eve, in the joy and wonder of the birth of her first child, Cain (Gen. 4:1).

From time to time God will even intervene in the interests of his greater glory and power to prove how closely his blessing is bound up with bodily fruitfulness, as on the occasion of those births which, in a framework of awe and wonder, bring home more pointedly the reality of the covenant with Abraham. It was not by chance that Abraham himself, and after him his son Isaac and his grandson Jacob, had wives who were barren; the history of this people who are to become as numberless as the sands on the seashore and the stars of heaven is destined to begin with the very barrenness of Sara, Rebecca, and Rachel.[3] Was it a sign of his special love that God chose precisely the sorrow and humiliation of the childless woman as the setting in which the promise would be fulfilled?

In any case, it is this very sterility of human love that heightens the brilliance of the sudden creative outpouring of divine love; it is the very barrenness and sorrow of Sara that God will transform into a wellspring of fruitfulness and joy for Abraham. Nothing could more forcefully reveal the truth that Isaac, the son of the promise, was born not only of flesh and blood or of the will of man, but of the promise of God. As Psalm 112 will sing at a much later date, it is God alone who "establishes in her home the barren wife as the joyful mother of children."

B. THE MOTHERHOOD OF MARY

When resituated in this biblical perspective where it belongs, Mary's motherhood takes on a spiritual dimension of extraordinary depth. More than any other Jewish mother, even more than Sara, she views her motherhood as a gift of God, as his supreme blessing on the whole womanhood of Israel. Jesus, far from being simply the fruit of her virginal flesh, is seen first of all as the fruit of grace, bestowed with the infinite freedom of the divine giving. We can see to what degree the marvelous fruitfulness of Abraham and Sara served as a preparation for the miraculous fruitfulness of our Lady. Sara was unable to have children because she was barren and had passed the age of childbearing; Mary was unable to have children because she had resolved to remain a virgin:

Shall a son be born to one who is a hundred years old? Shall Sara who is ninety bear a child? (Gen. 17:17; cf. 18:12-13).	How shall this happen, since I do not know man? (Luke 1:34).

Isaac is the fruit of the divine omnipotence that fructifies the dead womb of Sara; Jesus is the fruit of the Almighty One, who draws Mary into the shadow of his divine power:

Is anything too wonderful for the Lord? (Gen. 18:14).	Nothing shall be impossible with God. (Luke 1:37).

If Yahweh makes Sara's barren womb fruitful, it is because Abraham has found favor before him; so too, if God makes Mary's virginal womb fruitful, it is because she has found favor in his sight:

. . . if I find favor with you (Gen. 18:3).	. . . thou hast found grace with God (Luke 1:30).

There is thus a profound resemblance between the marvel of Abraham's fatherhood and the miracle of Mary's motherhood. The former was a preparation for the latter; both have their source beyond the world of nature in the order of grace; both are a revelation of the creative power of the divine love.

But there is much more. Mary's motherhood is really the ultimate completion of Abraham's fatherhood, bringing it to a perfection surpassing the most daring expectations of the hope awakened by the ancient promise. For Abraham did not know that the son of the promise, in whom his name would live forever, would appear at the end of his line as the very Son of God. In Mary, the Daughter of Abraham, the seed of the patriarch, the seed of the people of the promise, will attain to a divine term. It is through her that Abraham becomes the forefather of Christ; the long series of generations, coming down through the entire history of the Chosen People, will be brought to final issue in the Son of God:

> The book of the origin of Jesus Christ, the Son of David, the son of Abraham. Abraham begot Isaac, Isaac begot Jacob, Jacob begot Judas and his brethren. . . . Matthan begot Jacob. And Jacob begot Joseph, the husband of Mary, and of her was born Jesus who is called Christ (Matthew 1:1-2, 15-16).

Jesus, Son of Abraham, Son of God. We can see with what spiritual plenitude God fulfilled his promise — the true posterity of Abraham is Christ himself: "The promises were made to Abraham and to his offspring. He does not say, 'And to his offsprings,' as of many; but as of one, 'And to thy offspring,' who is Christ" (Gal. 3:16).

This call that God addressed nearly four thousand years ago to an obscure chieftain was, in the eternal reality of the divine plan, a call to beget, one day, the human nature of Jesus. The Blood of the Son of God that redeems the world, the Blood in which the new and eternal covenant is sealed (Luke 22:20; Mark 14:24; Matthew 26:28), is also the blood of Abraham.

All nations are blessed in Abraham, because Mary, the Daughter of Abraham, gives birth to the One in whom all the nations are blessed (Eph. 1:3ff.). Through her, Abraham receives the inheritance of the true Promised Land, which is no longer the earthly land of Canaan but the heavenly realm of Jesus Christ. Through her, Abraham becomes the father of a people as numberless as the sands on the seashore and the stars of heaven, because she brings forth the One who is to gather all the world's redeemed into a new unity in his own Body: "I saw a great multitude which no man could number, out of all nations and tribes and peoples and tongues, standing before the throne and before the Lamb . . ." (Apoc. 7:9). Thus is revealed the meaning of our Lord's words: "Abraham your father rejoiced that he was to see my day. He saw it and was glad" (John 8:56).

The New Covenant succeeds the Old without a break: God is faithful to his word, more faithful than the wildest stretches of human hope could have conceived. The New Covenant is, moreover, far superior to the Old, as is Mary's calling to Abraham's. Mary does not merely supersede Abraham — she surpasses him. In her the promise is brought to fulfillment; in him it had its beginning. Her vocation differs from Abraham's in the same way that her motherhood, which is not only miraculous but divine, differs from his fatherhood, which, although miraculous also, issues only in the purely human person of Isaac. Both Isaac and Jesus are sons of the promise, but Jesus is also the Son of God. Isaac is indeed both the fruit of divine grace and the fruit of Abraham's body, but Jesus, though born according to the flesh, is by his very nature the Son of God. Abraham's fatherhood is miraculous in its mode, but nevertheless accomplished in the flesh; Mary's motherhood is accomplished in the flesh, but is also a divine motherhood.

"Blessed art thou among women and blessed is the fruit of thy womb!" (Luke 1:42). Yes, Mary is indeed blessed among women; in the fullness of her assent to Christ's coming, she receives him in whom all the promises have found their "yes," their fulfillment (cf. 2 Cor. 1:20). In her, God fulfills the ancient promise of Deuteronomy:

> . . . he will bless the fruit of your womb (Deut. 7:13).
> . . . blessed is the fruit of thy womb! (Luke 1:42).

In Mary, as she becomes the Mother of Jesus, God is mindful of Abraham:

> Blessed be the Lord, the God of Israel . . ." (Luke 1:68).
> . . . to show mercy to our forefathers and to be mindful of his holy covenant, of the oath that he swore TO ABRAHAM OUR FATHER, that he would grant us (Luke 1:72-73).

---

[1] See Gen. 12:2-3; 13:16; 15:5; 17:2-6; 22:17. We have here a regrouping of the different elements coming from the several sources. Criticism distinguishes the Yah-

wist account as dwelling more intensively on the spiritual blessing accorded in the promise of fruitfulness and posterity, the Elohist tradition as centered more particularly on the covenant, and the Priestly tradition as highlighting the reality of the divine election: God elects a tribe to whom he promises the land, with circumcision as the sign of this election (Genesis 13:16 does not belong to any of these three great traditions.) For a discussion of these sources, the reader may consult H. Cazelles, "The Torah (Pentateuch)," in A. Robert and A. Feuillet (eds.), *Introduction to the Old Testament* (New York, 1968), pp. 68ff.

[2] In this perspective it is easier to understand the ruse of Thamar, who, in order to conceive the children that Onan had refused her, has no scruples about offering herself to Juda (Gen. 38:8ff.); her desire to live on in her descendants is stronger than the fear of death (v. 24). Juda acknowledges that she is more in the right than he (v. 26), and Jewish tradition will acclaim her action as heroic (cf. Ruth 4:12).

[3] Gen. 16:2; 25:21; 29:31. See M. Allard, "L'Annonce à Marie," in *Nouvelle Revue Théologique*, 78 (1956), pp. 730–733.

Chapter 2

THE FAITH OF ABRAHAM
and
THE FAITH OF MARY

A. THE FAITH OF ABRAHAM

Abraham's response to God's call will be one of faith. Indeed, all the succeeding stages in his wandering life — that life which was at the same time an inward journey of spiritual discovery — bear the mark of that faith. We can, however, following the author of the Epistle to the Hebrews,[1] single out three events in which the response of that faith shines out with particular intensity.

1. The Departure from Ur

Abraham is to see God intervene and, in a single instant, change the entire course of his life. And this divine summons, which opens up a vista of such grandiose proportions — "I will make a great nation of you. I will bless you, and make your name great" — is also a summons to leave all: "your country, your kinsfolk and your father's house" (Gen. 12:1).

Abraham will obey: "Abram went away as the Lord had commanded him" (Gen. 12:4). He leaves everything behind — the country of his own roots and beginnings, the clan with its bonds of duty and affection — to enter into the unfolding mystery of this encounter that has set him on a completely different path. It is a departure strange to our human ways of thinking; we would set a destination and look forward to a welcome at our journey's end. Abraham does not know where this call is to lead him. Yahweh will give only the vaguest of signs to point out the way: "the land

10

which I will show you." Abraham knows only that there will be no one to meet him at his journey's end. From this time forward, the world of faith will be his homeland.

> By faith he who is called Abraham obeyed by going out into a place which he was to receive for an inheritance; and he went out, not knowing where he was going. By faith he abode in the Land of Promise as in a foreign land, dwelling in tents with Isaac and Jacob, the co-heirs of the same promise; for he was looking for the city with fixed foundations, of which city the architect and the builder is God (Heb. 11:8-10).

From the time of this first call, Abraham's faith is manifested, not so much as an intellectual assent to a set of dogmatic truths, but rather, and from the very first, as the surrender of his entire life, in a marvel of daring born of humility and trust. Yahweh, revealing himself, offers his promise; Abraham, obeying, makes the return offering of his faith. Yahweh becomes the God of Abraham; Abraham becomes the man of Yahweh. This is the very substance of the covenant: it is grounded on the divine promise and on the faith of the believer.

2. *The Birth of Isaac*

Isaac's birth was to mark a new occasion for Abraham to surrender to God in faith:

> By faith even Sara herself, who was barren, received power for the conception of a child when she was past the time of life, because she believed that he who had given the promise was faithful. And so there sprang from one man, though he was as good as dead, issue like the stars of heaven in number and innumerable as the sand that is by the seashore (Heb. 11:11-12).

Abraham was, in fact, seventy-five years old when he received the promise that a son would be born to him, and Sara was sixty-five. For one who had believed, at the simple promise of God, that he would become the father of a multitude innumerable as the sands on the seashore and the stars of heaven, it was certainly about time that he did have a son, one, at least, in whom the promise would be fulfilled. But God was to wait still longer.

> Time passed, the possibility was there, Abraham believed; time passed, it became unreasonable, Abraham believed. There was in the world one who had an expectation. There is no song of Lamentations by Abraham. He did not mournfully count the days while time passed, he did not look at Sarah with a suspicious glance, wondering whether she were growing old. Then came the fullness of time. If Abraham had not believed, Sarah surely would have been dead of

sorrow, and Abraham, dulled by grief, would not have understood
the fulfilment but would have smiled at it as at a dream of youth.[2]

Yet the fact could not be dismissed: Sara's womb was dead. Such
was the setting, one of complete faith, in which Yahweh was to
fashion a father's heart within him, he who was to be the father
of an innumerable multitude.

For another twenty-five years Abraham waited, in the solitude
of seeing the love of his marriage union remain sterile and without
fruit. We can appreciate the devout reflection inserted by the Yahwist into his account: "Abraham believed the Lord, who credited
the act to him as justice" (Gen. 15:6), and which centuries later
was to inspire this admiring commentary of Paul's:

> Abraham hoping against hope believed, so that he became the father
> of many nations, according to what was said, *So shall thy offspring
> be.* And without weakening in faith, he considered his own deadened
> body (for he was almost a hundred years old) and the deadened womb
> of Sara; and yet in view of the promise of God, he did not waver
> through unbelief but was strengthened in faith, giving glory to God,
> being fully aware that whatever God has promised he is able also
> to perform. Therefore it was credited to him as justice (Rom. 4:18-22).

And when that day of the "annunciation" of Isaac finally did come,
Abraham and Sara did not know whether they should laugh in joy
or astonishment:

> Abraham . . . laughed and said to himself, "Shall a son be born
> to one who is a hundred years old? Shall Sara who is ninety bear
> a child?" (Gen. 17:17).
> Sara laughed to herself and said, "Now that I am grown old and
> my husband is old, shall I have pleasure?" (Gen. 18:12).

The day of Isaac's birth was a beautiful one. What happiness
for the old father, as in those hands that had weathered a hundred
years he held this child that had finally come to them as their
golden wedding gift! He laughed aloud, and in his happiness chose
for the little one the name Isaac, meaning "he laughs." [3]

Isaac — the laughter born of faith, the thrilling wonder at this
tiny child, this belated flower that had blossomed from his old body.

And the smile of God. Yahweh has granted him his favor; the
benevolence of his gaze is resting upon him. Isaac is born, but
less as the fruit of their love than as the fruit of the power of their
faith. He is, to be sure, their son according to the flesh; but even
more than that, he is the son of faith.

3. *The Sacrifice of Isaac*

Yahweh is going to purify his servant's faith one final time, and this will be the most crucifying purification of all. It will involve the very person of Isaac, the son of his love for Sara, the son that has come to him as the gift of Yahweh's love:

> After these events God put Abraham to a test. He said to him, "Abraham." He answered, "Here I am." God said, "Take your only son Isaac whom you love and go into the district of Moria, and there offer him as a holocaust on the hill which I shall point out to you" (Gen. 22:1-2).

The hardness of these words of God is inexpressible. Hiding nothing of the greatness of the sacrifice that is demanded, they only cast it into starker relief.

> It is as if God, in order to strike with all the greater cruelty into the Patriarch's heart, is heaping words upon words like a litany of tenderness: your son, your only son, your beloved son, Isaac. . . . Isaac; the son of the Promise, the son so long awaited, and born counter to all human hope, he in whom alone, to all appearances, the fulfillment of God's promises was contained. Isaac: the only son, now that Ismael is no more; the single fruit of Abraham and Sara's long and faithful witness in their marriage-bond, the sole link to connect the Patriarch with the posterity that according to the promise was to be as innumerable as the stars of heaven and the sands on the seashore. [4]

Was God taking pleasure in this father's sorrow? Could he take any joy in this innocent victim? No, his pleasure is not in the victim offered, but rather in the offering of the victim, in the deepest movements of Abraham's devoted soul, the sentiments that both quickened and sustained him in his "obedience to faith" (cf. Rom. 1:5). Both this God who rends Abraham's heart asunder and this God who loves him are the same Lord, who "preserve(s) him resolute against pity for his child" (Wis. 10:5) and at the same time exacts from him the total abandonment of faith. From meditation on this sacrifice, the author of the Epistle to the Hebrews could write this passage of such striking power:

> By faith Abraham, when he was put to the test, offered Isaac; and he who had received the promises (to whom it had been said, *In Isaac thy seed shall be called*) was about to offer up his only-begotten son, reasoning that God has power to raise up even from the dead; whence also he received him back (Heb. 11:17-19).

And now, more than ever, is this son the son of his faith.

4. *The Significance of Abraham's Faith*

Abraham's faith is not simply a historical truth ordained to serve as an example to the faithful of the covenant. Besides its mere exemplary significance, what we must consider here are the general principles governing justification — not only that of Abraham, but that of all the faithful of the New Covenant and also that of Mary.

To be of Christ requires being an heir to the promise, a child of Abraham. Now how does this come about? To the Jewish mind, the only requirements involved were physical descent and the works of the Law. And in speaking to the Jews, Jesus gave them this answer: "If you are the children of Abraham, do the works of Abraham" (John 8:39). But the work of Abraham is faith. In his commentary on the text: "Abraham believed God, and it was credited to him as justice," Paul writes:

> Know therefore that the men of faith are the real sons of Abraham. And the Scripture, foreseeing that God would justify the Gentiles by faith, announced to Abraham beforehand, "In thee shall all the nations be blessed." Therefore the men of faith shall be blessed with faithful Abraham" (Gal. 3:6-9).
>
> . . . by the faith of Jesus Christ the promise might be given to those who believe . . . (Gal. 3:22).
>
> . . . if you are Christ's, then you are the offspring of Abraham, heirs according to promise (Gal. 3:29).

In order to be saved, it is thus required to belong to the Chosen People, to have a share in the promise made to Abraham. But this inclusion in the Israel of God is accomplished through faith in Jesus Christ. Salvation is not the monopoly of one special caste or race, even though that race have the blood of Abraham in its veins; it is a matter of faith. And it is by virtue of this faith that all those born strangers to the promise are grafted onto the holy root of Abraham (cf. Rom. 11:11-24); it is through faith that they are members of the Church, the spiritual lineage of Abraham.

B. The Faith of Mary

Mary is the Daughter of Abraham according to the flesh. She is even more his daughter in virtue of her faith. ". . . blessed is she who has believed . . ." (Luke 1:45).

1. *In the Mystery of Her Motherhood*

We have already said that it is in virtue of her very motherhood that Mary is blessed; the entire secret of her life and holiness is contained in these three words: Mother of Jesus. To this we must now add that she is blessed first of all because of her faith. But these two statements are not contradictory; rather, they complement each other. Mary believed in the accomplishment of what had been told her by the Lord (cf. Luke 1:45): she believed that the promise of her motherhood would be fulfilled, and that in her Jesus would become incarnate. Just as in the flesh of her virginal body she welcomed the coming of her Lord, so, too, in all the loving ardor of her faith, she opened her soul to embrace him totally. And Christ, in giving himself to her as her Child, was also giving himself to her as the Son of the Most High.

It was through her faith that she conceived Christ; her conception was the act even more of her soul than of her body, as St. Augustine says: *prius mente quam ventre.*[5] Her motherhood, while rooted in the pattern of physical life, attains to its full flowering in the realm of the spirit. Mary is not only the earthly clay from which the second Adam was fashioned; her role was not confined simply to contributing the human nature of the spiritual Logos, "He who has been born neither of blood, nor of the will of the flesh, nor of the will of man, but of God."[6]

It was in the totality of her person, not in her body alone but above all in her soul, that she welcomed the coming of the Lord. She is truly one of those who "received him, . . . [of] those who believe in his name" (John 1:12). All the love that accompanies human generation is found in Mary, but in a more sublime manner, purified through the burning faith of her charity, *fidei caritate fervente.*[7]

We can see Mary's claim to the title "Daughter of Abraham": she is his descendant not only according to the flesh, but according to the spirit. Abraham is "the father . . . of those who follow in the steps of the faith that was our father Abraham's" (Rom. 4:12). These words apply first and foremost to Mary, the Daughter of Abraham in virtue of her faith.

2. *The Presentation in the Temple and on Calvary*

Following the example set by Abraham before her, Mary will be asked to offer to God this Son, whom she has conceived in the burning faith of her charity. This offering will be made a first time in the Temple, the scene of the Presentation, and a second time on Calvary, the scene of the Passion.

At the presentation of Jesus in the Temple, Mary fulfills the ancient law according to which the first-born male child belonged to Yahweh, and because of this special status, had to be "redeemed":[8]

> And when the days of her purification were fulfilled according to the Law of Moses, they took him up to Jerusalem to present him to the Lord — as it is written in the Law of the Lord: *Every first-born male must be consecrated to the Lord** (Luke 2:22-23).

This presentation is a recapitulation, so to speak, of all the "presentations" made under the Old Law, including Abraham's offering of Isaac: Jesus is the First-Born [9] *par excellence*, of all the people of Abraham.

Here again, we see the superiority of the new dispensation, signified by Mary's offering of Jesus, to the Old Law, prefigured by Abraham's offering of Isaac.

What is the ultimate meaning of the offering of first fruits? Here it should be recalled that God has absolutely no need of either our first fruits or our gifts; he has called our attention to this truth in regal tones that have an almost disdainful ring:

> If I were hungry, I should not tell you,
>   for mine are the world and its fullness.
> Do I eat the flesh of strong bulls,
>   or is the blood of goats my drink? (Ps. 49:12-13).

To offer to God the first fruits of the land, or the first fruits of flock and herd, or to go even further and offer the first fruits of married love, and even to offer him Isaac, is meaningless in terms of any divine need and renders him no service. What God is really saying is that he wants an interior offering, an offering of the heart, the "devotion" of the one who offers. What constitutes the sacrifice that is acceptable to Yahweh is not the victim offered, but rather the offering of the victim, the homage of faith and love. This was true of all the sacrifices of the Old Law, including that of Isaac.

But all these considerations are completely obliterated in our Lady's offering of Jesus. For here the Victim itself has a value that is infinite. And God receives, in a twofold act of homage, both Christ who is presented to him and the heart of her who is presenting him. It is here, for the first time in the history of the world, that the value of the Victim offered outweighs the value of the homage of the one offering. It is here, for the first time in the salvation history of the people of the covenant, that totally pure and spotless hands offer a totally pure and spotless Victim, a Victim who does truly render service to God.

As Mary makes her way to the Temple to offer Jesus, the entire Old Covenant with its innumerable sacrifices is in a real sense marching forward with her, to find its ultimate fulfillment in her offering. When Mary becomes the Mother of Jesus, the fruitfulness of the people of Abraham is, so to speak, utterly spent in this ultimate actualization of its power, since this fruitfulness has a divine Person for its term. In like manner, with Mary's offering of Jesus in the Temple, the offering power of the people of Abraham is totally embodied and consumed in this final oblation of oblations.

This offering of Jesus in the Temple will attain to its ultimate degree of perfection in the offering of Jesus on the Cross; the mystery of the Presentation will be completed in the mystery of the Cross. The aged Simeon will direct Mary's spiritual vision toward this future event with his uttering of these prophetic words: "And thy own soul a sword shall pierce" (Luke 2:35).

On the Cross the sacrifice of Isaac will be renewed;[10] Mary will take Abraham's place.[11] But whereas on the mount of Moria God supplied a victim to be substituted for Isaac and spared both the life of the son and the heart of the father, on Calvary God will fully accept both the sacrifice of his Son and the broken heart of the Mother: "For God so loved the world that he gave his only-begotten Son" (John 3:16).

In these two offerings, that of the Presentation and that of Calvary, we can readily discern the paternity motif that locates them in the spiritual context of the covenant made with Abraham. The first rights over the child do not belong to the love that fathered him, but to God who has blessed this love; the child is received in faith and love as God's gift, and in the same faith and love is given back to God. The virginal birth of Jesus, which brings blessedness to his Mother's heart, and his death on the Cross, which breaks that same heart, are only the ultimate consequences of the principles that governed the joyful birth of Isaac and the sorrowful sacrifice on the mount of Moria.

3. *During the Public Life*

If this spiritual dimension of our Lady's motherhood is taken into account, it becomes easier to understand certain passages in the Gospel where Jesus at first sight seems somewhat lacking in the affection and tenderness that in the purely human order he rightfully owed to his Mother. When she finds him again in the Temple, he affects an unawareness of her anguish: "Behold, in sorrow thy father and I have been seeking thee," and replies: "How is it that you sought me?" (Luke 2:48-49). As if it were not the most natural thing for parents to look for their lost child!

At Cana, some seventeen years later, when she intervenes with such delicate concern for the unfortunate bridal couple, he calls her "Woman" and adds these words that seem to strike such a jarring note: "What to me and to thee?" (literal translation of the Greek). As if their bond of Mother and Son did not unite them in the same love!

One day while Jesus was preaching, his mother and his brothers [12] came to see him. "They could not get to him," explains Luke, "because of the crowd" (Luke 8:19). He was told:

> "Behold, thy mother and thy brethren are outside, seeking thee." And he answered and said to them, "Who are my mother and my brethren?" And looking round on those who were sitting about him, he said, "Behold my mother and my brethren. For whoever does the will of God, he is my brother and sister and mother" (Mark 3:32-35. Cf. Matthew 12:46-50; Luke 8:19-21).

These texts may strike the superficial reader as somewhat puzzling. In reality, however, they are only the application of the messianic principle: the kingdom Jesus has proclaimed is a spiritual kingdom, composed of those who believe in him and who keep his Word. Hence, without belief in Jesus, mere physical descent from Abraham avails nothing.

By the same token, the fact that Mary was the Mother of Jesus would have profited her nothing if she had not from the very first listened to his Word. To the Jews who were only too inclined to acclaim a temporal Messias who would fulfill their nationalistic hopes, whose incessant cry was "Our father Abraham," it was necessary to point out that the people of Abraham were first of all the people of faith, and that it was precisely because of her faith that Mary had been declared blessed.

C. Conclusion

God's covenant with Abraham is the covenant of faith: Yahweh will reveal himself to Abraham and give himself to him as his God; Abraham will give himself to Yahweh and become his faithful believer.

This covenant is to have circumcision for its external rite:

> God also said to Abraham, "You shall keep my covenant, you and your descendants after you throughout their generations. This is my

covenant which you shall keep, between you and me and your descendants after you: Every male among you shall be circumcised. . . . My
covenant shall be in your flesh as a perpetual covenant" (Gen. 17:9-
10,13).

Circumcision was not the covenant itself, but only its outward
ritual sign, the symbol of one's interior incorporation into it through
faith and the observance of the Law. [13]

By his own reception of the circumcision of Abraham (Luke 2:21),
Jesus will officially declare himself the son of Abraham. Yet in this
very act whereby he ratified the prescription of the ancient rite,
he also changed it. For in the New Covenant, circumcision, as
Paul explains, will give way to baptism:

In [Christ] you have been circumcised with a circumcision not wrought
by hand, but through putting off the body of the flesh, a circumcision
which is of Christ. For you were buried together with him in Baptism,
and in him also rose again through faith in the working of God who
raised him from the dead. . . . he brought [you] to life along with
him (Col. 2:11-13).

Jesus, having received both circumcision and baptism, thus
stands at the central point of the salvation history of God's people.
All the circumcisions of the Old Law derived their value from their
reference to Abraham and their orientation toward Christ; all the
baptisms of the New Testament derive their value from their reference to Christ's baptism, and thus are the prolongation of the mystery
of his death and resurrection.

And it is precisely this central position that Mary's motherhood
holds: it encompasses both the fulfillment of the Old Testament
tradition and the inauguration of the messianic era. Mary is to Christ
and to the New Testament what Abraham is to Isaac and to the
time of the promise. In the Old Testament, all motherhood derived
its value from its reference to Abraham and its orientation toward
Christ; it was a preparation for the coming of the Messias, a harbinger
of Mary's motherhood. In the New Testament, all motherhood
derives its value from this same reference to Christ, and thus is
a prolongation of both the mystery of Jesus and, at the same time,
of the mystery of Mary's motherhood.

In this connection it might be said that all human motherhood
is a participation in Mary's vocation, insofar as it is called to
reproduce, in a mysterious way, Mary's own motherhood. To express
it somewhat differently, parents are called upon to view themselves,
as each of their children is born to natural life and reborn to the

supernatural life of grace, as the parents of another Christ who has been given to them to "bring up," in the deepest and most beautiful sense of the word, and finally to offer to the Father.

Taking stock of the implications of this ecclesial dimension of Mary's motherhood, we can draw these conclusions:

— Christ stands at the center of the salvation history of the human race and of the people of Abraham, in that he is God's gift of himself to the human race;

— Mary stands at the center of the salvation history of the human race and of the people of the covenant, in that she receives Christ totally in his coming and gives herself to him in the surrender of faith.

We have now, perhaps, a fuller understanding of the bond that so intimately unites these words:

> Blessed art thou because thou hast believed!
> All generations shall call me blessed!

---

[1] See Heb. 11:8-19. The Epistle to the Hebrews, written after 63 and before 70 A.D. (it makes use of the Pauline captivity Epistles, but contains no reference to the destruction of the Temple), permits us to grasp the significance of the place occupied by Abraham in the spirituality of the earliest Christians, during the period when Luke was compiling his sources for the redaction of his Gospel. (Luke's Gospel must have made its appearance during the same period, or at the most only a few years later; on this subject see J. Huby, "The Books of the New Testament," in Robert and Tricot [eds.], *Guide to the Bible*, 2nd ed. [Paris: Desclée, 1960], pp. 403–404).

[2] S. Kierkegaard, *Fear and Trembling*, translated by Walter Lowrie (Garden City, N.Y.: Doubleday, 1954), pp. 32–33.

[3] Isaac, an abridged form of Yshq-El, means "may God smile," namely, grant his favor.

[4] J. Lécuyer, "Abraham notre Pére," *L'Esprit Liturgique*, VIII (Paris, 1955), p. 118.

[5] *Sermo 215, In redditione Symboli*, 4; PL 38, 1074. English translation: *Writings of St. Augustine* (Sermons on the Liturgical Seasons), Vol. 17, translated by Sister Mary Sarah Muldowney, R.S.M., *The Fathers of the Church*, Vol. 38 (New York: Christian Heritage, Inc., 1959), pp. 145–146.

[6] John 1:13. On the justification for this translation and its interpretation, see Braun, "Qui ex Deo natus est," in *Mélanges M. Goguel* (for the sources of Christian tradition), pp. 22ff.

[7] *Sermo 214, In traditione Symboli*, 6; PL 38, 1069. (English translation: *op. cit.*, pp. 135–136). St. Augustine is particularly insistent on the role of faith in the generation of Christ: "Faith in her soul, Christ in her womb: *fides in mente, Christus in ventre*" (*Sermo 196, In natali Domini*, 1; PL 38, 1019. English translation, *op. cit.*, pp. 43–45). "The Virgin conceived Christ not through fleshly concupiscence, but through spiritual faith: *virgo Christum non carnaliter concupiscendo, sed spiritual-*

iter credendo concepit" (*Enarr. in Ps.* 67, 21; PL 36, 826); also see *Sermo 69*, 3;
PL 38, 442 — *Sermo 241*, 5; PL 38, 1319 (English translation, *op. cit.*, pp. 259–
261) — *Sermo 215*, 4; PL 38, 1074 (English translation, *loc. cit*) — *Enchiridion,
sive de fide, spe et caritate*, 34; PL 40, 249 — *De peccatorum meritis et remissione,*
lib. 2, 24; PL 44, 175 — *Contra Faustum*, lib. 29, 4; PL 42, 490. In these affirmations
St. Augustine is the seeming heir to the thought of St. Justin, St. Irenaeus and
Tertullian, who in the Eve-Mary parallel had set Mary's faith in opposition to Eve's
disobedience. (Cf. Excursus I, pp. 199–208).

⁸ Cf. Exod. 13:11-16; 22:28-29; 34:19-20. The term "first-born" does not imply
the existence of other children. On this subject see J.B. Frey, "La signification
du terme πρωτότοκος, d'apres une inscription juive,"*Biblica*, 10 (1930), pp. 373–390.
(The reference is to a young woman who had died giving birth to her "first-born"
son).

* *Translator's note*: We have followed here the phrasing of the *Jerusalem Bible*.
In this book Scriptural passages are quoted from the Confraternity-Douay version,
unless otherwise noted.

⁹ Cf. Rom. 8:29; Col. 1:18; Apoc. 1:5.

¹⁰ 2 Par. 3:1 identifies Mount Moria with Mount Sion, on which Solomon built
the Temple.

¹¹ Papal teaching often takes up the idea that the Virgin present on Calvary offers
her Son: "When she professed herself the handmaid of the Lord for the mother's
office, and when, at the foot of the altar, she offered up her whole self with her
Child Jesus — then and thereafter she took her part in the painful expiation offered
by her Son for the sins of the world. . . . she . . . offered generously to Divine
Justice her own Son, and in her Heart died with him, stabbed by the sword of
sorrow" (Leo XIII, Enc. *Jucunda Semper*, Sept. 8, 1894. English translation in
Papal Teachings: Our Lady, selected and arranged by the Benedictine Monks of
Solesmes, translated by the Daughters of St. Paul (Boston, 1961), pp. 126–127).
" . . . for the salvation of mankind she renounced her mother's rights and, as
far as it depended on her, offered her Son to placate divine justice" (Benedict
XV, Letter *Inter Sodalicia*, May 22, 1918. English translation, *op cit.*, p. 194).
"On Calvary [she] offered him as a Victim for us" (Pius XI, Enc. *Miserentissimus
Redemptor*, May 8, 1928. English translation published by Burns Oates and
Washbourne, Ltd., London, p. 16). " . . . as another Eve she offered Him on
Golgotha to the Eternal Father . . . and her mother's rights and mother's love
were included in the holocaust" (Pius XII, Enc. *Mystici Corporis*, June 29, 1943.
English translation provided by the Vatican, N.C.W.C., Washington, D.C. Pius
XII will return to this text in the encyclical *Ad coeli Reginam*, October 11, 1954.
English translation in *Papal Teachings: Our Lady*, pp. 384–399. Passage in question,
p. 393). In commenting on these texts, we must always be mindful of the hierarchical
relationship between the sacrifice of Christ and that of his Mother: Jesus is the
principal offerer (the "one Mediator," 1 Tim. 2:5), but he makes the Virgin his
associate in his offering. Hence the comparison with Abraham's sacrifice must not
be forced.

¹² These were near relatives (cousins, for instance), who among the Semites were
called brothers; see Gen. 13:8; 14:16; 29:15.

¹³ Scripture will insist on "circumcision of the heart" in contradistinction to that
of the flesh: cf. Deut. 10:16, 30:6; Jer. 4:4; Ez. 44:6-9.

Part II

MARY, DAUGHTER OF DAVID

> *The Lord God will give him*
> *the throne of David his father,*
> *and of his kingdom*
> *there shall be no end.*
> (Luke 1:32-33)

Chapter 3

THE COVENANT WITH DAVID

A. The Prophecy of Nathan

Nine centuries separate David and Abraham, yet God's covenant with David introduces nothing contrary to the promise made to Abraham. Matthew will preface his Gospel with these words: "The book of the origin of Jesus Christ, the Son of David, the son of Abraham" (Matthew 1:1). Israel's religion is in effect a historical religion. Having taken on flesh-and-blood existence in the salvation history of the Chosen People, it will wind its way along the paths by which Yahweh leads his people continuously being "revealed," ever progressing toward a more complete fulfillment. The appearance with David of a royal house will introduce no break in this sacred history; rather, it will perpetuate the very essence of the covenant, and at the same time both renew it and raise it to a loftier dimension. In the words of A. Gelin:

> The new element of a royal house was historically integrated with a pre-existing conception of a theocracy and assigned a role to play in the fulfillment of the Covenant, which henceforth became a truly *royal* Covenant. From the time of its institution, this royal line was to bear the burden of responsibility for fidelity to the Covenant, and by the Covenant would be judged. It is precisely within this perspective that its importance and special character are seen: the points of resemblance that it does undeniably share with the other monarchies of the Near East will appear as unequivocally superficial when viewed in the light of this essential element, which clearly manifests the unique transcendency of the religion of Israel.[1]

With the kingship of David, the covenant will become a truly "royal" covenant, its charter embodied in the words of Nathan's prophecy.

In a short time, through alliances and military successes, David had scored a definitive victory over the Philistines, pushing them back within the confines of their former possessions in the southern half of the coastal plain. Subsequently leaving Hebron, which, although the capital of the state of Juda, was too distant from the geographical center of Israel to be a suitable seat of government, he chose Jerusalem for his capital. This ancient Jebusite city was, at this period, only a small town of no importance; with the aid of his mercenaries he carried out the cunning plan (2 Kings 5:6-9) by which he conquered it and made it the "city of David." To confer on it a still greater dignity, he had the ark of the covenant, which had been resting in the Canaanite city of Cariathiarim, brought to Jerusalem and ceremoniously installed there (2 Kings 6:1-19). From then on Jerusalem was the headquarters from which he governed all the territory lying between the "great Sea" and the Euphrates, between the river of Egypt and the borders of Emath.

It was at this time that David conceived the idea of building a temple to Yahweh. Prompted as it was by a genuine piety, it was also motivated by considerations of a most practical nature. As the center of worship, the Temple would serve as a unifying force to draw the northern and southern halves of the kingdom more closely together. David sought counsel from the prophet Nathan:

> "Dost thou see that I dwell in a house of cedar, and the ark of God is lodged within skins?" And Nathan said to the king: "Go, do all that is in thy heart, because the Lord is with thee." But it came to pass that night, that the word of the Lord came to Nathan, saying: "Go, and say to my servant David: 'Thus saith the Lord: Shalt thou build me a house to dwell in? Whereas I have not dwelt in a house from the day that I brought the children of Israel out of the land of Egypt even to this day, but have walked in a tabernacle, and in a tent. In all the places that I have gone through with all the children of Israel, did ever I speak a word to anyone of the tribes of Israel whom I commanded to feed my people Israel, saying: Why have you not built me a house of cedar?'
>
> "And now thus shalt thou speak to my servant David:
>
> 'Thus saith the Lord of hosts: I took thee out of the pastures from following the sheep to be ruler over my people Israel. And I have been with thee wheresoever thou hast walked, and have slain all the enemies from before thy face; and I have made thee a great name, like unto the name of the great ones that are on the earth. And I will appoint a place for my people Israel, and I will plant them, and they shall dwell therein, and shall be disturbed no more; neither shall the children of iniquity afflict them any more as they did before, from the day that I appointed judges over my people Israel. And I will give thee rest from all thy enemies. And the Lord foretelleth to thee, that the Lord will make thee a house. And when

thy days shall be fulfilled and thou shalt sleep with thy fathers, I will raise up thy seed after thee, which shall proceed out of thy bowels, and I will establish his kingdom. He shall build a house to my name, and I will establish the throne of his kingdom forever. I will be to him a father, and he shall be to me a son. . . . And thy house shall be faithful, and thy . . . throne shall be firm forever'" [2] (2 Kings 7:2-16).

This prophecy constitutes the charter of the Davidic kingdom, and it will be the point of reference for the greater part of the later prophecies. At this stage it will be worthwhile to single out the following points:

1) The covenant with David is a covenant of grace and mercy. The power by which David occupies his throne is Yahweh's free gift. He has been, to be sure, a shrewd manipulator, a skilled and wily diplomat, fighting to his position with courage and cunning. But it is Yahweh who has given him the victory and freed him from the harassment of his enemies; it is Yahweh who has taken him out of the pastures "from following the sheep," to make him head over all Israel. Now David has thought to build him a house; but again, it is rather Yahweh who will raise up a *house* for David, namely, a dynasty.

2) This dynastic house will last forever: "Thy house shall be faithful, and thy kingdom forever before thy face, and thy throne shall be firm forever." The fatuous dream which so possessed the old monarchs of the East, of founding a kingdom that would endure for a thousand years, will now become a reality, through the power of the Lord's mercy. [3]

3) This kingship is set in a context that is by its very nature religious: "I will be to him a father, and he shall be to me a son." The House of David is to be governed, so to speak, by Yahweh himself; the royal sovereignty is in some manner a divine sovereignty. David belongs to Yahweh as a son to his father. As it will be expressed in Psalm 2, the king is "begotten" by God; on the day he takes possession of his throne, God pronounces over him the ritual formula of adoption: "The Lord said to me, 'You are my son; this day I have begotten you'" [4] (Ps. 2:7).

In Psalm 109, this divine enthronement will be likened to a sacerdotal consecration. David in fact possesses the throne of the ancient king Melchisedec, the king of Jerusalem:

Yours is a princely power in the day of your birth, in holy splendor; before the daystar, like the dew, I have begotten you.
The Lord has sworn, and he will not repent:

"You are a priest forever, according to the order of Melchisedec" [5]
(Ps. 109:3-4).

4) King and priest of his people, David is equally their savior.
In the name of the king whom he has enthroned in the midst of
his people, Yahweh will deliver the land from all enemies and the
"children of iniquity" (2 Kings 7:10-11); Israel will be "planted"
in the Promised Land and forever protected from the invasions
that were a periodic threat to her security. The people will acknowledge David as their savior, saying: "The king delivered us
out of the hand of our enemies, and he saved us out of the hand
of the Philistines" (2 Kings 19:9). The king's enthronement thus
ushers in an era of material prosperity and spiritual well-being;
Psalm 71 will sing of the royal accession that will free the soul
of the poor man and cover the land with an abundance of grain
(Ps. 71:13-16).

From this time onward, the Davidic dynasty is Yahweh's own
kindred, his own "house," and in some manner the vehicle of the
promises of the covenant. The most exalted of titles, the very titles
which fostered the high-spirited sense of exclusiveness and the pride
of the Chosen People — son of God, king, priest, savior — are
here assimilated and unified in the person of the king.

However the prophecy was one thing, its fulfillment, another.
God has made his promise, but it will be fulfilled according to
his own plan. In actual fact, the fullest extension of the Davidic
kingdom was never to be realized, and even in David's lifetime
was seen only as something to be hoped for. Indeed, the "son
of God" was to suffer betrayal and persecution by his own family
and friends; as God's protege, he was forced to seek protection
from others. Absalom's rebellion was an especially bitter sorrow
to him, and certain features of his own life are a foreshadowing
of the passion of the Messias: fleeing from Jerusalem, he "went
up by the ascent of mount Olivet, going up and weeping" (2 Kings
15:30).

B. SOLOMON

With Solomon's accession to the throne, [7] it might well have
seemed that Nathan's prophecy was beginning to be definitively
fulfilled. The Chronicler's account is enthusiastic:

Solomon sat on the throne of the Lord as king instead of David
his father, and he pleased all; and all Israel obeyed him. And all

the princes, and men of power, and all the sons of king David gave
their hand, were subject to Solomon the king. And the Lord magnified
Solomon over all Israel, and gave him the glory of a reign such as
no king of Israel had before him (1 Par. 29:23-25).

But only at its inauguration was his reign so eulogized; its last
days were lamentable. All the sumptuousness of the royal court
was unable to hide the interior weakness of the kingdom — the
countless taxes, the hordes of conscripted labor, the idol-worship
that was brought in with the innumerable foreign women acquired
for the royal harem and installed on "the mountain of scandal" — all
these practices discredited the regime in the eyes of the people
and rendered it utterly detestable in the eyes of God. One cannot
with impunity play at being Pharao in a kingdom consecrated to
Yahweh.

Hardly had Solomon died when his kingdom collapsed. The two
sisters, Ohola and Oholiba — the North and the South — went
their separate ways. Soon they were mere vassals, passing alternately
under the control of Egypt and Assyria.

C. THE BOOK OF EMMANUEL

It is, however, during this period of utter political decadence
that we find, in the Book of Emmanuel, the most celebrated of
the prophecies concerning the Davidic line.

The date was approximately 732, after the invasion of Theglath-
phalasar III. The inhabitants of Galilee, manacled and bent under
the goads of their Assyrian captors, had trod the hard road of deportation. Yet it is just at this time that Isaias appears, with his announcement of the great light that is to arise and shine upon this people
who are stumbling in the darkness. With prophetic foresight he
heralds the freedom that is to come through the birth of a royal
child; in place of the shoulder-pole and the oppressor's rod, the
royal child will receive on his shoulders the empire of David his
father:

> First he degraded the land of Zabulon and the land of Nepthali;
> but in the end he has glorified the seaward road, the land west
> of the Jordan, the District of the Gentiles (Is. 8:23).
>
> The people who walked in darkness have seen a great light; upon
> those who dwelt in the land of gloom a light has shone. You have
> brought them abundant joy and great rejoicing, as they rejoice before
> you as at the harvest, as men make merry when dividing spoils.
> For the yoke that burdened them, the pole on their shoulder, and

the rod of their taskmaster you have smashed, as on the day of Madian (Is. 9:1-3).

For a child is born to us, a son is given us; upon his shoulder dominion rests. They name him Wonder-Counselor, God-Hero, Father-Forever, Prince of Peace. His dominion is vast and forever peaceful, from David's throne, and over his kingdom, which he confirms and sustains by judgment and justice [8] (Is. 9:5-6).

Throughout, the oracle is dominated by the theme of Nathan's prophecy: the reign of the House of David is still a living reality. But whereas the promise had at the beginning been made to the dynasty as a whole, it here has a much more personal application: "a child is born to us, a son is given us." And it is in the person of this child that the ideal of the Davidic kingdom will in some manner be fulfilled, that ideal which David's descendants had never been able fully to realize.

No less astounding is the child's very name; his titles place him on the border between the human and the divine. He will direct the community as a "Counselor," namely, with the wisdom requisite for government,[9] but he also is to be a "Wonder-Counselor," in whom Yahweh can work anew the wonders of old.[10] He is to be a "Hero," but so like a "God" that he will be like the "mighty God" whose name is "Lord of Hosts";[11] he is to be a Father after the manner of the ancient patriarchs and the descendants of David,[12] but his kingdom transcends time and is written in the book of eternity; his birth, finally, is to inaugurate an era of endless peace,[13] in judgment and in justice.[14]

The religious character of these lines is affirmed even more strongly in the prophecy of the "just king":

But a shoot shall sprout from the stump of Jesse, and from his roots a bud shall blossom. The spirit of the Lord shall rest upon him: a spirit of wisdom and of understanding, a spirit of counsel and of strength, a spirit of knowledge and of fear of the Lord . . . (Is. 11:1-2).

Justice shall be the band around his waist, and faithfulness a belt upon his hips. Then the wolf shall be a guest of the lamb, and the leopard shall lie down with the kid; the calf and the young lion shall browse together, with a little child to guide them. The cow and the bear shall be neighbors, together their young shall rest; the lion shall eat hay like the ox. The baby shall play by the cobra's den, and the child lay his hand on the adder's lair. There shall be no harm or ruin on all my holy mountain; for the earth shall be filled with knowledge of the Lord, as water covers the sea[15] (Is. 11:5-9).

The kingdom of David has been placed in a prophetic perspective that is becoming more and more spiritualized; the stump of Jesse will blossom in the sunlight of a life-giving spirit; the kingdom now lies wholly within the dimension of the prophetic. The Spirit that had rested on the prophets of old, on Moses, David, and Elias,[16] now rests on David's successor. The coming of this future king will be the sign of a great religious reawakening; he will fill the land with the knowledge of Yahweh and will inaugurate an era of peace like that of man's first paradise.

D. The Mother of Emmanuel

During this same period, more explicit mention is made also of the mother of the future king. We know the familiar prophecy of Isaias:

> Listen, O house of David! . . . the maiden is with child and will soon give birth to a son,* and shall name him Emmanuel (Is. 7:13-14).

A few years later,[17] Micheas will give a similar description of the mother of the future king:

> But you, Bethlehem-Ephratha, too small to be among the clans of Juda, from you shall come forth for me one who is to be ruler in Israel; whose origin is from of old, from ancient times. (Therefore the Lord will give them up, until the time when she who is to give birth has borne, and the rest of his brethren shall return to the children of Israel.) He shall stand firm and shepherd his flock by the strength of the Lord, in the majestic name of the Lord, his God; and they shall remain, for now his greatness shall reach to the ends of the earth; he shall be peace (Mich. 5:1-4).

For the first time, the Mother of the Davidic Messias is associated with the future deliverance that the House of David will accomplish.[18] The linking of the royal Child and his Mother, which Luke and Matthew will present to us, is thus seen to have been proclaimed seven centuries before their time.

E. Sedecias

The final day of the earthly sovereignty of the House of David came in August of 587. Sedecias had occupied the throne for the past eleven years. An air of gloom hangs over the description of him left us by the Chronicler:

He did evil in the eyes of the Lord his God, and did not reverence
the face of Jeremias the prophet speaking to him from the mouth
of the Lord. He also revolted from king Nabuchodonosor, who had
made him swear by God. And he hardened his neck and his heart
from returning to the Lord the God of Israel (2 Par. 36:12-13).

Nabuchodonosor sent his army to surround Jerusalem. The city
held out for a year and a half (with a short period of relief provided
by aid from Egypt); the siege actually lasted from the tenth day
of the tenth month of the ninth year of Sedecias' reign until the
ninth day of the fourth month of the eleventh year. On the evening
of that day, the Chaldean battering rams concentrated all their
strength to make a breach in the walls of the Holy City.

Under cover of night Sedecias, the last descendant of the Davidic
line, together with his men tried to escape the slaughter, fleeing
eastward through the Judean desert and making for the land across
the Jordan. As he was passing through the Jordanian depression
near Jericho, he was sighted by the Chaldeans, who apprehended
him and took him to Nabuchodonosor. The latter had set up his
general headquarters at Reblatha, in central Syria. Upon the revolted
vassal he pronounced a terrible sentence: "He slew the sons of
Sedecias before his face, and he put out his eyes, and bound him
with chains, and brought him to Babylon" (4 Kings 25:7). The bloodstained bodies of his children — such was the last sight to meet
the eyes of this most unfortunate of David's descendants before
they were plunged into darkness, the vision that he would carry
with him into the night of his captivity.

F. AFTER 587

This date marks the end of the earthly kingdom of the Davidic
line. The dynasty whose eternal rule Nathan had prophesied with
such solemnity had lasted in all only four centuries. It was never
to rise again. The Temple that had perished in the flames would
be rebuilt; the walls that Nabuchodonosor had razed would rise
again; but no direct descendant of David would ever again mount
the throne of Jerusalem.

The dynasty of David would indeed rise again; its new throne,
however, would not stand in an earthly Jerusalem but in a new
Jerusalem built by faith. If God's word abides eternally — and God
is forever faithful, even going beyond the terms of his promises — then this kingdom cannot be one of this world. When

the line of human issue fails, we must look to the generative power of the divine. As an example, in the captivity of Babylon royal messianism was purified and spiritualized. Considered in themselves, the deportation and captivity were no school of spirituality, but they were the medium in which the Israel of God, the tiny remnant who would return, was led to a new vision of things to come. The disaster of 587 was not in itself, and magically, as it were, a proof that Nathan's prophecy referred to a spiritual reality, but at least it demonstrated, and in a manner that was irrefutable, that the domain of its fulfillment would not be of this world. This fact alone was a considerable step forward.

In justice to the people of God, it must be said that in Israel there had always existed men whose faith in the divine Word remained unshakable, even when this Word, in the eyes of the world, seemed only foolishness; men who, as the Epistle to the Hebrews will assert much later, "by faith conquered kingdoms" (Heb. 11:33). In the darkest moments of misery and failure, the Book of Jeremias foretells a glorious future for the House of David:

> Behold, the days are coming, says the Lord, when I will raise up a righteous shoot to David; as king he shall reign and govern wisely, he shall do what is just and right in the land [19] (Jer. 23:5).
>
> On that day, says the Lord of hosts, "I will break his yoke from off your necks and snap your bonds." Strangers shall no longer enslave them; instead, they shall serve the Lord, their God, and David, their king, whom I will raise up for them (Jer. 30:8-9).

The prophecy borders on paradox. But it is precisely in the most paradoxical of situations that God's plan is fulfilled with a logic that surpasses all human wisdom. The promise of an eternal reign for the House of David remains firm, even though it is now only a "fallen hut" (Amos 9:11). The vigorous lines of Psalm 88 portray what to all appearances is only contradiction:

> "I will keep my love for him always,
> my covenant with him shall stand,
> I have founded his dynasty to last for ever,
> his throne to be as lasting as the heavens."
> And yet you have rejected, disowned
> and raged at your anointed;
> you have repudiated the covenant with your servant
> and flung his crown dishonoured to the ground.
> You have stripped him of his glorious sceptre,
> and toppled his throne to the ground (Ps. 88:28-29, 38-39, 44).[20]

G. Ezechiel

Ezechiel, whose prophetic activity dates from 593 to 571, will be quick to seize upon the lessons of history. Yahweh will himself take up the sceptre that has fallen from David's hand and lead the flock scattered in Babylonia back to the pastures of Israel. The dethronement of the Davidic line is presented as the prelude to the inauguration of a new kingdom, which will be the very theocracy of old (cf. Ez. 34:2-16). David will remain, but his royal sceptre from henceforth is to be the crook of the Good Shepherd:

> I will appoint one shepherd over them to pasture them, my servant David; he shall pasture them and be their shepherd. I, the Lord, will be their God, and my servant David shall be prince among them. I, the Lord, have spoken. I will make a covenant of peace with them (Ez. 34:23-25).
>
> Thus they shall know that I, the Lord, am their God, and they are my people, the house of Israel, says the Lord God. You, my sheep, you are the sheep of my pasture, and I am your God, says the Lord God (Ez. 34:30-31).

In direct contrast to the kings who had been unfaithful to the covenant, the future Messias will be, like David, "the servant of the Lord," [21] the title that designates the spirit of his total fidelity. He will not reign as a king, but will dwell simply as a prince in the midst of his people: Ezechiel is harking back to the ideal time — or rather, the idealized time — of the entrance into the Promised Land [22] when the tribes were still without a king. We have here, in fact, a turning away from the concept of a flesh-and-blood perpetuation of the Davidic kingship; and this rise of an anti-royalist prophetism is at the same time the sign of a more spiritual messianism.

Ezechiel preserves all his profound feeling for the new Jerusalem and the new Temple,[23] and likewise for the new covenant which God is to write in the hearts of his faithful.[24] Those dry bones that the spirit of Yahweh is going to bring to life are the Israel of the promise; [25] is not the "fallen hut of David" [26] the true city of God? It is the new Temple filled with the glory of Yahweh,[27] the new Jerusalem whose name means "Yahweh is here." [28]

With the passage of the thousand years of history given to Jewish piety for meditation on the meaning of Nathan's prophecy, the Davidic theme accumulated a weight of biblical reflections. Through the prophecies of Isaias, Jeremias and Ezechiel, and the contributions of Psalms 2 and 109, the little shepherd of Bethlehem, having become king, arrives at the threshold of the New Testament, reclothed in a garment whose rich spiritual hues display some striking contrasts. God, at last, is about to draw all these prophecies to their complete fulfillment by unifying them in the person of Christ Jesus. To the Old Testament, with its ceaseless cry: "Remember, O Lord, for David" (Ps. 131:1), God, in the Son of Mary, will give his answer; in Jesus, he will be mindful of David, in accordance with his promise:

> I will make a horn to sprout forth for David;
> I will place a lamp for my anointed . . .
> upon him my crown shall shine (Ps. 131:17-18).

[1] A. Gelin, "Messianism," *Dict. Bibl.*, *Suppl.*, fasc. 28 (1955), col. 1174–1175. We shall be making frequent allusion to the resemblances between God's Word and profane royal literature. It will be well here at the outset to take stock of the attendant ambiguities; for there are, it seems to us, two errors to avoid. The first would be to reduce the Bible to a simple copying of profane texts, and thereby to forget the transcendence of God's Word, which comes to us from above while yet incarnate in a well-defined historical context. The second error would consist in denying to the Bible all resemblance to these same texts, and thereby to forget the immanence of the Word, which, although it comes from above, is uttered by man. God's Word is in some way a participation in the very mystery of Christ: just as Christ is truly God, so the Word (*Parole*) is fully divine, that is to say, inspired by the Holy Spirit. And just as Christ is perfect man, so equally the Word (*Parole*) is fully human, that is to say, uttered by man, although under the action of the Holy Spirit. On this subject see Pius XII, Enc. *Divino Afflante Spiritu*, Sept. 30, 1943. On inspiration in general, see the article of P. Benoît, in Robert and Tricot (eds.), *Guide to the Bible*, 2nd ed (Paris: Desclee, 1960), pp. 9–52.

[2] Verse 13 is doubtless an addition intended to justify Solomon's construction of the Temple.

[3] Nathan's prophecy is marked by the style of the court literature of the period. Hence it will be well to interpret the promised "forever" and "divine sonship" in a sufficiently broad sense. This having been said, it must be added that Christ will fulfill the prophecy on a level far above that of its first sense.

[4] In Assyria-Babylonia, the king was thought to possess kinship with the divine. Cf. P. Dhorme, *La religion assyro-babylonienne*, pp. 166–168; J. de Fraine, *L'aspect religieux de la royauté israelite. L'institution monarchique dans l'Ancien Testament et dans les textes mésopotamiens* (Rome, 1954); R. de Vaux, *Ancient Israel: Its Life and Institutions*, translated by John McHugh (New York: McGraw-Hill, 1961), pp. 111–113. In the Code of Hammurabi, 170 and 171, the formula "You are my son" is the ritual formula of adoption (see V. Scheil, *La loi d'Hammourabi* [Paris, 1906], p. 38). On Psalm 2, an enthronement psalm, see E. Podechard, *Le Psautier*, I (Lyons, 1949), pp. 13ff.; A. Robert, "Considerations sur le messianisme du Psaume 2," *Recherches de Science Religieuse*, XXXIX, pp. 88–98.

[5] Here it must be recalled that the ancient kings of Egypt, Assyria, and Phoenicia were at the same time priests. David will share this idea of royal priesthood: he erects the first altar at Jerusalem (2 Kings 24–25) and decides to build the Temple

there; on the occasion of the ark's translation to Jerusalem he offers sacrifices (2 Kings 6:13, 17, 18), blesses the people (v. 18), and wears the linen loincloth, the vestment of officiating priests (v. 14).

The idea of one's consecration from birth is also reminiscent of the election of the prophets: Jeremias (Jer. 1:5) and the Servant of Yahweh (Is. 42:6; 44:24; 49:1) were consecrated from their mother's womb.

On the priesthood of the king, see R. de Vaux, *Ancient Israel*, pp. 113–114, and H. H. Rowley, "Melchizedek and Zadok," *Festschrift Bertholet* (Tübingen, 1950), pp. 461–472. On Psalm 109 (110): L. Durr, *Psalm 110 im Lichte der neueren alttestamentlichen Forschung* (Münster, 1929); Podechard, *Le Psautier*, II (Lyons, 1954), pp. 167–183; J. Coppens, "La portée messianique du Psaume CX," *Ephemerides Theologicae Lovanienses*, XXXII (1956), pp. 5–23.

⁶ These ideas are reminiscent of the traditional clichés of profane royal literature. Thus, in the text of Assurbanipal we read: "From the moment that Assur, Sin, Shamash, Adad, Bel, Nabon, Ishtar of Nineveh, goddess and queen of all things, Ishtar of Arbele, Nin-ib, Nergal and Nusku placed me with happiness on the throne of the father who sired me, Adad made his rain fall, Ea opened her springs, the wheat grew five cubits high, the corn in the ear grew to five-sixths of a cubit. The harvest is rich, the grain abundant, the jiparu bear their fruit in due season, the trees are laden with luscious fruits, the herds swell with new offspring; in short, under my government the abundance is extraordinary, and throughout my years, the fertility is splendid!" (Translated by Dhorme, *op. cit.*, pp. 171–172).

Another text, doubtless referring to the same Assurbanipal, relates: "Good government, length of days, years of justice, rain in abundance, plentiful waters, flourishing trade! (. . .) Old men leap, children sing, maidens rejoice, women conceive . . . and in their joy say to their children: our lord the king has brought us life! Those who for years were prisoners, you have freed! Those who for years were sick, enjoy health! The hungry are filled, the thin grow fat, the naked are clothed" (cf. Dhorme, *op. cit.*, pp. 172–173). See also the prologue to the Code of Hammurabi (Scheil, *op. cit.*, pp. 1–4). On the king as savior, see R. de Vaux, *op. cit.*, pp. 110–111, and R. Meyer, "Der Erlöserkönig des Alten Testaments," *Münchener Theologische Zeitschrift*, III (1952), pp. 221–243 and 367–384.

⁷ On the messianic significance of Solomon's succession to David, the reader may consult Y. M.-J. Congar, "David et Solomon, Types du Christ en ses deux Avènements," *Vie Spirituelle*, 91 (1954), pp. 323–340. On the messianic significance of Solomon, see H.-M. Féret, "L' économie providentielle. . . ," *Forma Gregis* (March, 1951), pp. 57–70.

⁸ The lands referred to in 8:23 are those that were to form the Assyrian provinces of Dor, Megiddo, and Galaad. Verse 3: "you have smashed, as on the day of Madian" refers back to the Book of Judges 7:15-25. For the historical context, see J. Steinmann, "Le Prophète Isaïe. Sa vie, son oeuvre son temps," Coll. *Lectio divina*, 5 (Paris, 1950), pp. 120ff.

⁹ Cf. Mich. 4:9.

¹⁰ Cf. Ps. 76:12.

¹¹ Cf. Is. 10:21; Jer. 32:18; Ps. 23:8 and especially Soph. 3:14-17, which announces the saving presence of the God-Hero in the womb of the Daughter of Sion; see Chapter 5 and the translator's note.

¹² Cf. Is. 22:21.

¹³ On the messianic peace, see J. Bonsirven, *Le Judaïsme Palestinien*, I (Paris, 1934), pp. 442–444.

¹⁴ On the judicative role of the King-Messias, see J. Bonsirven, *op. cit.*, pp. 500–503. See also M.-J. Lagrange, "Le Judaïsme avant Jésus-Christ," Coll. *Études bibliques* (Paris, 1931), pp. 363ff., for the author's study of the various features of the expected Savior. Also H. Riesenfeld, *Jésus Transfiguré: l'arriére-plan du*

récit évangélique de la transfiguration de Notre-Seigneur (Lund, 1947), pp. 66–80 (the various functions of the Messias).

[15] Verses 6-8 describe the restoration of the peace of paradise; on this subject see Bonsirven, *op. cit.*, I, pp. 511–516.

[16] See Num. 11:17 (Moses); 2 Kings 23:2 (David); and 4 Kings 2:9 (Elias).

* Translator's note: We have here used the version of the *Jerusalem Bible*. See footnote 18.

[17] Isaias' vocation dates from about 740; Micheas exercised his ministry before and after the fall of Samaria in 721.

[18] Resetting the subject in its historical context, A. Gelin notes: "In the mind of the times a theological value was attached to the role of the mother of the dynastic heir. The representations at Luxor and Deir el Bahari show the royal child as born not of the father, but of the union between the god and the mother. Similar conceptions seem to have been entertained at Jerusalem, although full account was taken of the moral and invisible nature of Yahweh" ("Messianisme," *loc. cit.*, col. 1181). As a matter of fact, we find the formula "The Almah will give birth to a son" in the Phoenician texts of Ras Shamra (Gordon, *Ugaritic Handbook* [Rome, 1947], text 77).

This should be no stumbling block for us. If later on in history the Logos took a human nature into hypostatic union with himself, he could just as well have taken a text of Ras Shamra and integrated it into God's Word. Indeed, we have only admiration for the divine pedagogy which in such a marvelous way prepared the Jewish conscience for its later acceptance of an idea more wonderful still — that of the dwelling of a totally spiritual God in the womb of the Virgin Mary. So likewise, when later on the Septuagint editors translate the word *almah* (maiden) by παρθένος (virgin), it is only to stress the marvelous character of David's future descendant; they will be more faithful to the spirit of the prophecy than to its letter (on Is. 7:14, see also pp. 93–94).

[19] The name "shoot" will designate the Messias in Zach. 3:8 and 6:12.

[20] This psalm is composed of three clearly distinct parts:

— the first (vv. 1-9, excepting vv. 4-5 and 16-19) is a hymn of praise, written before 722 in the northern kingdom (cf. Podechard, *Le Psautier*, II, *op cit.*, p. 115).

— the second (vv. 20-46) recalls the choice of David (vv. 20-28), the promises made to his posterity (vv. 29-38), and declares, finally, the actual fall of the dynasty (vv. 39-46). "There can be no doubt," writes Podechard (*ibid.*, p. 117), that the author was thinking of Sedecias himself, the last successor of David."

— the third part is a personal prayer of supplication (vv. 47-53). *Translator's note*: We have here used the version of the Jerusalem Bible.

[21] Cf. 4 Kings 8:19; Ps. 17:1; Ps. 88:4, 21.

[22] Cf. Ez. 47:13–48:29.

[23] Cf. Ez. 40:1ff.

[24] Cf. Ez. 36:26-27.

[25] Cf. Ez. 37:1-14.

[26] Amos 9:11. This text, which has been placed in the Book of Amos, can be presumed to belong to the same period as that of Ezechiel's oracles.

[27] Cf. Ez. 43:5.

[28] Cf. Ez. 48:35.

Chapter 4

MARY, MOTHER OF THE
SON OF DAVID

A. THE GOSPEL THEMES

With the birth of Jesus dawns the new messianic era, the renewal of the entire royal history of David and his line. But this renewal is at the same time a fulfillment: Christ is truly the "yes" in whom the Father fulfills all his promises (cf. 2 Cor. 1:20).

This contains the explanation of the special place that David occupies in the narratives of Christ's infancy, above all in that of the Annunciation. At the end of the list of marvelous titles which the angel enumerates for Mary, David's own name is to be found, forming a conclusion, as it were, to the array of titles bestowed upon the Messias:

> He shall be great, and shall be called the Son of the Most High; and the Lord God will give him the throne of David his father, and he shall be king over the house of Jacob forever; and of his kingdom there shall be no end (Luke 1:32-33).

This mention of David is all the more important in that it occurs in a context which recalls the promise that Nathan had made to David a thousand years before:

2 Kings 7:3-15	*Luke 1:28-33*
the Lord is with thee (v. 3)	the Lord is with thee (v. 28)
I have been with thee (v. 9)	
my mercy I will not take away from him (v. 15)	thou hast found grace with God (v. 30)
Yahweh will make you great* (v. 11)	He shall be great (v. 32)
I will be to him a father, and he shall be to me a son (v. 14)	and shall be called the Son of the Most High (v. 32)

38

thy house shall be faithful, and thy kingdom forever before thy face, and thy throne shall be firm forever (v. 16)	the Lord God will give him the throne of David his father (v. 32)
	of his kingdom there shall be no end (v. 33)
to be ruler over my people Israel (v. 9)	he shall be king over the house of Jacob forever (v. 32).

It can readily be seen that Nathan's prophecy is the predominant element of the Annunciation message. But we must go beyond the factor of parallelisms — which has only a relative importance — and see what lies much deeper: the continuity between the promise and its fulfillment. What Luke is trying to bring out here is not merely the resemblance of wording, but the similitude of themes and ideas. Simply to say that Jesus is the Son of God would be far too little; we must draw out all the richness of meaning that this title conveys.

1. Mother of the King

Christ, the Son of David, is King. Mary is the Mother of the King, the Mother of the true Son of David.

The angel's message gives manifest emphasis to Jesus' royal character: ". . . the Lord God will give him the throne of David his father, and he shall be king over the house of Jacob forever; and of his kingdom there shall be no end" (Luke 1:32-33). Like David, Jesus possesses the throne of Jerusalem and at the same time is king over the house of Jacob. The unification of the North and the South achieved under David was thus a prophetic foreshadowing of the spiritual unification that Jesus would accomplish, a thousand years later, in the messianic kingdom.

The royal character of the new Son of David is brought out by a combination of several other themes. Thus does Zachary, drawing on the inspiration of Psalm 131:17, see "a power of salvation" (literally: "a horn of salvation") "raised up . . . in the house of David his servant; as he promised through the mouth of his holy ones, the prophets from of old." His exegesis is sound and invites our confidence. Luke is careful to point out that Zachary was indeed speaking under the inspiration of the Holy Spirit (Luke 1:67-70).

The evangelist also notes that Joseph, Mary's husband, was "of the house and family of David" (Luke 2:4), and that Jesus was born in Bethlehem, the place of David's own birth: "I bring you good news of great joy which shall be to all the people; for today in the town of David a Savior has been born to you, who is Christ the Lord" (Luke 2:10-11).

The annunciation to the shepherds is patterned after the annunciation to Mary:

The Annunciation to Mary	*The Annunciation to the Shepherds*
Do not be afraid	Do not be afraid
Rejoice*	I bring you good news of great joy
thou . . . shalt bring forth a son Jesus (i.e., Savior)	a Savior has been born to you
He shall be great, and shall be called the Son of the Most High	Christ the Lord
God will give him the throne of David his father	in the town of David

It can readily be seen that here we are confronted with a regrouping of themes, borrowed from, among others, Isaias 9:1-7. In the prophecy "a child is born to us," we in effect find the theme of joy, the announcement of deliverance to come through the birth of the infant-savior, the attestation of his royal Davidic ancestry; the very song of the angels: "Peace on earth to men whom God loves" (Luke 2:14) is a careful reference to Isaias 9:6: "His dominion is vast and forever peaceful."

Matthew, in his habitual concern to stress the fulfillment of the prophecies, will focus particular attention on the Bethlehemic, i.e., Davidic, origin of Jesus, and in this context recalls the prophecy of Micheas 5:1: "And thou, Bethlehem, of the land of Juda, art by no means least among the princes of Juda; for from thee shall come forth a leader who shall rule my people Israel" (Matthew 2:6).

There is a certain liberty in the evangelist's citation; the refinements of textual criticism are obviously not his present concern.[1] What to him is of central importance is the bearing of the passage on the Davidic origin of Jesus, the Messias: he is born in Bethlehem, the city of David; moreover Joseph, Mary's husband, is also for him a "son of David" (Matthew 1:20). In view of these considerations, we can understand why he began his Gospel with the genealogy of Jesus "the Son of David, the son of Abraham."[2]

The royalty of the Davidic line thus confers on Mary's motherhood a new dignity, a royal dignity. Mary is not simply the Mother of the "Child Jesus"; she is also the Mother of the King. Her motherhood is a royal motherhood.

Here it would be well to call attention to the fundamental difference that exists between ordinary human motherhood and the unique motherhood that is Mary's. After having conceived her child, a woman's knowledge of him is confined to little more than a faint awareness of his existence; she can neither foresee the circumstances of his birth nor know him as a person, nor can she divine the secret of his future. The common expression we all use, "she is expecting *a* child," reflects a deep psychological truth.

Mary, on the contrary, knows even before she has conceived her Son what his vocation is to be. Her *Fiat* is more than merely her consent to motherhood; rather, it is principally her consent to being made the Mother of Christ Jesus. It is with full awareness of the mystery of Jesus that she becomes his Mother; not that she had fully understood this mystery, but she did fully understand that this mystery was being wrought in her. And so it is that her "yes" extends to the very royalty of Jesus. Jesus is the only child who has ever chosen his own Mother, and Mary is the only Mother who has ever chosen her own Son. And this is why, in choosing her for his Mother, Jesus has equally enthroned her as Queen, "the Mother of the Lord" (Luke 1:43).

2. *Mother of the Savior*

Jesus, the Son of David, is the Savior. Mary is the Mother of the Savior.

In the message of the Annunciation, the angel Gabriel had said to Mary: "thou shalt call his name Jesus" (Luke 1:31); and later, at the time of the circumcision, Luke notes: "his name was called Jesus, the name given him by the angel before he was conceived in the womb [of his mother]" (Luke 2:21; cf. Matthew 1:25).

In Hebrew custom the name is a synonym of the person who bears it; and when God himself bestows a name, he brings to pass at the same time what the name signifies. To decree that Christ was to be called *Jesus* was to affirm that he was truly *Jesus*, namely, Savior.[3] Matthew will be more explicit: "And she shall bring forth a son, and thou shalt call his name Jesus; for he shall save his people from their sins" (Matthew 1:21).

Such an explanatory gloss is not to be found in Luke's narrative; but by means of numerous allusions[4] Jesus is portrayed for us as the fulfillment of the messianic salvation promised to the House of David. Thus we read in the *Benedictus* of Zachary:

> Blessed be the Lord, the God of Israel . . .
> He has raised up a horn of salvation

in the house of David his servant. . . .
Salvation from our enemies, and
from the hand of all who hate us (Luke 1:68-71).

Remaining within the perspective of Nathan's prophecy, these lines evoke the image of the enemies that will be crushed by the exploits of the battlefield. However, Zachary is not unaware of the concept of a purely spiritual liberation that we have already encountered in the prophecy of the just king (Is. 11:1-9) — the deliverance from sins. In effect, he is proclaiming that God, being mindful of his holy covenant, is granting to his people that they will serve him in holiness and justice; that he is giving them knowledge of salvation (namely, Jesus the Savior) through the forgiveness of sins (Luke 1:72, 75, 77).

In the annunciation to the shepherds, the angel gives another sign of the messiaship of the Davidic Child and his role of Savior: ". . . in the town of David a Savior has been born to you, who is Christ the Lord (Luke 2:11). In this connection it will be remembered that the parallel noted between this scene and that of the annunciation to Mary brought out the correspondence of the name Jesus to the term Savior.

Finally Simeon, as he holds the infant Jesus in his arms, proclaims that his eyes have seen

the salvation prepared before the face of all peoples:
A light of revelation to the Gentiles,
and a glory for thy people Israel" (Luke 2:30-32).

The perspective has widened to embrace the whole world. Here Luke displays his fondness for one of his favorite themes, the universality of salvation. He thus shows himself as the faithful disciple of Paul, who had already cited the Book of Emmanuel (Is. 11:10) in Romans 15:12: "There shall be the root of Jesse, he who arises to rule the Gentiles . . . in him the Gentiles shall hope."

All these texts and allusions are designed to highlight the special vocation of Jesus: he is the Savior of his people and the very Savior of all nations. He thus assumes in his own person, and at the same time magnifies to far vaster dimensions, the vocation of the Savior-King, that vocation to which David and all his successors had failed to measure up. In the light of this comprehensive glance at the history of the kingship, it can even be affirmed that the Davidic line had brought the people as much in the way of misery as it had of salvation and glory; at the end it had led it to the captivity of Babylon. David the savior was in reality only a prophetic type of Jesus the Savior; the definitive salvation was the messianic achievement of Jesus.

At this point we should return to the fact that Mary's motherhood does not terminate simply in the Child Jesus; as we have said above, this motherhood was fully aware that it was to find its consummation not only in the "Child," but in the fulfillment of his messianic vocation. As the Mother of Jesus, of the true Son of David, Mary is thus also, and in the fullest sense of the word, the Mother of the Savior, and she willed and desired this salvation inaugurated by the birth of her Child as much as she willed and loved Jesus himself.

3. *Mother of the Son of God*

Jesus, the Son of David, is the Son of God. Mary is the Mother of the Son of God.

On the level of the prophecy taken in itself — "I will be to him a father, and he shall be to me a son" (2 Kings 7:14) — the king's "divine" sonship had a purely moral signification: Yahweh will treat the king as a father treats his son.[5] But on the level of its ultimate realization — "He shall be called the Son of the Most High" (Luke 1:32) — Jesus' divine sonship is an absolutely perfect sonship: God is the Father of our Lord Jesus Christ. We can see the plenitude with which Nathan's prophecy is fulfilled in Jesus: David is magnified in Jesus, who is not only his son but also the Son of God. Jesus is the Lord *par excellence*, not solely in virtue of his royal ancestry, but more precisely in virtue of his eternal divine sonship.

Moreover, the idea of the divine sonship[6] of David's descendant comes to the Lucan text charged with all the richness of the intervening history of Scripture. It undergoes development particularly in Psalm 2, that eminently royal psalm; in Psalm 109, where, as elsewhere, it is vested in the concept of the royal priesthood; and in Isaias 9:1-6, with the array of human-divine features portrayed in its announcement of the mystery of the Man-God.[7] All these texts, which so strongly emphasize the glorious and triumphant character of the Son of God, are an annunciation of Jesus' royal glory, the same glory which the angel is to prophesy to our Lady.

But alongside this properly royal aspect, the texts of the more recent past also bear witness to a son of God who is humble and poor. The divine sonship is not the exclusive possession of the victorious king who "makes his enemies his footstool" and "heaps up the corpses" of his adversaries (Ps. 109:1, 6); it belongs equally to the just man who is humble and persecuted,[8] to him who fulfills the ideal of the *'anawim*, the poor of Yahweh.[9] The "memoirs of the Virgin" do not leave us without a picture of Jesus as the Poor Man *par excellence*, who was born in a stable because there was no room for him at the inn, who had humble shepherds for his first worshippers, and who was redeemed in the Temple by the offering prescribed for the poor.[10] To augment this, Simeon's prophecy will announce the mystery of the Passion of the Poor Man of Israel in these veiled terms, which at the same time announce the mystery of the compassion of his Mother: "And thine own soul a sword shall pierce" (Luke 2:35).

These two traditions, one of a son of God who is triumphant and victorious, the other of a son of God who is humble and poor, far from being mutually contradictory, converge to form a sublime unity in the vocation of the "holy servant Jesus" (Acts 4:27), humiliated in his Passion and glorified in his resurrection. As Luke writes in the Acts of the Apostles:

> The promise made to our fathers, God has fulfilled to our children, in raising up Jesus, as also it is written in the second Psalm, *Thou art my son, this day have I begotten thee.* And to show that he has raised him up from the dead, never again to return to decay, he has said thus, *I will give you the holy and sure promises of David.* Because he says also in another Psalm, *Thou wilt not let thy Holy One undergo decay* [11] (Acts 13:32-35).

We can see the intimacy of the link between Christ's divine sonship and his resurrection; we are confronted here with one of the oldest themes in the theology of the primitive Church, according to which Jesus is established fully as the "Son of God" through the triumph of the Cross and the resurrection.[12]

These reflections can lead us to a more precise understanding of the divine Word: "He shall be great, and shall be called the Son of the Most High." Ordinarily we think of these words in terms of the divine sonship as Christ will lay claim to it later on in the Gospels. In reality, however, it is a new dimension which Luke's text opens up to us, a dimension which certainly announces the mystery of the Man-God, but which above all centers on the Davidic sonship of Jesus together with his enthronement through the mystery of his resurrection.

If we rise beyond the partial conclusions that theology can draw from these texts, we see above all else that the title "Son of David" is charged with all the weight of the sacred history of God's people — that royal history which, in the person of Jesus, enters the dimension of the divine. All the different royal themes are gathered up but at the same time spiritualized, and in this divinization are brought to their ultimate perfection.

In coming down to us from his Father, Jesus comes no less equally from David; his appearance is not a disruption of human history, but an evolving to full flower in the richness of God's own life. The earthly kingdom of Daivd is thus the preparation for the spiritual kingdom of Jesus, which "is not of this world."

David, the savior of his people, is the herald of Jesus, the Savior of the world. The eternal dynasty promised to David — in a context reminiscent of the forceful court style of the East — stretches to the sands of the divine eternity in Jesus. The "divine sonship" in terms of which Yahweh would treat David as his son attains its fulfillment in the divine sonship of Jesus; the priesthood of the ancient king of Jerusalem becomes the priesthood of Melchisedec according to the new and eternal covenant; the little shepherd boy whom Yahweh had taken from behind the flocks of Jesse heralds the coming of the true Shepherd to the sheepfold that will encompass the entire world; the insignificant Jebusite village that David had seized with a handful of wily mercenaries now becomes the symbol of the new Jerusalem of the Apocalypse, which is coming down from heaven from God (Apoc. 21:2-4), which is reigned over by "the root and the offspring of David," and shines in the light of "the bright morning star" (Apoc. 22:16).

In taking on human flesh in the Virgin Mary, Jesus also took on the flesh of the line of David; he took on the flesh, we can even say, of the entire sacred history of God's people. He took upon himself the whole content of that history — its glories and its failures, its smallness and occasional shabbiness, even its very sinfulness. The blood of Bethsabee the adulteress, of Ruth the Moabitess, the daughter of the unknown God, of Thamar, who played the prostitute, and of Rahab, who really was one — all these names, in themselves so lowly, are glorified in Jesus; they are part of his genealogy (Matthew 1:3-6). These persons, in their contrition and repentance, prepared the way for his coming; and they are also the flesh-and-blood link of God's Son with the human race.

Our intense interest in the Davidic ancestry of our Lord is not simply a historical or archeological concern; it is inspired by the truth that beneath the features of David and his descendants we can begin to trace the figure of Jesus.

B. CONCLUSION

Where is Mary's place in this perspective? At its very center, for it is precisely through her that David himself becomes what he really is: the forefather of Christ. She stands at the very point in the sacred history of God's people where the royal line of David issues in the history of the Logos. She is the place of meeting between God and David, not merely because she gave God's Son the shelter of her womb, but above all because she begot him equally in her heart and in her soul, and devoted herself, with all the ardor of her faith and her love, to this motherhood of hers that was at once both Davidic and divine.

This history of the new David, which begins at the Annunciation, will continue throughout the entire public life of Jesus. Each time that some unhappy soul will cry out: "Jesus, Son of David, have mercy on me!" and will be cured, Jesus will fulfill his vocation as the Savior-King; he will deliver both the body from disease, and the soul from sin.[13]

This history of David will finally reach its full term in the mystery of the Cross. In writing "Jesus of Nazareth, the King of the Jews" on the placard for the Cross (John 19:19), the Jews had no idea of how literally true these words really were; unwittingly, they were reminding his mother of the angel's words: "The Lord God will give him the throne of David his father, and of his kingdom there shall be no end" (Luke 1:32-33); unwittingly, they also were announcing the mystery of the new David's royal resurrection. In his first sermon, Peter will bring out this very truth:

> The patriarch David . . . both died and was buried, and his tomb is with us to this very day. . . . [But] this Jesus God has raised up, and we are all witnesses of it. Therefore, exalted by the right hand of God, and receiving from the Father the promise of the Holy Spirit, he has poured forth this Spirit which you see and hear. For David did not ascend into heaven, but he says himself, *The Lord said to my Lord: Sit thou at my right hand, until I make thy enemies thy footstool* [Ps. 109]. Therefore, let all the house of Israel know most assuredly that God has made both Lord and Christ, this Jesus whom you crucified (Acts 2:29-36).

The mystery of David will continue in the life of the Church until the Parousia. Each time that a child will be presented for baptism and receive the royal anointing, he will become a sharer in the vocation of the true Son of David, and a member of the royal and priestly people of the New Testament: "You, however, are a chosen race, a royal priesthood, a holy nation, a purchased people; that you may proclaim the perfections of him who has called you out of darkness into his marvellous light" (1 Peter 2:9). And to this people Mary is what she was to Christ — she is its Mother.

Translator's note: From the *Jerusalem Bible.*

[1] Micheas had actually written: "But you, Ephratha, the least among the clans of Juda. . . ." Matthew's re-reading is as follows: "And you, Bethlehem, of the land of Juda, are not the least among the cities of Juda. . . ." Such arrangements of the text, provided that the essential content was left untouched, were admitted by rabbinical exegesis at the time of Christ.

[2] Matthew 1:1. Notice that Peter cites Psalm 15:8-11 and Psalm 109:1 in Acts 2:25-36 to establish the truth of the resurrection and the kingship of Jesus, the Son of David.

[3] The Greek Ἰησοῦς is the transcription of the Hebrew *Yeshua*, an abridged form of *Yehoshua*, which means "Yahweh saves." In Israel the name was in itself a fairly common one, even as late as the second century after Christ. Cf. Foerster, "Ἰησοῦς," *Theological Dictionary of the New Testament*, 3, pp. 284ff.

[4] See R. Laurentin, "Traces d'allusions étymologiques en Luc 1–2," *Biblica*, 37 (1956), pp. 444–447; in the original Hebrew (or Aramaic) these allusions would have been easily discernible; in the Greek translation they have disappeared.

[5] This interpretation is dictated by what follows in the text: "if he commit any iniquity, I will correct him with the rod of men, and with the stripes of the children of men" (2 Kings 7:14).

[6] The expression "sons of God" covers a rather wide range of meanings. Thus the angels can be called "sons of God" because they form the court of the Most High (Pss. 29:1; 88:7; Job 1:6; 38:7); but Yahweh is equally the father of the entire nation of the Chosen People to which he has given national existence and which he protects, rears, and loves as a father does his son (Exod. 4:22; Deut. 14:1; Osee 11:1; Jer. 31:20; Is. 63:16; cf. Is. 49:15-16). From contact with the Babylonian religions, in which each man had his own personal god, a sort of protecting *jinn*, and even from the distinction that had to be drawn in Israel between those who were just and those who were unfaithful to the covenant, the divine sonship became the privilege of the faithful alone (cf. Tob. 13:4; Ps. 102:13; Mal 1:6; Wis. 2:13-18; 5:5). On this subject see Lagrange, "La paternité de Dieu dans l'Ancien Testament," *Revue Biblique* (1908), pp. 481–499.

[7] The theological reflection of the author of the Epistle to the Hebrews (Heb. 1:3-4) will mark the term of this Christological evolution in its application to Christ, the universal Lord, of the royal prophecies made to David and his descendants (2 Kings 7:14; Ps. 2:7 = Heb. 1:5; Ps. 44:7-8 = Heb. 1:8-9; Ps. 109:1 = Heb.1:13). The divine sonship is distinctly affirmed in terms clearer than those we find in Luke 1. Moreover the first ten chapters, as we know, establish the transcendent priesthood of Christ.

[8] Wis. 2:13-18; 5:5.

[9] See pp. 113ff.

[10] Luke 2:24; cf. Lev. 12:8.

[11] The text cites Ps. 2:7; Is. 55:3 and Ps. 15:10.

[12] Also see Acts 2:25-31.

[13] In the biblical mentality, sickness is often regarded as the consequence of sin.

In curing maladies, the consequence of sin, Jesus is thereby orienting minds toward the idea that he can likewise forgive sins, the cause of sickness. In certain miracles (like that of the cure of the paralytic in Mark 2:3-12; Matthew 9:2-7; Luke 5:18-26), Jesus himself explicitly establishes the relation between the cure of the body and the forgiveness of sins.

Part III

THE VIRGIN OF THE
ANNUNCIATION

> *Joy be to thee, full of grace!*
> *The Lord is with thee!*
> *The Holy Spirit shall come upon thee*
> *and the power of the Most High*
> *shall overshadow thee.*
> (Luke 1:28, 35)

INTRODUCTION TO PART III

Up to this point we have been considering Mary as the Daughter of Abraham and the Daughter of David. In these first two sections we have seen that Jesus, by taking on flesh in Mary, took on the flesh, so to speak, of the entire sacred history of Israel, and that in fact the totality of this history can be summed up in these two titles, the very words with which Matthew will introduce his genealogy of Christ: "Jesus Christ, the Son of David, the son of Abraham" (Matthew 1:1). The mystery of Mary was defined in terms of its reference to the mystery of Christ; it is precisely because Jesus, her Son, has fulfilled the promises made to Abraham and to David that Mary has appeared before us as the Daughter of Abraham and the Daughter of David. These reflections had Jesus for their center.

However, while we must not lose sight of this absolute preeminence of our Lord, we can make a more direct study of Mary's personal role in the Incarnation. For in Mary, the Annunciation narrative in fact shows us the DAUGHTER OF SION, the personification of the Church.

The Annunciation narrative, part of the section of Luke's Gospel (1:5–2:52) dealing with Christ's childhood and called "the memoirs of the Virgin,"[1] is constructed along the lines of the special literary genre known as "midrash."[2] Meditating on the ancient texts of Scripture, Luke collates them with the totally new situation which brings about Christ's coming into this world. Thus does he perceive, with the light of the Holy Spirit, the continuity between the marvels of past history and the incarnation of Christ, while at the same time centering attention on the transcendency of God's Word, which ceaselessly affirms its eternal presence above and beyond the particular circumstances of its utterance in time.

In contrast to Matthew, who introduces his biblical citations with the solemn formula "that what was spoken by the Lord through the prophet might be fulfilled,"[3] Luke proceeds rather by way of

51

allusions so delicate as to nearly veil them. His text is overflowing
with citations, to the point that the Greek translation is a belaboring
of the original Hebrew. But these citations are hardly ever under-
lined or formally inserted;[4] he leaves to the reader the joy of discover-
ing the profound harmonies which his text weaves with the divine
Word that is ancient and yet ever new. If we would enter into
the interior spiritual world of the Virgin's story, we must, as she
did, ponder over all these things which she kept in her heart.[5]

The Annunciation Narrative

Now in the sixth month the angel Gabriel was sent from God to
a town of Galilee called Nazareth, to a virgin betrothed to a man
named Joseph, of the house of David, and the virgin's name was
Mary. And coming in to her, he said: "Joy be to thee,* full of grace,
the Lord is with thee. Blessed art thou among women."

When she had heard him she was troubled at his word, and kept
pondering what manner of greeting this might be. And the angel
said to her, "Do not be afraid, Mary, for thou hast found grace with
God. Behold, thou shalt conceive in thy womb and shalt bring forth
a son; and thou shalt call his name Jesus. He shall be great, and
shall be called the Son of the Most High; and the Lord God will
give him the throne of David his father, and he shall be king over
the house of Jacob forever; and of his kingdom there shall be no
end."

But Mary said to the angel, "How shall this happen, since I do
not know man?"

And the angel answered and said to her, "The Holy Spirit shall
come upon thee and the power of the Most High shall overshadow
thee; and therefore the holy [child] to be born shall be called the
Son of God. And behold, Elizabeth thy kinswoman also has conceived
a son in her old age, and she who was called barren is now in her
sixth month; for nothing shall be impossible with God."

But Mary said, "Behold the handmaid of the Lord; be it done
to me according to thy word." And the angel departed from her
(Luke 1:26-38).

Few passages in Scripture bear a heavier load of divine revelation.
Luke has a unique manner, distinguished by a high degree of intellectual finesse, of bringing out the divinity of Christ, the action
of the Holy Spirit, and the virginity of Mary. But although these
different elements present an array of theological riches, they are
not the object of our present study. What directly concerns us,
and to which we shall devote all our attention, is the ecclesial dimension of the mystery of Mary.

¹ Mary was actually the first and, at times, the only witness to the recounted facts; hence she is, directly or indirectly, the first source of Luke 1:5–2:52. Moreover, Luke has followed up all things carefully (ἀκριβῶς) from the very first (Luke 1:3); he has had access to the Hebrew (or Aramaic) account and has translated it in accordance with the vocabulary and spirit of the Septuagint, underlining his favorite themes in the process.

² The word *midrash* has the root meaning "to seek out or investigate." On the midrashic genre, see A. Robert, "The Literary Genres," in Robert and Tricot (eds.), *Guide to the Bible*, 2nd ed. (Paris: Desclée, 1960), pp. 505–509. (Paris, 1954), pp. 305–309. On Luke's use of the midrashic genre, see R. Laurentin, *Structure et Théologie de Luc I–II* (Paris, 1957), pp. 96ff.

³ Cf. Matthew 1:22; 2:15.

⁴ With the exception of Luke 2:22-24, where it is a question of "the Law of Moses" and "the Law of the Lord," all the other citations are incorporated into the structure of the narrative.

⁵ "Mary kept in mind all these things, pondering them in her heart" (Luke 2:19). The verb "to ponder" is a translation of the Greek συμβάλλειν, meaning literally "to throw together," hence to collect and meditate upon; "word" is a translation of the Greek ῥῆμα, in turn a translation of the Hebrew *dabar*, meaning both "word" and "thing."

Translator's note: This is the personal translation of the author. See p. 54.

Chapter 5

JOY BE TO THEE

And coming in to her, [the angel] said:
"Joy be to thee, full of grace!" (Luke 1:28).

In the translation that we are proposing, we have chosen the formula "Joy be to thee" to convey the meaning of the Greek χαῖρε, which the Vulgate translates by *Ave*, and the majority of translations simply by "Hail."

Literally, χαῖρε really does mean "Joy be to thee," or, also, "Rejoice." But in common speech the formula had lost its pristine color and was simply the equivalent of our "Good morning" or "Good afternoon." Such is the fate that befalls all words of very frequent usage: they are employed and depersonalized to the point where they lose their literal meaning. This is true in the case of the Greek χαῖρε as we find it in the Gospels when Greek is the native language of the person speaking (Mark 15:18; Matthew 27:29; John 19:3); in these instances it is only a casual salutation. But when a Semite is speaking, the Gospel text ordinarily has εἰρήνη, i. e., "Peace" (John 20:19, 21; Luke 24:36).

In the context of the Annunciation, however, we think that the full literal meaning of the expression should be restored by translating it as "Joy be to thee!" In the Septuagint, χαῖρε is employed four times — Soph. 3:14; Joel 2:21; Zach. 9:9; Lam. 4:21. If exception is made for the last of these instances, where it occurs within an ironic apostrophe referring to Edom, the χαῖρε of the Septuagint regularly corresponds to the announcement of the joy of the messianic era. The same is true in the case of the Annunciation.

Various prophecies appear to have been used by Luke as the biblical foundation upon which he has built his own narrative.

1) The most important is that of Sophonias.[1] Sophonias is the prophet of the "Day of the Lord": "A day of wrath is that day, a day of anguish and distress, a day of destruction and desolation, a day of darkness and gloom" (Soph. 1:15), "the day of the Lord's wrath, when in the fire of his jealousy all the earth shall be consumed" (Soph. 1:18). One hope remains, however — that of conversion and repentance — and the prophet entreats his people: "O nation without shame . . . Seek the Lord, all you humble of the earth" (Soph. 2:1, 3).

This is why the Day of the Lord is not solely a proclamation of terror and destruction; it is also an announcement that "the remnant of Israel," "a people humble and lowly" (Soph. 3:12-13), will in their love for Yahweh seek and find him. It is precisely this image, that of a day all-radiant with joy, resplendent in the sun of God's presence in the midst of his people, that Sophonias evokes as the conclusion to his message:

> Shout for joy, O Daughter of Sion! sing joyfully, O Israel! Be glad and exult with all your heart, O Daughter of Jerusalem! The Lord has removed the judgment against you, he has turned away your enemies; the King of Israel, the Lord, is in your midst, you have no further misfortune to fear. On that day, it shall be said to Jerusalem: Fear not, O Sion, be not discouraged! The Lord, your God, is in your womb*, a mighty savior; he will rejoice over you with gladness, and renew you in his love, he will sing joyfully because of you, as one sings at festivals (Soph. 3:14-18).

The following points can be singled out for special attention:

a) The message is addressed to the "Daughter of Sion," the "Daughter of Jerusalem." Ever since the time of Osee, Yahweh's covenant with his people has been presented as a marriage covenant: the Daughter of Sion, the personification of Israel, is the bride of Yahweh. No other image could convey more forcefully, or with deeper tenderness, the truth that Yahweh's relationship with Israel is not simply a juridical relationship, but a relationship of love. With the help of this imagery, sin can be seen to consist primarily, not in unfaithfulness to a law or prescription, but in unfaithfulness to love. Israel belongs totally to her God as a woman to her husband. In the New Testament this marriage symbolism will reach its full flowering in the image of the Church as the chaste virgin who is betrothed to Christ (2 Cor. 11:2).

b) The joy to which the Daughter of Sion is invited is brought by the coming and the presence of Yahweh: he is "in her midst," he is "in her womb."

c) He is coming to the Daughter of Sion to renew her in his love and to save her.

d) Finally, we have the affirmation of God's royal sovereignty over Sion: "the King of Israel, the Lord, is in your midst."

These are exactly the same points that Luke will take up in the Annunciation message. The parallelism between the "annunciation" to the Daughter of Sion and the "annunciation" to Mary could be shown as follows:

Sophonias 3:14-18	*Luke 1:28-33*
Be glad	Rejoice
Daughter of Sion	Full of grace
the Lord is in your midst	the Lord is with thee
Fear not, O Sion	Do not be afraid, Mary
The Lord, your God, is in your womb	thou shalt conceive in thy womb
a mighty savior	Jesus (i.e., Savior)
the King of Israel, the Lord	he shall be king . . .

Our admiration cannot pay adequate tribute to the extraordinary concordance between the prophecy to the Daughter of Sion and its fulfillment in the Virgin of the Annunciation. The two choirs, that of the Old and that of the New Testament, combine their harmonies to form a symphonic orchestration of the very mystery of the Church; here this symphony reaches one of its climactic heights. Gabriel's message takes up nearly word for word the prophecy of Sophonias: in the Virgin of the Annunciation we are shown the daughter of Sion whom Yahweh is renewing in his love. Mary is the representative of the "tiny remnant" of Israel, that chosen few of the true Israel who have never broken their fidelity to God, and to whom God will be ever faithful in the fulfillment of his promise.

2) The cause of this exultation is the presence of Yahweh in the midst of his people. Sophonias had said: "Shout for joy, O Daughter of Sion! The Lord, your God, is in your womb." Luke will repeat this theme even more strongly: "Rejoice, full of grace, thou shalt conceive in thy womb. . . ."

The pleonasm "thou shalt conceive in thy womb" is all the more marked in view of the fact that it is not to be found in the account of the annunciation to Zachary, which is constructed on the same plan as the annunciation to Mary:

Luke 1:13	*Luke 1:31*
thy wife Elizabeth	thou shalt conceive in thy womb
shall bear thee a son	and shalt bring forth a son;
and thou shalt call his name John.	and thou shalt call his name Jesus.

It seems most likely that the addition of the words "in thy womb" is a deliberate choice — premeditated, so to speak. Yahweh, in the very name of the covenant, was understood as present *in the womb* of his people, *in the midst* of his people. The very word employed in the texts, which ordinarily we translate as "in the midst of" or "in the womb of," in its literal sense means "inner organs" (Exod. 12:9; Lev. 1:13), "heart" (1 Kings 25:37), and "maternal womb" (Gen. 25:23).[2]

In the same way, the hymn in Isaias 12 sings of the joy resulting from Yahweh's presence "in the womb" of his people: "Shout with exultation, O city of Sion, for great in your womb is the Holy One of Israel!" (Is. 12:6). This same imagery again figures in Luke's text: "Rejoice, full of grace, thou shalt conceive in thy womb the Holy One to be born [of thee]"[3] (Luke 1:28, 31, 35).

3) Zacharias 2:14 is inspired by the prophecy-source of Sophonias and issues a further invitation to the Daughter of Sion: "Sing and rejoice, O Daughter of Sion! See, I am coming to dwell in your midst,* says the Lord." The phrase "in your midst" obviously lacks the warmth of the expression "in your womb." The Septuagint gave fresh color to the text, but by employing an image which in its very richness shifted the meaning of the original: "See, I am coming and will pitch my tent in your midst." This image will be taken up by John, who in the prologue to his Gospel will write: "The Word was made flesh and pitched his tent among us"* (John 1:14).

4) This presence of God in the midst of his people will be a *saving* presence. The very name of Jesus means "Savior": ". . . thou shalt call his name Jesus; for he shall save his people from their sins" (Matthew 1:21).

Here again the Old Testament has served as a prelude to the New. In the texts from the post-exilic period, the announcement of the joy of the return from captivity was linked to the manifestation of God's salvation:

Sing out, O heavens, and rejoice, O earth, break forth into song,
you mountains. For the Lord comforts his people . . . (Is. 49:13).
All mankind shall know that I, the Lord, am your savior (Is. 49:26).

5) In this connection Psalm 97 is particularly interesting. A com-

parison between it and the Lucan text will help us to see how much the latter is seeking to re-create the spiritual atmosphere of the return from the exile — the joy of Yahweh's coming, the revelation of his salvation, the mindfulness of his love, and the proclamation of his royal sovereignty:

Psalm 97	*Luke 1–2*
Sing to the Lord a new song (v. 1)	Rejoice (1:28)
Sing joyfully to the Lord, all you lands; break into song; sing praise (v. 4)	
For he has done wondrous deeds (v. 1)	He has done great things for me (1:49)
The Lord has made his salvation known (v. 2)	(Jesus = Savior)
His right hand has won victory for him (v. 1)	He has shown might with his arm (1:51)
his holy arm (v. 1)	Holy is his name (1:49)
in the sight of the nations he has revealed his justice (v. 2)	A light of revelation to the Gentiles (2:32)
He has remembered his kindness (v. 3)	mindful of his mercy (1:54)
toward the house of Israel (v. 3)	He has given help to Israel (1:54; cf. 2:34)
the King, the Lord (v. 6)	he shall be king (1:32-33)

Our study of this parallelism should not be too forced. The spiritual content of these passages is more important than their material resemblance. It is not so much that Psalm 97 is a prophecy (in the exegetical sense of the word) of Luke 1–2; rather, it is Luke who is endeavoring to build his narrative on the various themes of the post-exilic period, showing us that Jesus is "the Lord who comes" (Ps. 97:9).

6. There is, finally, a second passage in the book of Zacharias, considerably later in date than the one cited above, which appears to have been inspired by Sophonias 3:14-18:

> Rejoice heartily, Daughter of Sion, shout for joy, Daughter of Jerusalem! See, your king shall come to you; a just savior is he (Zach. 9:9).

We know from Matthew 21:5 and John 12:15 that this text is messianic. When Jesus made his solemn entry into Jerusalem on Palm Sunday, acclaimed by the wildly cheering crowd who cried out:

> Hosanna to the Son of David! (Matthew 21:9)
> Blessed is the kingdom of our father David that comes! (Mark 11:10)

Matthew solemnly notes:

> Now this was done that what was spoken through the prophet might
> be fulfilled, *Tell the Daughter of Sion: Behold, thy king comes to
> thee.* . . (Matthew 21:4-5).

The prophecy had proved to be of such importance to the first
Christian catechesis that John, when drawing up his Gospel some
thirty years after the Greek redaction of Matthew, will consider
it necessary to include it in his, along with the following reflections
of his own:

> These things his disciples did not at first understand. But when Jesus
> was glorified, then they remembered that these things were written
> about him, and that they had done these things to him (John 12:16).

But there can be no question that it is Luke whose account sug-
gests the richest insights, for it is the one that gives full value to the
fundamental themes of the Infancy Gospel: joy, praise, the kingship
of Christ, the glory of God, peace:

> The whole company of the disciples began to rejoice ($\chi\alpha\acute{\iota}\rho o\nu\tau\epsilon\varsigma$)
> and to praise God with a loud voice for all the miracles that they
> had seen, saying, "Blessed is he who comes as king, in the name
> of the Lord! Peace in heaven, and glory in the highest!" (Luke 19:37-
> 38).

The phrase "Peace in heaven, and glory in the highest" (i.e.,
in the highest heaven) is a clear re-echoing of the song the angels
had sung in praise of God — $\alpha\grave{\iota}\nu o\acute{\upsilon}\nu\tau\omega\nu$ $\tau\grave{o}\nu$ $\Theta\epsilon\grave{o}\nu$: "Glory to God
in the highest, and peace on earth to men [who have his] good
will." [4]

---

[1] Sophonias' ministry took place in the years around 630 during the reign of Josias
(638–609). The reign of Manasses had been absolutely lamentable; "he did evil
in the sight of the Lord," with power and perversity of will (cf. 4 Kings 21:1-16).
Unhappily he ruled for more than a half-century (691–638), thus bringing the reform
of Ezechias to ruin. If his son Amon did not commit as many sins as did his father,
it was only because he was not given enough time; he died in the second year
of his reign (642–640), assassinated by his own officials. Josias his son succeeded
him, ascending the throne at the mere age of eight. It was during this disturbed
and checkered period that the word of Yahweh was addressed to Sophonias (Soph.
1:1); it had not been proclaimed for almost sixty years.

* *Translator's note:* The French phrase *en ton sein*, like the Hebrew *beqerebh*
which it translates, can be used to denote either "in your midst" or "in your womb,"
and therefore admirably lends itself to the rendering of the rich nuances of the
original Hebrew. For lack of an equivalent word in English, we have, therefore,

while reproducing the Confraternity version of the passage cited above, replaced the reading of the word "midst" with that of "womb," following the French translation in the *Bible de Jérusalem*. The text of Isaias 12:6 and the other Old Testament passages to which reference is made in these footnotes can be approached in the same manner.

² See also Deut. 6:15; 7:21; Osee 11:9; Mich. 3:11; Ps. 45:6; 1 Kings 4:3; Jer. 14:9.

³ This is almost certainly a reference to Isaias 12:6 or even to Osee 11:9 (I am the Holy One in your midst; *literally*: in your womb), which is the basis for the importance, and also the exegetical difficulties, of the passage in Luke 1:35: "the Holy One to be born [of thee] shall be called the Son of God."

⁴ Luke 2:13-14. Following certain texts and reading $εὐδοκία$ in place of $εὐδοκίας$, we could also translate this as: "Glory to God in the highest — and on earth peace — his good will towards men." This translation would be more in accord with Luke 19:38 and Luke's own theology, in which the messianic times are the times in which God bestows his $εὐδοκία$ on men. Among the studies on Luke 2:13-14, the following should be consulted: E. R. Smothers, "Ἐν ἀνθρώποις εὐδοκίας," *Rech. Sc. Rel.*, 24 (1934), pp. 86–93; U. Holzmeister, "*Pax hominibus bonae voluntatis*," *Verb. Dom.*, 18 (1938), pp. 353–361; H. T. Henry, "Men of Good Will," *Hom. Past. Rev.*, 41 (1940), pp. 241–249; C. H. Hunzinger, "Neues Licht auf Lk II, 14, 'ἄνθρωποι εὐδοκίας'," *Zeitschrift für die neut. Wissenschaft*, 44 (1952), pp. 85–90; E. Vogt, "*Pax hominibus bonae voluntatis*," *Biblica*, 34 (1953), pp. 427–429.

Chapter 6

FULL OF GRACE

"Joy be to thee full of grace" (Luke 1:28).

A. The Expression and Its Meaning

"And the virgin's name was Mary" (Luke 1:27); that was the name that men had given her. The name that God gives her has a meaning which is totally new and profound: "Joy be to thee, κεχαριτωμένη, full of grace" (Luke 1:28).

In the history of the Chosen People, God often imposes names on those whom he singles out for a special vocation. Such, for example, is the case with Abraham and his wife Sara, with Isaac, and with Israel.[1] According to Semitic custom, the name is in effect a synonym of the person who bears it.[2] When God bestows a name, he not only imposes it, but at the same time brings what it signifies to fulfillment:

> God spoke to [*Abram*] thus, "This is my covenant with you: You shall be the father of a multitude of nations; you shall no longer be called Abram, but your name shall be Abraham; for I will make you the father of a multitude of nations" (Gen. 17:3-5).

This equivalence between name and person will continue into New Testament times. Thus the expression "to baptize in the name of Christ" has the same meaning as "to baptize into Christ."[3] When we read that Jesus is "called" the Son of the Most High, the Son of God, the Word of God, and Faithful,[4] it is to signify that he really is the Son of the Most High, the Word of God, and the Faithful One.

In the annunciation to Mary, the angel Gabriel addressed the Virgin as κεχαριτωμένη. What is this word's exact meaning?

Κεχαριτωμένη is the perfect passive participle of the verb χαριτοῦν, which derives from the substantive χάρις. This word designates first of all loveliness, beauty, and all those qualities that could be expressed by the word "grace," to which the Greek spirit was so finely sensitive. Thus does the Septuagint speak of a woman as fair and charming (Nahum 3:4 — ἐπιχαρής); and Proverbs 5:19 reads: "Have joy of the wife of your youth, your lovely hind, your graceful doe."

Always careful to present his Greek readers with a Christ possessed of all that is attractive and noble, Luke does not fail to remark on the captivating power and beauty of our Lord's words: "all bore him witness, and marvelled at the words of grace that came from his mouth" (ἐπι τοῖς λόγοις τῆς χάριτος — Luke 4:22).

From this first level of meaning it is only a step to the spiritual level;[5] the Greek mind can hardly separate the beautiful from the good. In the Septuagint, χάρις occurs most frequently as the translation of the Hebrew word *hén*,[6] which is employed to designate the favor and good pleasure with which a person of distinction inclines toward someone he loves. Luke employs the word to designate the loving watchfulness of the divine favor that rested on the Child Jesus: "The child grew and became strong. He was full of wisdom and the grace (χάρις) of God was upon him" (Luke 2:40).

These expressions recur further on as a kind of refrain or *ritornello* with which to conclude all the thematic strands of Christ's childhood: "And Jesus advanced in wisdom and age and grace (χάριτι) before God and men" (Luke 2:52). The angel spoke in a similar way to Mary: "Do not be afraid, Mary, for thou hast found grace (χάριν) with God" (Luke 1:30). We can readily conjecture that the underlying meaning of the Greek is just this connotation of the Hebrew word *hén*. Moreover, the Virgin herself will take up this same idea when in her Magnificat she sings: "He has regarded the lowliness of his handmaid" (Luke 1:48).

On occasion Luke expands the connotation of χάρις to include the totality of the gifts of the redemption (Acts 11:23; 13:43; 15:11) In these instances the author of Acts clearly shows the influence of his master, Paul. It is precisely the verb χαριτοῦν that we find in the hymn forming the introduction to the letter to the Ephesians:

> Such was the good pleasure of the Father's will, *
> unto the praise of the glory of his grace,
> with which he has *favored* us in his beloved Son.
> In him we have redemption through his blood . . . (Eph. 1:5-7).

This agreement between the vocabularies of Paul and of Luke is even more easily explained in view of the fact that both the redaction of the Epistle to the Ephesians and that of Acts date from the same period, the years 62–63.

To sum up: in Luke's vocabulary χάρις means chiefly not only outward loveliness and beauty, but also the divine good pleasure and favor, and finally, in a broader sense, the totality of all God's gifts. In the narrative sections devoted to the childhood of Jesus, the word recurs three times, twice in reference to Christ and once in reference to Mary. In each of these three cases it manifestly conveys the meaning of the Hebrew word *hén* and designates the divine good pleasure and favor. We would not presume, of course, to confuse the "grace" that the Father bestows on his Son with that which he bestows on the Virgin; but neither do we, on the other hand, presume to separate the Son from his Mother.

The meaning of χαῖρε κεχαριτωμένη can thus be interpreted as "Joy be to thee, thou who art all-lovely, upon whom the divine good pleasure rests." The aptness of the Vulgate translation, *gratia plena*, is thus clearly evident. If, moreover, we bear in mind that the word "grace" has the same ambivalence of meaning as does *cháris* (beauty and good pleasure) and that the determination of all the differing accepted meanings of the Greek word is a highly speculative undertaking, we shall even more readily agree that the received translation "full of grace" is a particularly happy one.

B. The New Name of the Daughter of Sion

Call her: "Not-loved," "Not-my-people":[7] such was the former name of the Daughter of Sion, the "captive daughter" (Is. 52:2), "the outcast" (Jer. 30:17), the "rebellious daughter" (Jer. 31:22). But there had also been the announcement of that day to come, when Yahweh would renew his love for his bride:

> I will espouse you to me forever; I will espouse you in right and in justice, in love and in mercy; I will espouse you in fidelity, and you shall know the Lord (Osee 2:21-22).
> I will love "Not-loved." I will say to "Not-my-people," "You are my people," and she shall say, "My God!" (Osee 2:25).

And he will give a new name to the Daughter of Sion when he comes to her as her Savior:

> Say to the Daughter of Sion, your savior comes! . . . They shall be called the holy people, the redeemed of the Lord, and you shall

be called "The-sought-after," "City-not-forsaken" * (Is. 62:11-12).
No more shall men call you "Forsaken," or your land "Desolate,"
but you shall be called "My Delight," and your land "Espoused."
For the Lord delights in you, and makes your land his spouse (Is.
62:4).

Untiringly, the prophetic message keeps returning to the name
of the new Jerusalem:

. . . you shall be called city of justice, faithful city (Is 1:26). They
shall call you "City of the Lord," "Sion of the Holy One of Israel
(Is. 60:14).

You shall call your walls "Salvation" and your gates "Praise" (Is. 60:18).

Lo, I am about to create new heavens and a new earth . . . I now
create Jerusalem "Joy" and her people "Gladness" * (Is. 65:17-18).

Jerusalem, take off your dress of mourning and of misery,
put on the beauty of the glory of God forever,
wrap the cloak of the justice of God around you,
put the diadem of the glory of the Eternal on your head:
since God means to show your splendor to every nation under heaven,
since the name God gives you forever will be:
"Peace of justice," and "The glory of God's worship" * (Bar. 5:1-4).

The name that Yahweh is to give will itself contain the complete
fulfillment of its meaning. Man can easily give a name, but this
effects no change in the person who receives it. On the contrary,
when God himself bestows a name, it is through the creative power
of his word. Through her God's love, the Daughter of Sion will
truly be "The sought-after"; sanctified by the Holy One of Israel,
she will become the "City of Justice"; when her Lord comes to
save her, she will be radiant with joy and gladness.

We would not, of course, presume to posit an absolute equivalence
between the names of the new Jerusalem and the "Joy be to thee,
full of grace" of Luke. But it remains no less true that these texts
form a sublime prelude to the name of the true Daughter of Sion,
the Virgin Mary. For when God did begin to fulfill the ancient
promises in all their plenitude, was this not precisely with the incarnation of Jesus?

C. BRIDE AND TEMPLE

We can see how easily the theme of the Daughter of Sion, the
betrothed of Yahweh, ties in with that of the Temple and the new
Jerusalem. This is not the work of mere chance. We find a parallel
in the Church of the New Testament, which is the chaste virgin

betrothed to Christ Jesus (2 Cor. 11:2), the Bride radiant with the glory of Jesus (Eph. 5:27), and also the holy Temple which is built together in Christ, into a dwelling place for God (Eph. 2:21-22).

In reality, these two themes seem to go as far back as the Book of Genesis. The Yahwist account, in fact, portrays God as fashioning — or more strictly speaking, constructing — Eve as a building:

> And the rib which the Lord God took from the man, he made into (*banah*) a woman, and brought her to him. Then the man said, "She now is bone of my bone, and flesh of my flesh; she shall be called Woman, for from man she has been taken" (Gen. 2:22-23).

It is in precisely this mystery of Adam and Eve that we see the prefiguration of the mystery of Christ and his Church, who herself is also both the Bride and the Temple of God (Eph. 5:32).

In the Canticle of Canticles, the Bridegroom unceasingly compares his Beloved to a city, i.e., to Jerusalem:

> Your neck is like David's tower girt with battlements (Cant. 4:4).
> You are as beautiful as Thersa, my beloved, as lovely as Jerusalem (Cant. 6:4).
> Your neck is like a tower of ivory. Your eyes are like the pools in Hesebon by the gate of Bath-rabbim. Your nose is like the tower on Lebanon that looks toward Damascus (Cant. 7:5).

The Beloved does not remain unmoved by the compliment; she accepts and confirms it:

> I am a wall, and my breasts represent its towers; and under his eyes I have found true peace * (Cant. 8:10).

While the Bride remains faithful to her God, she finds peace; but when she becomes an adulteress, he leads her enemies right up to her walls. It is during the siege of 588–587, at the very moment that the Assyrians were breaching the walls of Jerusalem, that the restoration is announced by Jeremias. For it is not her enemy's battering rams that have brought her walls to the ground, but Yahweh himself who has "brought grief on wall and rampart" (Lam. 2:8); and it is Yahweh, too, who in his love will rebuild his Bride:

> With age-old love I have loved you; so I have kept my mercy toward you. Again I will restore you, and you shall be rebuilt, O virgin Israel; carrying your festive tambourines, you shall go forth dancing with the merrymakers (Jer. 31:3-4).

Here is the point at which the themes of the marriage covenant and the restoration of Sion can be seen to overlap. It will be in the sufferings of the exile that the Israelites will arrive at a deeper understanding of how the eternal love whose forgiveness was unceasing would also never cease in its rebuilding of Sion: "As a young man marries a virgin, your Builder shall marry you" (Is. 62:5).

It will be in Mary that this eternal love will at last raise up the true Daughter of Sion; it will be in her who is "full of grace" that he will fill Sion with the treasures of faithfulness and justice (Is. 1:27); it is in her that he will bring to fulfillment the prophecy of the Canticle of Canticles:

> You are as beautiful, . . . my beloved, . . . as Jerusalem (Cant. 6:4),
> You are beautiful, my beloved, and there is no blemish in you (Cant. 4:7).

The mystery of Mary thus prefigures, in still another way, the mystery of the Church, the new Jerusalem, the holy City which comes down out of heaven from God, made ready as a bride adorned for her husband (Apoc. 21:2).

---

[1] Cf. Gen. 17:5, 15; 17:19; 35:10.

[2] See H. Lesètre, "Nom," *Dict. Biblique*, 4, col. 1671ff.

[3] Cf. Matthew 28:19; Acts 2:38; 19:5; Rom. 6:3; Gal. 3:27.

[4] Cf. Luke 1:32-35; Apoc. 19:11-13.

[5] The adjective καλός can likewise signify something as being either beautiful or good. The substantive καλοκαγαθία (beauty-goodness) is an excellent illustration of this tendency in Greek thought.

[6] In Genesis alone, the translation *hén-χάρις* recurs twelve times: in 6:8; 18:3; 30:27; 32:6; 33:8, 10, 15; 34:11; 39:4, 21; and 47:25, 29.

* *Translator's note*: From the French, which is a literal translation of the Greek.

[7] This is the meaning of "Lo-ruhama" and "Lo-ammi," the symbolic names that Yahweh had imposed on Osee's children (Osee 1:6-9).

* *Translator's note*: Here we are following the wording of the *Jerusalem Bible*.

* *Translator's note*: The wording of the *Jerusalem Bible*.

* *Translator's note*: The wording of the *Jerusalem Bible*.

Chapter 7

THE LORD IS WITH THEE

"Joy be to thee, full of grace, the Lord is with thee"
(Luke 1:28).

At first sight, the expression "the Lord is with thee" does not present any special difficulty, and we might be tempted to interpret it along the lines of the tract on grace: God is with the Virgin as an object of knowledge and love. Certain authors have not been able to resist this temptation; and from the dogmatic standpoint, the result of their analyses is perfectly acceptable. It is clear that in virtue of the fullness of grace flowing from the privilege of the Immaculate Conception, God is *with* the Virgin. The deficiency of this interpretation lies in the fact that it neglects to take into account the *Scriptural* use of the words *Dominus tecum*, an expression that figures prominently in the vocabulary of the Old Testament. It is impossible to grasp all the wealth of meaning that this phrase contains unless we study it within its proper biblical context.

In a carefully detailed study, Fr. U. Holzmeister has singled out all the passages which contain the expression *Dominus tecum* or its equivalents.[1] The conclusions of his investigation present themselves as follows:

1. "In all the cases we have cited, this formula is never applied to a man placed in ordinary circumstances; on the contrary it refers either to the people of God who are the object of the special divine election and protection, or — more commonly — to a particular man whom God has entrusted with a mission of singular importance. . . ."

2. "By the preposition 'with' is affirmed a certain mode of the divine presence: and a presence which is by no means inoperative,

but active and oriented toward the work that the man in question is called upon to accomplish." [2]

Formulated in different terms, the expression clearly pertains to the very mystery of the Church; it denotes not so much God's presence in the individual faithful as it does his guiding presence in the midst of the covenant community; and it also signifies the assistance given by God to the individual man of faith whom he deputes to accomplish a work directed toward the welfare of the Chosen People taken as a whole.

Let us go on to examine the texts that bear most closely on the study of the *Dominus tecum* in Luke 1:28.

A. THE VOCATION OF SERVANT TO THE PEOPLE OF THE COVENANT

First of all we are confronted with the examples of vocations that involve a special calling, such as that of Moses. We know the subterfuges to which Moses resorted, and the reticence with which he finally accepted the mission that Yahweh was imposing on him: "Moses, however, said to the Lord, 'If you please, Lord, I have never been eloquent, neither in the past, nor recently, nor now that you have spoken to your servant; but I am slow of speech and tongue. . . . If you please, Lord, send someone else!" (Exod. 4:10, 13). When in the end he does accept it, it is because God has conferred a miraculous power on him and assured him of his presence: "I will be with you; and this shall be your proof that it is I who have sent you" (Exod. 3:12).

The calling of Jeremias is also a case in point. It is he, Jeremias, the most gentle of all the prophets and a true son of his race whom he loved with all the tenderness of his sensitive heart, that God chooses for a "prophet to the nations." Jeremias tried to evade these demands: "Ah, Lord God! I know not how to speak; I am too young." But Yahweh confirms him in his mission: "Say not, 'I am too young.' To whomever I send you, you shall go; whatever I command you, you shall speak. Have no fear before them, because I am with you to deliver you" (Jer. 1:6-8).

These examples indicate the context for the interpretation of the *Dominus tecum*: If God is "with" Isaac (Gen. 26:3, 24), with Jacob (Gen. 31:3), with Moses, with Josue (Jos. 1:5, 9; 3:7), with David (2 Kings 7:9), with Jeroboam (3 Kings 11:38), with Jeremias, it is not solely as their God, the Holy One who makes them holy. He is "with" Isaac, Jacob, Moses, Josue, David, Jeroboam, Jermias and Mary herself because of their mission as servants of God's people. Hence the *Dominus tecum* tells not so much "the story of a soul" as the story of a soul who is a servant of the Israel of God. With the very opening words of his message, Gabriel makes known to the Virgin that she is chosen for a special vocation, a mission whose fullness will embrace the entire people of God.

B. THE COVENANT WITH ABRAHAM

The *Dominus tecum* occurs with particular frequency in Genesis, where it is bound up with the covenant made with Abraham (cf. Gen. 26:3; 46:3). In the theophany at Bersabee, Yahweh spoke these words to Isaac: "I am the God of your father Abraham; fear not, for I am with you. I will bless you and multiply your descendants for the sake of my servant Abraham" (Gen. 26:24). Already this passage is a foreshadowing of Luke's narrative:

Genesis 36	Luke 1
Fear not (v. 24)	Do not be afraid, Mary (V. 30)
For I am with you (v. 24)	The Lord is with thee (v. 28)
I will bless you . . . for the sake of my servant Abraham (v. 24)	to Abraham and to his posterity forever (v. 55)

The story of Jacob at Bethel follows the same pattern.[3] Jacob had left Bersabee to return to Haran, his brother Esau having uttered against him the terrible threat: "The time of mourning for my father is coming; then I will kill my brother Jacob" (Gen. 27:41). In his headlong flight, Jacob spent the night under the stars. He has a wondrous dream: a ladder, reaching down to earth from heaven, with angels upon it in continuous ascent and descent. He hears strange words:

> I am the Lord, the God of Abraham your father, and the God of Isaac. I will give you and your descendants the land on which you lie. They shall be as the dust of the earth. You shall spread abroad to the west, to the east, to the north, and to the south; in you and in your descendants, all the nations of the earth shall be blessed. I will be with you and protect you wherever you go. I will bring you back to this land; indeed I will not forsake you till I fulfill my promise (Gen. 28:13-15).

Jacob is overcome with awe at what has happened to him: "This is none other than the house of God; this is the gate of heaven" (Gen. 28:17). He knows that the divine covenant made with Abraham now rests upon his shoulders, that Yahweh is with him to bring all the promises to their fulfillment. In the New Testament we shall be shown the fulfillment of the true Bethel: "Amen, amen, I say to you, you shall see heaven opened, and the angels of God ascending and descending upon the Son of Man" (John 1:51). God's true dwelling-place among men is Christ himself. Mary will see brought to fulfillment in her the promises that had been made to Isaac and to Jacob. The theophanies of Bersabee and Bethel are the prelude to the theophany of the Annunciation.

C. IN THE BOOK OF DEUTERONOMY

In its Deuteronomic context, the expression "I am with you" is readily evocative of the divine protection with which Yahweh was sustaining his people throughout the numerous battles they were waging against their turbulent neighbors. Israel's wars — and her victories — are also God's.

> When you go out to war against your enemies and you see horses and chariots and an army greater than your own, do not be afraid of them, for the Lord, your God, who brought you up from the land of Egypt, will be with you. When you are about to go into battle, the priest shall come forward and say to the soldiers: "Hear, O Israel! Today you are going into battle against your enemies. Be not weakhearted or afraid; be neither alarmed nor frightened by them. For it is the Lord, your God, who goes with you to fight for you against your enemies and to save * you" (Deut. 20:1-4).

The accounts in the Book of Judges, which paint the strategy of this holy war in such bright colors, are real tales of the people. When Yahweh is with his people, victory is certain; when Yahweh abandons his people, there is slaughter. The number of men fighting matters little; in fact, it must not be raised too high: "The Lord said to Gedeon, 'You have too many soldiers with you for me to deliver Madian into their power, lest Israel vaunt itself against me and say, "My own power brought me the victory" ' " (Judg. 7:2). And when Gedeon was left with no more than some three hundred soldiers, then it was that his army was close to victory, for God had said: "I shall be with you, and you will cut down Madian to the last man" (Judg. 6:16).

In this perspective it will be helpful to review Psalm 45 (undoubtedly composed at the time of the victory over Sennacherib [4] in 701), which celebrates the reality of Yahweh's presence in the midst of Sion, the holy city; she cannot be disturbed, for God is inside

her! (v. 6). How joyful is the psalm's rhythmic refrain to this ode
of triumph, as it rings out like a battle cry: "The Lord of hosts
is with us; our stronghold is the God of Jacob!"

> God is our refuge and our strength,
>   an ever-present help in distress.
> Therefore we fear not, though the earth be shaken,
>   and mountains plunge into the depths of the sea;
> Though its waters rage and foam
>   and the mountains quake at its surging.
> The Lord of hosts is with us;
>   our stronghold is the God of Jacob.
> There is a stream whose runlets gladden
>   the city of God,
>   the holy dwelling of the Most High.
> God is in its midst; it shall not be disturbed;
>   God will help it at the break of dawn.
> Though nations are in turmoil, kingdoms totter,
>   his voice resounds, the earth melts away.
> The Lord of hosts is with us;
>   our stronghold is the God of Jacob.
> Come! Behold the deeds of the Lord,
>   the astounding things he has wrought on earth:
> He has stopped wars to the end of the earth:
>   the bow he breaks; he splinters the spears;
>   he burns the shields with fire.
> Desist! and confess that I am God,
>   exalted among the nations, exalted upon the earth.
> The Lord of hosts is with us;
>   our stronghold is the God of Jacob [5] (Ps. 45).

There can be no question that a whole new dimension of St.
Luke's *Dominus tecum* opens up when we see the richness of these
affinities between the two texts. The very color and historical meaning of this biblical passage places the Virgin, if we may venture
the expression, on the open battlefield. If the Lord is with her,
it is not simply by reason of a personal indwelling as an object
of knowledge and love; the horizon that opens out before her has
a vastness of another dimension entirely. She appears as entering
into direct combat with the enemies of Yahweh, a contest that will
be brought to an end with the victory of God the Savior. The parallel
with the text of Deuteronomy is particularly illuminating:

Deuteronomy 20:1-4	*Luke 1:28-31*
Do not be afraid	Do not be afraid, Mary
Be not afraid	
The Lord, your God, will be with you	The Lord is with thee

The Lord, your God, goes with you
To save you.   (Thou shalt bring forth)
                                Jesus (= Savior).

Such is the profound harmony between the two Testaments: just as Yahweh is with his people to save them from their enemies, so likewise is the Lord with Mary to save his people from their sins. The text of Deuteronomy is not, to be sure, a Marian prophecy, but it does permit us to grasp the unity and the continuity between the two Testaments.

Here it should be pointed out that the Emmanuel prophecy, which Matthew explicitly refers to Mary (Matthew 1:23), is set in precisely the same perspective: "The maiden is with child and will soon give birth to a son, and shall name him Emmanuel" (Is. 7:14), that is to say, "God with us." It is possible that Catholic exegesis has let itself become unduly absorbed in the problem of the virginity of the "maiden"; proof had to be furnished to support a dogma, that of Mary's virginity. The real context of Isaias is in fact quite different. In the time of Achaz, the kings Rasin and Phacee were advancing on Jerusalem to take the city of David. "The heart of the king and the heart of the people trembled, as the trees of the forest tremble in the wind" (Is. 7:2). Yahweh intervenes and sends Isaias to Achaz: the king is to have no fear of Rasin and Phacee, "these two stumps of smoldering brands" (Is. 7:4); but: "Unless your faith is firm you shall not be firm!" (Is. 7:9).

It is at this juncture that the Emmanuel prophecy intervenes. The immediate import of the sign is its announcement that the continuity of the dynasty will not be broken, thanks to Ezechias, Achaz' son, and that the city will be spared: ". . . for 'With us is God!' " (Is. 8:10). The name Emmanuel that will be given to the child will signify this presence of God among his people and the protection that will defend them against the enemy nations:

> Know, O peoples, and be appalled! Give ear, all you distant lands! Arm, but be crushed! Arm, but be crushed! Form a plan, and it shall be thwarted; make a resolve, and it shall not be carried out, for "With us is God!" [6] (Is. 8:9-10).

Emmanuel thus appears simultaneously as a battle cry and a cry of faith: God is with his people, but on the condition that this people be with God. They must renounce all assistance from outside powers, their alliance with Egypt — in short, all human resources that hold out a promise of safety — and rely on God alone. The salvation of the House of David lies neither in warriors nor in chariots nor in horses, but solely in faith in Yahweh who is with his people.

Beyond these immediate historical events, the Emmanuel prophecy and the oracles which follow (particularly chapters 9 and 11) afford a future glimpse of a definitive intervention on God's part in the interests of the messianic kingdom. It is this intervention that Matthew sees fulfilled in the birth of the Lord when he cites the following passage from the Septuagint translation: "Behold, the virgin shall be with child, and shall bring forth a son, and they shall call his name *Emmanuel*, which is, interpreted, 'God with us'" (Matthew 1:23).

D. In the Exilic Literature

In the literature of the exile and the post-exilic period, the formula "I will be with you" makes a quite natural reappearance in conjunction with the great themes of the return and the restoration. There is, for instance, Jeremias' prophecy in the Book of Consolation:[7]

> But you, my servant Jacob, fear not, says the Lord, be not dismayed, O Israel! Behold, I will deliver you from the far-off land, your descendants, from their land of exile; Jacob shall again find rest, shall be tranquil and undisturbed, for I am with you, says the Lord, to deliver you (Jer. 30:10-11).

The Book of Consolation in Isaias will take up these same themes, at times in identical terms. It is readily evident that the expression "Fear not, I am with you" is an integral element in the literature of the Return:

> But you, Israel, my servant, Jacob, whom I have chosen, offspring of Abraham my friend — (Is. 41:8)
>
> . . . fear not, I am with you; be not dismayed; I am your God. I will strengthen you, and help you, and uphold you with my right hand of justice (Is. 41:10).
>
> For I am the Lord, your God, who grasp your right hand; it is I who say to you, "Fear not, I will help you." Fear not, O worm Jacob, O maggot Israel; I will help you, says the Lord; your redeemer is the Holy One of Israel (Is. 41:13-14).

And further on:

> But now, thus says the Lord, who created you, O Jacob, and formed you, O Israel: Fear not, for I have redeemed you; I have called you by name: you are mine. When you pass through the water, I will be with you; in the rivers you shall not drown. When you

walk through fire, you shall not be burned; the flames shall not con-
sume you. For I am the Lord, your God, the Holy One of Israel,
your savior. . . . Because you are precious in my eyes and glorious,
and because I love you, I give men in return for you and peoples
in exchange for your life. Fear not, for I am with you (Is. 43:1-5).

All these texts widen the dimensions of the interpretation of the
Dominus tecum of Luke. They close the door to a narrower interpretation which would see Mary only as the favored one whom special
grace has set apart; they open the way for an exegesis oriented
toward the identification of Mary with the Church. The grace-favored
one — this Mary is indeed, but to such a degree that the promise
"I will be with you" which God had in the past made to all his
people is now brought to fulfillment in the Virgin herself, who
alone not only stands in the place of this people, but embraces
them in their totality within the fullness of her own person.

E. Judith

There will be even further evidence to support this conclusion
if we take into consideration the fact that, outside of the case of
the Annunciation, the *Dominus tecum* was never addressed to a
woman. The only exception that we should take into account is
that found in the Book of Judith. As the young woman is leaving
the town of Bethulia to go to Holofernes, Ozias, "the prince of
Juda," says to her: "Go in peace, and the Lord be with thee[8] to
take revenge of our enemies" (Judith 8:34).

But this text has a special meaning. The story of Judith represents
the very history of the Jewish nation, who with the favor of divine
protection is victorious over all its traditional enemies.[9]

F. In the New Testament

If we would set Luke's *Dominus tecum* in the perspective of
the New Testament, we should be open to seeing its connection
with the Pauline teaching of God's indwelling in his Church:

You are the temple of the living God, as God says, *I will dwell
and move among them, I will be their God and they shall be my
people* (2 Cor. 6:16).

and also its connection with the Johannine theme of the new
Jerusalem:

And I saw the holy city, New Jerusalem, coming down out of heaven from God, made ready as a bride adorned for her husband. And I heard a loud voice from the throne saying, "Behold the dwelling of God with men, and he will dwell with them. And they will be his people, and God himself will be with them as their God" (Apoc. 21:2-3).

Before his ascension, Christ had promised to remain with his Church until his return (Matthew 28:20); here, at the Annunciation, Mary personally receives what belongs to the Church as a whole. So is the mystery of the Emmanuel, God-with-us, continued in Mary and in the Church.

[1] "Dominus tecum," *Verb. Dom.*, 23 (1943), pp. 232—237; 257–262. This study takes up and develops an article that Fr. Holzmeister had already presented in the same periodical: 8 (1928), pp. 363–369.

[2] *Op. cit.*, pp. 259–260.

[3] Gen. 28:10-19. In reality the Genesis narrative seems to be a fusion of two distinct narratives: that of the dream (Elohist tradition: vv. 10-12, 17-18, 20-22) and that of God's promise (Yahwist tradition: vv. 13-16).

[4] "The angel of the Lord went forth and struck down one hundred and eighty-five thousand in the Assyrian camp. Early the next morning, there they were, all the corpses of the dead" (Is. 37:36; cf. 4 Kings 19:35-36).

* *Translator's note*: the translation "save" is used in the *Jerusalem Bible*.

[5] Verse 6: "The Lord is in her womb" is a retouching to reproduce the image of the Hebrew text. On this subject see what we have said above, pp. 56–58.

[6] For the historical setting of the Book of the Emmanuel, see J. Steinmann, "Le Prophète Isaïe. Sa vie, son oeuvre et son temps," *Lectio Divina*, 5 (Paris, 1950)., pp. 81ff.

[7] The Book of Consolation of Jeremias (Jer. 30:1–31:32) was written between the reform and the death of Josias. The announcement of the return concerned the deportees of the North (Samaria, captured in 721). After the capture of Jerusalem, some further additions to the text of the Book extended the promise of the return to Juda as well.

[8] Literally, "The Lord God [is] before thee," ἔμπροσθέν σου.

[9] Certain commentators are averse to viewing the Book of Judith as a simple historical fiction; but the historical and geographical data are of such inconsistency, and the resemblances to the apocalypses are so profound, that it must readily be admitted that we are dealing with "an edifying narrative, freely composed with the careful intent to detach attention from a precise historical context in order to center it entirely on the lesson of the religious drama and its denouement." Barucq, "Judith," *Bible de Jérusalem* (Paris, 1952), Introduction, p. 14. "The disparate elements which in this narrative merge into a common flow serve to bring out the purpose of the author. He has made no pretensions to writing a history. . . . We are not to suppose that the inspired writers and their readers are more naive than other people. . . . We lack a term to designate this literary genre that has not counterpart in our own literature. What the apocalypses proclaim in prophetic language, our author conveys in the simple style of a narrative." A. Le Fèvre, "Judith," *Dictionnaire de la Bible Suppl.*, 4 (1949), col. 1319–1320; by the same author, "Judith," *Introduction to the Old Testament* (Robert-Feuillet, New York, 1968), pp. 520ff. See also J. Steinmann, *Lecture de Judith* (Paris, 1953); L. Soubigou, *La Sainte Bible*, 4 (1949), pp. 481ff.; A. Miller, *Das Buch Judith* (Bonn, 1940).

Chapter 8

THE TEMPLE OF GOD'S GLORY

"The holy Spirit shall come upon thee,
and the power of the Most High shall overshadow thee"
(Luke 1:35).

Luke is fond of associating the concepts of spirit and power. Thus in 1:17 he writes that John "shall himself go before him in the spirit and power of Elias"; in 4:14 he shows us Jesus returning into Galilee "in the power of the spirit"; in Acts 10:38 Peter says that Jesus "was anointed with spirit and with power." This last text, moreover, bears considerable affinity to Luke 1:35; the word "spirit" should not be placed in a Trinitarian context, but rather should be understood as signifying the life-giving breath of God. From the very outset, in virtue of the parallelism of the two phrases:

> The holy Spirit shall come upon thee,
> and the power of the Most High shall overshadow thee,

it seems that the level of meaning of the expression "holy Spirit" is not higher than that of the word "power." This lesser signification likewise would impose a new interpretation on the succeeding lines of the text: ". . . therefore the holy [child] to be born of thee shall be called the son of God." Jesus would be holy in the same way that the prophets were holy (cf. Luke 1:70), and his divine sonship would be only an adoptive sonship.

If we confine our consideration to verse 35, this exegesis would impose itself as the surest. Luke would have been employing terms which, taken in themselves, do not implicate the divine transcendence, but simply provide other modes for our understanding of it. This interpretation would not affect the dogma of the virginal conception, since, viewed from any angle, the conception of Jesus is the work of God. But it would place the dogma of Christ's divinity in jeopardy, for Jesus would no longer appear to be the Son of God, but only a son of God.[1] It is precisely here that this interpretation is at variance with all the rest of Luke's Gospel,[2] and even with the immediate context of the Annunciation itself;[3] it is then, inadmissible.

It may be, however, that the central message of the narrative does not hinge upon the meaning of the words "spirit" and "power," as we shall see from a more minute analysis.

A. The Power of the Most High Shall Overshadow Thee

In the phrase "The power of the Most High shall overshadow thee," the verb ἐπισκιαζειν can aptly be translated as "to cover with one's shadow" or "to overshadow." Thus Luke relates in Acts how the Apostles were working such prodigies that the sick were being carried into the streets "that, when Peter passed, his shadow might cover (ἐπισκιάσῃ) one of them" (Acts 5:15). Outside of this passage and the Annunciation narrative, Luke employs this verb only once — in the account of the Transfiguration. While the Apostles are witnesses to the glory of Jesus (Luke 9:32) and hear the Father's voice: "This is my beloved Son," the luminous cloud comes and overshadows them (ἐπεσκίαζεν, Luke 9:34).

In the Septuagint vocabulary the verb recurs four times: twice in the psalms, once in Exodus 40:35, and once in Proverbs 18:11 (this last passage, inasmuch as it has no bearing on our study, will not be considered here). In the psalms, the verb denotes the divine protection with which Yahweh surrounds the man of faith: "Lord, Lord, strength of my salvation, you have covered my head (ἐπεσκίασας) in the day of battle" (Ps. 139:8, as in the Septuagint). Psalm 90 holds a special interest for us, since we not only know that the New Testament utilizes it in a messianic context,[4] but find again in it the *Dominus tecum* with which we have already become familiar:

> You who dwell in the shelter of the Most High,
>   who abide in the shadow of the Almighty,
> Say to the Lord, "My refuge and my fortress,
>   my God, in whom I trust."
> With his pinions he will cover you (ἐπισκιάσει),
>   and under his wings you shall take refuge.

He shall call upon me, and I will answer him;
I will be with him in distress (Ps 90:1-2, 4, 15, as in the Septuagint).

The verb ἐπισκιάζειν appears in its specific technical sense in Exodus 40:35, where it is employed to describe the luminous cloud that overshadowed the Meeting Tent: "Moses could not enter the Meeting Tent, because the cloud settled down upon it and the glory of the Lord filled the Dwelling" [5] (Exod. 40:35). In this passage, the verb ἐπισκιάζειν translates the Hebrew *shakan*, a technical term designating the dwelling of God among men.

To conclude: we find the verb ἐπισκιάζειν twice in the Psalter, to signify the divine protection, once in the Book of Exodus as the translation of the verb "to indwell," and once in the Gospel account of the Transfiguration theophany.[6] In these last two cases the verb is associated with the luminous cloud and the glory of God. The text of John's prologue can be seen to harmonize with this schema: "The Word was made flesh, he pitched his tent among us,* and we saw his glory, the glory that is his as the only Son of the Father, full of grace and truth" (John 1:14).

If we recall that in Johannine symbolism Christ is the new Temple, the place of meeting between man and God, and bear in mind that the verb ἐπισκιάζειν is the technical term used to signify this divine presence, the following parallel will emerge:

John 1:14	Luke 9:32-35
The Word was made flesh	there came a cloud and
he pitched his tent among us	overshadowed them (v. 34)
and we saw his glory	they saw his glory (v. 32)
the glory that is his as the only Son of the Father	This is my beloved Son (v. 35)

Although we should not exaggerate the importance of such concordances, neither may we fail to take them into account, for in any case they do furnish an attractive basis on which we can place Luke's passage "the power of the Most High shall overshadow thee" in an Old Testament perspective of rather broad dimensions.

The glory of Yahweh (ἡ δόξα κυρίου) is manifested for the first time to the desert Church after its deliverance from servitude in Egypt and its passage through the Red Sea: ". . . lo, the glory of the Lord appeared in the cloud!" [7] (Exod. 16:10). It made a subsequent appearance at Sinai when Yahweh made his covenant with his people: ". . . a cloud covered the mountain. The glory of the Lord settled upon Mount Sinai" (Exod. 24:16). It also filled the

Meeting Tent (Lev. 9:6, 23; Num. 14:10), where Moses was holding familiar conversation with God. At a much later date in history, when Solomon had the ark of the covenant and the Meeting Tent brought into the Temple which he had built, God took possession of the sanctuary:

> . . . a cloud filled the house of the Lord . . . the glory of the Lord had filled the house of the Lord. Then Solomon said: The Lord said that he would dwell in a cloud. Building I have built a house for thy dwelling, to be thy most firm throne forever (3 Kings 8:10-13).

B. The New Temple

The "eternity" of Solomon's Temple will in fact last only four centuries. In 587 the Assyrian armies will lay siege to Jerusalem, and Sion's walls will give way to their battering rams; the Temple in all its fabled splendor will be looted, torn down, and burned. But in their hearts the exiles, although deported to Babylon, will continue to cherish their hopes for a Sion renewed in all her splendor. Aggeus must have found a ready audience when he foretold that in its splendor the new Temple would surpass that of Solomon's:

> I am with you, says the Lord of hosts . . . and my Spirit continues in your midst; do not fear (Aggeus 2:4-5).
>
> Greater will be the future glory of this house than the former, says the Lord of hosts; and in this place I will give peace, says the Lord of hosts! [8] (Aggeus 2:8-9).

The prophet's solemn affirmation is fulfilled to the letter on the day of the Annunciation. As the Virgin welcomes into her womb him who is the substantial glory of the Father's splendor (Heb. 1:3), she becomes the Temple of the New Covenant that is filled with the divine glory:

Aggeus 2	*Luke 1*
I am with you, says the Lord of hosts (v. 4)	the angel said (to Mary), ". . . the Lord is with thee" (v. 28)
do not fear (v. 5)	"Do not be afraid"
my Spirit continues in your midst (v. 5)	"The holy Spirit shall come upon thee" (v. 35)
I will fill this house with glory (v. 7).	". . . the power of the Most High shall overshadow thee" (v. 35).

We shall find these same themes in Isaias 35, the song of the exiles' return. The return to Sion will be like a new Exodus, when Yahweh's glory will shine in new splendor on the caravan of the redeemed; new flowers will bloom in the desert, that desert in which God had sealed his covenant and given his love to "Not Loved" (Osee 1:25); he will come to save his people:

> The desert and the parched land will exult;
>   the steppe will rejoice and bloom.
> They will bloom with abundant flowers,
>   and rejoice with joyful song.
> The glory of Lebanon will be given to them,
>   the splendor of Carmel and Saron;
> They will see the glory of the Lord,
>   the splendor of our God.
> Strengthen the hands that are feeble,
>   make firm the knees that are weak,
> Say to those whose hearts are frightened:
>   Be strong, fear not!
> Here is your God,
>   he comes with vindication;
> With divine recompense
>   he comes to save you.
>
> Those whom the Lord has ransomed
>   will return and enter Sion singing,
>   crowned with everlasting joy;
> They will meet with joy and gladness,
>   sorrow and mourning will flee (Is. 35:1-4, 10).

The extraordinary lyricism of this poem makes us even more sensitively aware of the ideas that underlie the Annunciation message. The theme of joy, introduced by Luke's "Rejoice," here is developed to grandiose proportions and painted in dazzling colors. The presence of Yahweh's glory, which is delicately woven into the fabric of Luke's text, is described in language that evokes the epic-event of the Exodus; even the name of Jesus-Savior is paraphrased by "he comes to save you." Gabriel's message, it is true, is less lyric in character than Isaias', but the fundamental realities are the same. It opens us to the perception that Mary, the Daughter of Sion, is a participant, and in a very intense way, in the glory of the theophanies of the past, that she is the new Jerusalem, radiant with the splendor of the divine light.

Does Mary, at the time she receives the angel's invitation to joy and his announcement that she is filled with the fullness of the divine favor and covered by the shadow of the power of the Most High, comprehend the extraordinary dimension of her supernatural vocation? Is she aware of the ecclesial dimension of the mystery that is being wrought within her? This much, at least, is certain: she does know that she is blessed among all women; and she recognizes herself as the one whom all nations will call "blessed:" ". . . behold, henceforth all generations shall call me blessed" (Luke 1:48).

Our thoughts can only turn to this prophecy from the Book of Isaias: "I will make you the pride of the ages, a joy to generation after generation" (Is. 60:15). And this prophecy is found precisely in the poem of Isaias 60 that describes for us the brilliant resurrection of the new Jerusalem, shining with the splendor of Yahweh's glory, all lovely in God's own beauty, and the mother of countless sons and daughters:

> Rise up in splendor! Your light has come,
> the glory of the Lord shines upon you.
> See, darkness covers the earth,
> and thick clouds cover the peoples.
>
> Raise your eyes and look about;
> they all gather and come to you;
> Your sons come from afar,
> and your daughters in the arms of their nurses.
> Once you were forsaken,
> hated and unvisited,
> Now I will make you the pride of the ages,
> a joy to generation after generation.
>
> No longer shall the sun be your light by day,
> nor the brightness of the moon shine upon you at night;
> The Lord shall be your light forever,
> your God shall be your glory (Is. 60:1-2, 4, 15, 19).

C. Conclusion

As we come to the end of these notes on the Annunciation, Mary stands before us as the Daughter of Sion whom Yahweh is renewing in his love (Sophonias); the Church full of grace; the "Sought-after" of God (Isaias), enjoying the presence of God promised to the people of Abraham (Deuteronomy); the tiny remnant coming back from captivity on whom the divine light is shining (Isaias); the new Temple filled with God's glory (Aggeus). All these images serve to illumine the ecclesial aspect of our Lady's vocation: she is the personification of the Church, *the most perfect fulfillment of the most perfect Church.*

But Christ is also this Church. How can these two affirmations be brought into harmony with each other? Would Mary come to take our Lord's place? In order to arrive at a proper understanding of Luke's theme, it will be helpful here to introduce a distinction which, elementary though it may be, is nevertheless of capital importance.

The Church can be considered as the community of Christ and the redeemed. This community is presented to us under the image of God's betrothal to the Daughter of Sion:

— If we consider the Head of this community, that is to say Christ, we must on one hand affirm the absolute transcendence of the Lord; and on the other, the illuminative power of his grace. As St. Paul says, the Father has established Christ over all things, "as head over all the Church, which indeed is his body, the completion of him who fills all with all" [9] (Eph. 1:22-23).

— But if we consider the members of this community, we must affirm both their total dependence in relation to Christ, and at the same time their possession of the obediential power to receive, through the medium of this total dependence, all the plenitude of divinity.

In terms of this last consideration, Mary's condition is no different from that of the other members. She is not a feminine hypostasis of royalty reigning at the side of the one and only Lord; she is not a priestess at the side of the one and only Priest, or a new mediatrix placed at the side of the one and only Mediator; she is simply the Daughter of Sion whom Christ renews through the all-holiness of his love. [10] The exceptional nature of her vocation, indeed, entails the affirmation of her need for an exceptional grace: that she is redeemed *sublimiori modo*, in a more sublime manner. [11]

But it is precisely when we consider the other members of the Church that we see the position of absolute privilege that Mary does enjoy:

— In the singleness of her own person, she comprises the entire people of God in their expectant hope for grace; in the singleness of her own person, she represents the entire Church that is filled with the fullness of grace. She is the individual, and also the highest and most perfect, realization of all that this Church possesses, namely, the power to receive from Christ and the actualization of this power by Christ. If Luke's texts have any meaning, they can be understood only as conveying this mystery of the fullness of God, which, in the Church, exists first of all in Mary, the Daughter of Sion;

— Because it is in Mary that this mystery is consummated in

its perfect fullness, [12] it must also be added that she prefigures the imperfect condition of the other members. Thus we see that the entire Church as a whole is made holy through the coming of Jesus-the-Savior. The transformation of the mass of sinful humanity into the chaste virgin betrothed to Christ [13] — this is precisely the miracle that Christ has wrought. To use the picturesque language of St. Ambrose, the Church is pure with her impurities, *ex maculis immaculata*, [14] she is the *casta meretrix*, [15] the chaste harlot; her chastity is the chastity of Christ who dwells within her; her harlotry was her sins. But of all the members of the Church, Mary — and she alone — is perfect holiness, and in this she prefigures the Church that is all-holy; the mystery of her person thus both represents and announces that of the other members of the Church.[16]

What is the bond, in Luke's thought, which unites the mystery of the Church's holiness with the holiness of Mary's divine motherhood? In his description of Christ's incarnation in Mary, Luke turns to the Old Testament texts that contain the theme of the restoration of the Daughter of Sion; accordingly he establishes that it is precisely through the motherhood of Mary that the Church is renewed and made holy. It is in this perspective, above all others, that the predication *Mary is the Daughter of Sion* takes on an extraordinary realism. The Incarnation, in effect, was promised to the entire community of Israel; but Mary — and she alone — became the Mother of Jesus. And this motherhood was a total one, a motherhood that although rooted in the physical reality of her flesh, at the same time came to full flower in her soul.

By her flesh and blood Mary belongs to the Chosen People; she is the flower that blossomed on the rough stem of Jesse. She belongs equally by her whole soul to the people of God as she bears all their hopes within her heart, and in his mercy the Lord fulfills in her what was promised to Abraham and his posterity forever. But at the hour of the Incarnation, Mary stands alone before God's face: she alone, then, participates in the Incarnation of the Logos; she alone conceives and gives birth to the Man-God; and the other members of the Church are saved in the measure of their communion in the mystery of Jesus born of Mary.

And there is something more. In reading the angel's message as "Joy be to thee, full of grace!" we now know that at the same time we are reading our own history. The joy and grace that were announced to the Virgin are also our messianic joy and our messianic grace. Not that we have received them from Mary, as though she were their highest source; indeed, let us repeat, there is only one joy and only one grace — that which is Christ's and which comes to us from Christ (cf. John 15:11) — but it is in Mary that we receive them. She is, as it were, the receptacle of all the spiritual treasures with which the Lord has filled his Church and of which, in Mary, we come to enjoy our own share. If we are so vitally concerned with the message of the Annunciation, it is because this message was addressed to us as well, and because, with our Lady, we must also let it speak to us.

* *Translator's note*: The author here has given his personal translation of the text. See the following note.

[1] The text has "son of God" without the article; but as Laurentin notes: "The omission of the article in Luke I–II is to be imputed to the Hebraisms which ordinarily are lost in translation" (*Structure et théologie de Luc I-II, op. cit.*, p. 75). The author refers to Luke 1:25, where the word "Lord" occurs without the article.

[2] See, for example, the theophanies of the Baptism (Luke 3:21-22) and the Transfiguration (Luke 9:34-35).

[3] In the parallels between Luke's narrative and the source-texts, especially Sophonias 3 (cf. p. 56), Christ holds the place of Yahweh-Savior; this constitutes an affirmation of his divinity. Whether Mary was aware of her Son's divinity at the moment of the Incarnation is another question; on this subject see S. Lyonnet, *Le récit de l'Annonciation et la maternité divine de la sainte Vierge* (Rome : Pontifical Biblical Institute, 1954); this study is reproduced in *Ami du Clergé*, 66 (1956), pp. 33–48. R. Laurentin, *op cit.*, notes annex 1, pp. 165ff.

[4] Psalm 90:11-12 is cited in regard to the messianic temptation of Christ in Luke 4:10-11 and Matthew 4:6; this psalm was possibly (on the earliest occasion of its use) one of royal investiture.

[5] In Numbers 9:18-22 and 10:34 and in Wisdom 19:7, we find the verb $\sigma\kappa\iota\acute{\alpha}\zeta\omega$ used in the same sense.

[6] On the relationship between the Transfiguration and the divine cloud, see especially H. Riesenfeld, *Jesus Transfiguré* (Lund, 1947); the author studies the symbolism of the cloud in Chapter IX, pp. 130–145.

* *Translator's note:* "He pitched his tent among us" is the literal meaning of the Greek. For the remainder of the passage we have quoted the translation of the *Jerusalem Bible*.

[7] In the Pentateuch the column of cloud, associated with the column of fire (Yahwist tradition), the dense mist and the cloud (Elohist tradition), and the glory of Yahweh (Priestly tradition) are different manifestations of the divine presence (cf. Exod. 13:21-22; 19:9, 18; 24:16; 33:9, 10; Num. 12:5; 16:19; Deut. 31:15). Here in Exodus 16:7 the glory of Yahweh is associated with the cloud. On the meaning of the word $\delta\acute{o}\xi\alpha$ as it is employed in the Septuagint, see Kittel, "$\delta\acute{o}\xi\alpha$," *Theological Dictionary of the New Testament*, 2, pp. 242–245.

[8] Cf. also Ez. 10:3, 4; 43:1-5.

[9] P. Huby comments as follows: The Church "is the perfect receptacle of Christ's graces and gifts; she is totally filled by them, and in her they display all their divine energy" (*Épîtres de la captivité*, pp. 167–170). In the same vein see L. Cerfaux, *The Church in the Theology of St. Paul*, translated by Geoffrey

Webb and Adrian Walker (New York:Herder and Herder, 1963), pp. 321–325.

[10] From time to time Mary has been compared to a secondary head of the Church (see the texts from earlier periods gathered by P. Barré in "Marie et l'Église, De Bède à saint Albert le Grand," *Bulletin de la Société Française d'Études Mariales*, 9 (1951), pp. 92–93. In our opinion, the image is not a particularly happy choice and gives rise to a certain uneasiness; it overturns the traditional symbolism of the Church as the Body and Bride of Christ and fosters the awkward notion that there are two heads in the nuptial community of Christ and his Church, as if Christ were the Head of Mary and that Mary in turn were the Head of the Church! On this subject see the reflections of G. Roschini, *Mariologia*, 2 (Rome, 1948), pp. 352–357, and those of R. Laurentin, *Marie, l'Église et le sacerdoce*, 2 (Paris, 1953), p. 76.

[11] Pius IX, *Ineffabilis Deus*, December 8, 1854.

[12] Clearly it is here a question of the relative perfection of which a creature is capable.

[13] Here it will be suggestive to compare 1 Corinthians 6:9 with 2 Corinthians 11:2: "Fornicators, idolaters, adulterers, the effeminate, sodomites, thieves, the covetous, drunkards, the evil-tongues, the greedy" — see what the Corinthians were; "a chaste virgin," "betrothed to Christ" — and see what they have become!

[14] *In Lucam I*, 17; PL 15, 1540–1540 C.

[15] *In Lucam III*, 23; PL 15, 1598 B; CSEL 32/4, 115.

[16] Here is how St. Augustine presents these relationships: "Let us honor [the Church] because she is the bride of so great a Lord. And what shall I say? Great and unique is the condescension of her Spouse; He found her a courtesan and made her a virgin. She should not deny that she was a courtesan, lest she forget the mercy of her Liberator. How was she not a courtesan when she committed fornication in the pursuit of idols and demons? Fornication of heart was in all; of the flesh in a few, but of the heart in all. And He came and made her a virgin; He made the Church a virgin. She is a virgin in faith. He has a few nuns, virgins in the flesh; He ought to have all, women and men alike, virgins in the faith. For there chastity, purity, and holiness ought to exist.

"Do you wish to know how the Church is a virgin? Hear the Apostle Paul; hear the friend of the Bridegroom who is zealous, not for himself, but for the Bridegroom: 'I betrothed you to one spouse.' He spoke to the Church. To which Church? To all, whithersoever his letter could reach. 'I betrothed you to one spouse, that I might present you a chaste virgin to Christ. But I fear lest,' he said, 'as the serpent seduced Eve by his guile. . .' That serpent never physically defiled Eve, did he? Yet he did destroy her virginity of heart. On that account Paul said: 'I fear lest . . . your minds may be corrupted from that chastity which is in Christ.'

"Therefore, the Church is a virgin; she is a virgin, may she be a virgin. Let her beware of the deceiver, lest he turn out to be a corrupter. The Church is a virgin. Are you, perhaps, going to say to me: 'If the Church is a virgin, how does she bring forth children? Or, if she does not bring forth children, how did we give our names so that we might be born of her?' I answer: 'She is a virgin and she also brings forth children.' *She imitates Mary who gave birth to the Lord.* Did not the holy Mary bring forth her Child and remain a virgin? So, too, the Church both brings forth children and is a virgin. And if you would give some consideration to the matter, she brings forth Christ, because they who are baptized are His members. 'You are,' said the Apostle, '*the body of Christ and his members.*' If, therefore, the Church brings forth the members of Christ, *she is very like to Mary.*" — Sermon 213, 7; PL 38, 1063–1064. English translation: *Writings of St. Augustine* (Sermons on the Liturgical Seasons), Vol. 17, translated by Sister Mary Sarah Muldowney, R.S.M., *The Fathers of the Church*, Vol. 38 (New York:Christian Heritage, Inc., 1959), pp. 126–127.

Part IV

THE VIRGIN OF THE VISITATION

*Blessed art thou among women
and blessed is the fruit of thy womb!*
(Luke 1:42)

Chapter 9

THE VIRGIN OF THE VISITATION

A. INTRODUCTION

At the time of the Annunciation, the angel Gabriel had given the Virgin a sign: "And behold, Elizabeth thy kinswoman also has conceived a son in her old age, and she who was called barren is now in her sixth month" (Luke 1:36). Mary had believed; but this happening had been so extraordinary, so marvelous, and even, might we say, so unbelievable, that it would have been entirely normal for her to think of comparing it with the sign that Gabriel had given her. Not that her faith would have faltered if no sign had been given; but this sign had been offered to her by God himself, and it was only natural that she should accept it. Elizabeth's motherhood did, moreover, have a certain relationship to her own: "Elizabeth thy kinswoman *also* has conceived a son." The two gifts of motherhood were bestowed within the same messianic framework.

There was, in addition, the very natural desire to seek out Elizabeth as an older relative who could be the confidante of her thoughts. For Mary had been the solitary witness to what had taken place; there is nothing in Luke's narrative to indicate that she would have spoken of it to Joseph her betrothed. Matthew (1:18-21) even testifies explicitly to the contrary: despite the extreme delicacy, and even the utter painfulness, of the situation with which she was to confront her betrothed husband, she maintained a complete silence; indeed from any angle such a disclosure would have been difficult. But with Elizabeth it was different — the bonds of kinship and the similarity of their circumstances were conducive to an easy and very natural exchange. Besides, Mary could be of help to her

89

cousin in her everyday tasks by offering the womanly services customary at such times, for Elizabeth was already in her sixth month.

Such is the setting of the Visitation, in all its simplicity. The
narrative is a joyful and utterly appealing one — so much so that
an over-hasty reader could see in it nothing more than the charming
scene of two women sharing the joy-filled secrets of their approaching
motherhood. But this setting of festive expectancy and simplicity
provides the backdrop, as it were, against which Luke, with delicate
skill, takes up the great themes that he had already begun to enlarge
upon in his narrative of the Annunciation.

The Visitation Narrative

> Now in those days Mary arose and went with haste into the hill
> country, to a town of Juda. And she entered the house of Zachary
> and saluted Elizabeth. And it came to pass, when Elizabeth heard
> the greeting of Mary, that the babe in her womb leapt. And Elizabeth
> was filled with the Holy Spirit, and cried out with a loud voice,
> saying, "Blessed art thou among women and blessed is the fruit of
> thy womb! And how have I deserved that the mother of my Lord
> should come to me? For behold, the moment that the sound of thy
> greeting came to my ears, the babe in my womb leapt for joy. And
> blessed is she who has believed, because the things promised her
> by the Lord shall be accomplished. . . . And Mary remained with
> her about three months and returned to her own house" (Lk 1:39-45,
> 56).

B. Elizabeth was Filled With the Holy Spirit

As soon as Elizabeth had heard Mary's greeting, the child she
was carrying leapt in her womb, and she was filled with the Holy
Spirit. As seen throughout the narrative of Christ's infancy and
in the Book of Acts — which is, it could be said, the narrative
of the Church's infancy — Luke has a special fondness for mentioning the presence and the effusion of the Holy Spirit; it is one of
his favorite themes.[1]

In fact, the personages who occupy the foreground of the
scene — Mary (1:35), Zachary (1:67), Elizabeth (1:41), John the Baptist (1:15), and Simeon (2:25) — are all filled with the Holy Spirit;
it is under his impetus and inspiration that they act and prophesy.
It could even be said that the central figure in this *dramatis personae*
is the Holy Spirit himself; the other characters are directed by
his designs, they speak according to his will. Luke's insistent repeti-
tion of this theme has a very specific function: the pouring-forth

of the Holy Spirit is, in effect, the sign of the messianic era. As Peter says in his first sermon: "But this is what was spoken through the prophet Joel: And it shall come to pass in the last days, says the Lord, that I will pour forth of my Spirit upon all flesh; and your sons and your daughters shall prophesy . . ." (Acts 2:16-17, citing Joel 3:1).

In the Acts of the Apostles, the evangelist continues to devote his interest to the principal messianic themes that he had set in relief in the "memoirs of the Virgin." He thereby shows that the mystery of Christ is reproduced in the living reality of the Church. The Acts, which are, as we said, the narrative of the infancy of the Church, are in a way a new edition of the narrative of the infancy of Christ. Mary is present with the Church as she was with Christ. In the Gospel, Elizabeth is filled with the Holy Spirit as Mary comes to meet her; in the Acts, it is again in Mary's presence that the Holy Spirit descends upon the Church of Pentecost (cf. Acts 1:14).

C. The Babe Leapt in Her Womb

As Elizabeth heard Mary's greeting, the child she was carrying leapt in her womb. This "leaping" of John the Baptist has been interpreted in various ways.[2] The simplest and surest interpretation is the one that Elizabeth herself gives of the event — John's leaping was a sign of joy: "For behold, the moment that the sound of thy greeting came to my ears, the babe in my womb leapt for joy" (Luke 1:44).

Here again we are in the presence of a theme close to Luke's heart, that of the messianic joy; the dawn of salvation is radiant with the joy of the Day of the Lord. So in the annunciation to Zachary does Gabriel prophesy that John is to bring "joy and gladness, and many will rejoice at his birth" (1:14); his annunciation to Mary opens with a like invitation to joy: "Rejoice, full of grace" (1:28); and the annunciation to the shepherds of Bethlehem takes up the same theme: "I bring you good news of great joy which shall be to all the people" (2:10). In the *Magnificat*, Mary's "spirit rejoices in God [her] Savior" (1:47); and finally, Simeon directs his canticle of praise to Jesus as "the consolation of Israel"[3] (2:25). All these texts converge on the same reality: the messianic time has come; it is now the Day of the Lord.

The verb σκιρτᾶν, translated by our verb "to leap," seems to have been chosen with this same design in mind. In its literal sense it means "to skip" and "to gambol." Thus, according to the paschal hymn which we read in Psalm 113, when Israel came forth from Egypt the mountains skipped (ἐσκίρτησαν) like rams, and the hills like the lambs of the flock "before the face of the Lord" (Ps. 113:4-7). Here Luke has perhaps let his thought be shaped by the use of σκιρτάν in Malachias' celebrated prophecy of the Day of Yahweh:

> But for you who fear my name, there will arise the sun of justice with its healing rays; and you will gambol (σκιρτήσετε) like calves out of the stall. . . . Lo, I will send you Elias, the prophet, before the day of the Lord comes, the great and terrible day, to turn the hearts of the fathers to their children (Mal. 3:20, 23).

The image introduced by the verb σκιρτάν is so attractive and unexpected that it seems somewhat out of character with the role John the Baptist is to play. But this impression is counterweighted by the last phrase concerning the return of Elias: "[he shall] turn the hearts of the fathers to their children," which is textually cited in the annunciation to Zachary (Luke 1:17). John is to go before the Messias, like a new Elias.[4] Again we are given warning that the messianic times are at hand.

D. How Have I Deserved That the Mother of My Lord Should Come to Me?

> Elizabeth was filled with the Holy Spirit, and cried out with a loud voice, saying, ". . . how have I deserved that the mother of my Lord should come to me?" (Luke 1:41-43).

Luke seems to have attached a special importance to Elizabeth's words. They are not merely an answer to Mary's greeting, a commonplace response that the aging woman would have uttered in a rush of feeling. Their entire exchange is marked, on the contrary, by a profound dignity, in a manner, we might say, that is almost liturgical. Elizabeth is filled with the Holy Spirit; she acknowledges the incomparable dignity of the Mother of the Lord; she proclaims her blessed because of her faith; she extols her as "blessed among women." The verb ἀναφωνεῖν that introduces this litany of praise is solemn in tone and has a specifically liturgical connotation. It is, in fact, the same word used in the Septuagint to denote the chanting of the Levites before the ark of the covenant:

> [David] appointed Levites to minister (λειτουργοῦντας), before the ark of the Lord, and to remember his works (ἀναφωνοῦντας), and

to glorify and praise the Lord God of Israel (1 Par. 16:4; cf. 16:6, 42).

The verb recurs once again in the account of the translation of the ark into the City of David:

> David and all the ancients of Israel, and the captains over thousands, went to bring the ark of the covenant of the Lord out of the house of Obededom. . . . And all Israel brought the ark of the covenant of the Lord with joyful shouting, and sounding with the sound of the cornet, and with trumpets, and cymbals, and lifting up their voices (ἀναφωνοῦντες) with the sound of psalteries and harps (1 Par. 15:25, 28; cf. 2 Par. 5:13).

With the exception of this passage and those of a parallel nature, the verb ἀναφωνεῖν is found nowhere else in either the Old or the New Testament; its specific link with the liturgical celebration of the Levites before the ark of the covenant is therefore evident. And it is precisely to this setting that Luke is alluding as he quotes Elizabeth's words: ". . . how have I deserved that the mother of my Lord should come to me?" (Luke 1:43). The passage is actually a reference to the sixth chapter of the Second Book of Kings. David has made the decision to transfer the ark from the house of Abinadab to Jerusalem. "David and all Israel played before the Lord on all manner of instruments made of wood, on harps and lutes and timbrels and cornets and cymbals" (2 Kings 6:5). And David cried out: "How shall the ark of the Lord come to me?" (2 Kings 6:9).

Luke, then, would here be suggesting a typological identification of Mary with the ark of the covenant. He thus is continuing, and with precise consistency, the typological identification of Mary with the Temple that he had already introduced with the Annunciation narrative.

Studying these parallels within the unitary structure of Luke 1–2, Laurentin makes this perceptive observation:

> These two chapters are the literary vehicle, as it were, of Jesus' "going up" to the Temple of Jerusalem. And the "going up" of the ark to Jerusalem is precisely what is described in the account of 2 Kings 6. Like the station of "the ark of the Lord" at the house of Obededom, the station of "the mother of the Lord" at the house of Zachary represents a stage in the course of the ascent to the City. In both cases, the sojourn is of *three months'* duration, and in a *house* which because of its presence there receives a *blessing*. The connection of the Visitation scene with 2 Kings 6 hence gives definitive substance to . . . the two key ideas of development: Jesus is ascending to his place, the Temple of Jerusalem; Mary, who is carrying him, is the type of the ark of the covenant." [5]

We can observe that John seems to have taken up this typology in the Apocalypse:

> And the temple of God in heaven was opened, and there was seen the ark of his covenant in his temple . . . (Apoc. 11:19).
>
> And a great sign appeared in heaven: a woman clothed with the sun, and the moon was under her feet (Apoc. 12:1).

In the actual redaction of the text, the sign of the woman clothed with the sun and crowned with stars immediately follows the appearance of the ark of the covenant.

E. BLESSED ART THOU AMONG WOMEN

> Blessed art thou among women and blessed is the fruit of thy womb!
> (Luke 1:42)

The expression "Blessed art thou among women" occurs for the first time in the Canticle of Debora (Judg. 5:2-31); it was addressed to Jahel, the wife of Heber the Cinite. The time was the period of settlement in Canaan, around 1125. At the utterance of Debora the prophetess, the tribes of Nephthali and Zabulon, under Barac's command, rose up against their Canaanite oppressors led by Sisara. Debora had said to Barac: "Be off, for this is the day on which the Lord has delivered Sisara into your power. The Lord marches before you" (Judg. 4:14).

The entire army of the enemy did actually fall under the sword (4:16); Sisara himself, who had succeeded in escaping the slaughter, went to Jahel seeking a hiding-place. Jahel gave him a warm welcome, but after he had fallen asleep in her tent, battle-weary and drowsy, she got up, took a tent-peg, grabbed a mallet, stealthily crept up to him, and drove a hole right through his temple (4:17-22). It is this feat that Debora is celebrating: "Blessed among women be Jahel, blessed among tent-dwelling women" (Judg. 5:24).

We may wonder how Jahel, the crafty woman with bloodstained hands, can be an image of the "sweet" Virgin Mary. Maertens' explanation goes to the heart of the matter:

> Behind Jahel's cunning and the particular setting of a local conflict between Israel and Canaan, we can see the first attacks of Yahweh upon the kingdom of Satan, with the aim of wresting the Promised Land from his grasp as an advance position, so to speak, from which he will strike out on his victorious conquest of the world. It was with the purpose of impressing on his people the truth that the periods of warfare in their history were above all periods of God's own re-

conquest of his empire on earth, that God made an ordinary woman the instrument of victory.[6]

It is, in fact, precisely the victory of Yahweh that Debora's canticle will celebrate, the all-powerful protection with which the Lord surrounds his people:

> That warriors in Israel unbound their hair, [7]
> that the people came forward with a will,
> for this, bless Yahweh!
>
> Listen, you kings! Give ear, you princes!
> From me, from me comes a song for Yahweh.
> I will glorify Yahweh, God of Israel.
>
> Yahweh, when you set out from Seir,
> as you trod the land of Edom,
> earth shook, the heavens quaked,
> the clouds dissolved into water. . . .
>
> Blessed be Jael among women
> (the wife of Heber the Kenite);
> among all women that dwell in tents may she be blessed.
>
> He asked for water; she gave him milk;
> in a precious bowl she brought him cream.
> She stretched out her hand to seize the peg,
> her right hand to seize the workman's mallet.
>
> She struck Sisara, crushed his head,
> pierced his temple and shattered it.
> At her feet he tumbled, he fell, he lay;
> at her feet he tumbled, he fell.
> Where he tumbled, there he fell dead. . . .
>
> So perish all your enemies, Yahweh!
> And let those who love you be like the sun
> when he arises in all his strength! * (Judg. 5:2-4, 24-27, 31).

All those who love you — despite its wild and warlike tone, this triumphal ode is already a love song.

Over a thousand years later, Jahel's story will be told afresh in Judith. History will give way to apocalypse, Judith will supplant Jahel, but the message will be the same. Two sides are in conflict, that of the people of God and that of the pagan nations; God's side seems doomed to extermination, but he intervenes anew to save his people through the hand of a woman. And when Judith brings the gory head of Holofernes to Bethulia, the songs of thanksgiving will take up the themes of Debora's canticle:

> And [all the people] adored the Lord, and said to her:
> "The Lord hath blessed thee by his power,

because by thee he hath brought our enemies to naught."
And Ozias the prince of the people of Israel, said to her:
"Blessed art thou, O daughter, by the Lord the most high God,
above all women upon the earth."
. . . they all blessed her with one voice, saying:
"Thou art the glory of Jerusalem,
thou art the joy of Israel,
thou art the honor of our people!
By doing all this with thine own hand
thou hast done well in the midst of Israel
and God hath approved what thou hast done.*
Therefore also the hand of the Lord hath strengthened thee,
and therefore thou shalt be blessed forever."
And all the people said: "So be it, so be it" (Judith 13:22-23; 15:10-12).

In saying that Mary is blessed among all women, Luke thereby
seems to be pointing out that it is she in whom God is bringing
the salvation of his people to fulfillment. Mary supplants Jahel and
Judith; but at the same time she also stands on a higher plane.
Jahel was the instrument of deliverance, Judith stood for the victory
of the nation; but Mary is at once both the woman blessed among
all women through whom God brings about salvation, and the
Daughter of Sion, the personification of the new Israel. Her combat,
her victory, her triumph — all are subsumed in one great reality:
she is the Mother of Jesus. Yahweh, who saves his people, has
become Jesus, "the blessed fruit of her womb":

Judith 13	*Luke 1*
Blessed art thou, O daughter. . . above all women upon the earth (v. 23)	Blessed art thou among women
Blessed be the Lord (v. 24)	and blessed is the fruit of thy womb! (v. 42).

In Mary, God is mindful of his covenant: ". . . the Lord, your
God, will keep with you the merciful covenant which he promised
on oath to your fathers. He will love and bless and multiply you;
he will bless the fruit of your womb" (Deut. 7:12-13). With Mary's
carrying of Christ within her womb, the prophecy of Deuteronomy
is fulfilled to the letter. She, too, is the woman of victory, and
precisely because she is the Mother of Jesus; her hour of triumph
is her bringing forth of the Christ. We thus come full circle and
rejoin the thought expressed in the proto-Gospel — the first Eve
will triumph over the serpent in the victory of her offspring: "I
will put enmity between you and the woman, between your seed
and her seed; he shall crush your head" (Gen. 3:15).

[1] For further texts besides the passages cited, see Luke 3:16, 22; 4:1, 18; 10:21; 11:13; 12:10, 12; 24:49. Luke 10:21 has a particular affinity with our present text: Jesus "thrilled with joy" (ἠγαλλιάσατο) under the action of the Holy Spirit (*Translator's note*: It is noteworthy that with the exception of this sentence which is peculiar to Luke, the account of this episode is almost identical to Matthew's.)

[2] Some have thought that at this moment the Precursor was given the use of reason in order that he could recognize the Messias, but the text is silent on this point. Others have even advanced the notion that he was purified from original sin; however, the perspective of original sin is utterly foreign to the spiritual climate of Luke 1–2.

[3] The expression "consolation of Israel" likewise designates the Messias; see J. Bonsirven, *Le Judaïsme Palestinien*, 1 (Paris, 1934), pp. 351–352.

[4] See T. Maertens, *Le Messie est là, op. cit.*, pp. 28ff.

[5] R. Laurentin, *Structure et théologie de Luc I–II, op. cit.*, p. 81.

[6] Maertens, *op cit.*, p. 60.

[7] This is a reference to a battle ritual.

* *Translator's note*: In quoting the Canticle of Debora, we have used the translation of the *Jerusalem Bible*.

* *Translator's note*: In verse 11 the Confraternity translation follows the Vulgate; we have translated here from the French.

Part V

THE MAGNIFICAT

INTRODUCTION TO PART V

Singing, joyous souls hold an especial attraction for Luke. He delights in showing us the joy and gladness that broke forth among the people at the coming of the Lord:

> . . . they glorified God . . . saying, "We have seen wonderful things today" (Luke 5:26).
>
> . . . the entire crowd rejoiced at all the glorious things that were done by him (Luke 13:17).
>
> And at once he received his sight, and followed him, glorifying God. And all the people upon seeing it gave praise to God (Luke 18:43).
>
> . . . the whole company of the disciples began to rejoice and to praise God with a loud voice for all the miracles that they had seen (Luke 19:37).

Clearly we can expect to find this atmosphere of joy and praise in the "memoirs of the Virgin," which form the preface of Luke's Gospel. In Luke 1–2 we really do find not only the spiritual climate of the remainder of his Gospel, but still more, the canticles which are the expression *par excellence* of these specially favored occasions of praise: the canticle of Mary (1:46-55); that of Zachary (1:67-79); that of the angels of Bethlehem (2:13-14); and finally that of Simeon (2:29-32). Among these, the canticle of the Mother of the Lord will receive our exclusive attention.

The Magnificat

My soul magnifies the Lord,
    and my spirit rejoices in God my Savior;
Because he has regarded the lowliness of his handmaid;
    for, behold, henceforth all generations shall call me blessed;
Because he who is mighty has done great things for me,
    and holy is his name;
And his mercy is from generation to generation
    on those who fear him.
He has shown might with his arm,
    he has scattered the proud in the conceit of their heart.
He has put down the mighty from their thrones,
    and has exalted the lowly.

> He has filled the hungry with good things,
>> and the rich he has sent away empty.
> He has given help to Israel, his servant,
>> mindful of his mercy —
> Even as he spoke to our fathers —
>> to Abraham and to his posterity forever (Lk 1:46-55).

The *Magnificat* can be seen as composed of three distinct parts: (1) a song of praise and victory; (2) the song of the poor of Yahweh; (3) the fulfillment of the promise made to Abraham. Since this last part has already been discussed in the chapter "Mary, Daughter of Abraham," [1] only the first two parts will be studied here.

By way of introduction, we would like to make three preliminary remarks:

1) It will be noted at first sight that there is an absence of concrete allusions to what has happened to Mary and to Elizabeth. The canticle is, in fact, made part of the structure of the Visitation narrative: Elizabeth has just recognized Mary as "the mother of the Lord, blessed among women"; she proclaims her blessed for having believed; she reveals to her that her own child had leapt for joy at the moment she had heard her greeting (Luke 1:41-45).

It therefore would have been the most natural thing for Mary to return the courtesy and to acknowledge, even if by only a single word, the greatness of her cousin. But she does nothing of the kind. As Gaechter remarks, with a touch of humor, Mary's reply, "as it were, goes against all the rules of etiquette; she makes no allusion to Elizabeth nor to what had happened to her, to the child she was carrying in her womb." [2]

It will readily be conceded that the Canticle of Mary is not a formula of human politeness; but courtesy at its supreme level of expression is that ordered by the love of God. And the *Magnificat* truly is consecrated in its very essence to the praise of God: it extols the holiness of his name, his mercy toward the lowly, his preferential love for the poor, the fulfillment of the promises made to Abraham and his offspring: "He has given help to Israel, his servant, mindful of his mercy" (Luke 1:54).

Here we uncover an aspect of our Lady's piety that is extremely interesting. This piety is oriented more along the lines of the history of the salvation that God is bringing to fulfillment in his Church than it is along the lines of the history of her own personal spiritual life. Exegesis in turn must be guided by this same orientation; analysis of the text must be centered on this praise of God who is fulfilling the promises made to Abraham and to his posterity.

2) In our consideration of this first aspect we must not, however, lose sight of the truth that it is precisely in Mary that God is bringing the salvation of his people to fulfillment. We might say that the Virgin has the lowliness to realize her own greatness: "He who is mighty has done great things for me" (Luke 1:49). She knows that the messianic age which is beginning in her will perpetuate her offering of praise forever: ". . . for, behold, henceforth all generations shall call me blessed" (Luke 1:48). Her act of thanksgiving is addressed to Jesus-the-Savior whom she is carrying within her womb: ". . . my spirit rejoices in God my Savior" (Luke 1:46).

If the *Magnificat* is therefore essentially the praise of God's salvation, it is also the praise of the salvation that God is bringing to fulfillment in Mary. It is in Mary that the people of God enter into possession of his promises.

It truly can be said of these two aspects that they are so completely interrelated that in places it is difficult to determine whether a particular passage should first be regarded as applying to Mary (as the representative of the entire people) or to the entire people (represented in Mary). The same holds true of the passages where exegesis seems a simple matter. As an illustration of this, the verse ". . . behold, henceforth all generations shall call me blessed (μακαριοῦσιν με)" evidently applies to the Virgin alone; the incomparable dignity of the divine maternity is uniquely hers, and it is because of this maternity that the generations to come will proclaim her blessed. But this exegesis, so self-confident while proceeding on Scriptural and theological grounds, becomes hesitant before the realization that a similar prophecy was addressed in equal measure to the entire people of the promise: "Then all nations will call you blessed (μακαριοῦσιν ὑμᾶς)" (Mal. 3:12).

Could not the *Magnificat* here be an echo of Malachias' text? We can readily conjecture that this ambivalence of meaning is fully intentional on Luke's part and even, so to speak, pre-meditated. If the *Magnificat* does seem to stand outside the immediate event-sequence of the Visitation, it nevertheless harmonizes, in a very perfect way, with the spiritual context of the narrative as a whole; the possibility may even be entertained that the Visitation narrative was designed simply as an introduction to the *Magnificat*.

3) Much has been made at times of our Lady's poetic gifts; her canticle would be seen to display a lavish imagery revealing the intensely lyric quality of her soul. Here, from the very start, it is of vital importance that we draw a distinction between the quality of an artistic creation and the dignity of the divine maternity. One

does not of necessity imply the other. As Fr. Lagrange has written, and with a pointed serenity: "In the canticle we do not find any striving after formulation of personal insights nor — and we shall be frank — any originality of imagery. Its literary value has, perhaps, at times been exaggerated; it is too predominantly reminiscent in content to rank as a major contribution of poetic talent. Why need we attribute to Mary a superiority of natural gifts for which her Son never displayed any esteem?" [3] In point of fact, a completely objective reading of the text will suffice to show that the imagery is hardly of high poetic caliber, not only remaining within the conventional but lacking in depth of color.

If we compare the Canticle of Mary with that of Debora: "By the unbound hair of Israel!" (cf. Judg. 5:2, *Jerusalem Bible* translation), it seems almost lifeless. What we have here is not, properly speaking, an artistic creation, but rather a cento, i.e., a selection of passages borrowed from other texts of Scripture. Hence we are not called upon to admire Mary's poetic gifts, but rather to the re-reading of the sources from which her own devotion drew its nourishment. The incomparable beauty of the Canticle of Mary lies not in its lines themselves, but in the setting of their utterance. What is new is not the lines but the setting — a milieu that in its very newness of dimension utterly surpasses the level of all the Old Testament texts.

Once again we encounter the midrashic genre with which Luke has already made us so familiar. The author tells us the story of the New Testment with the texts of the Old. He thereby shows us that the Word of God is always active in the present and, what is more, that it is only in the New Testament that the Old begins truly to be fulfilled.

[1] See pp. 3–21.

[2] Cf. Gaechter, *op cit.*, p. 41. It is this paucity of concrete allusions that has led certain authors to think either that the *Magnificat* was divorced from its original context or that it was not the utterance of Mary but of Elizabeth. This attribution to Elizabeth enjoyed a certain vogue in Modernist circles, especially at the turn of the century. Loisy launched the idea (under the pseudonym of F. Jacobé, *Rev. hist. littér. rel.*, 2 [1897], pp. 424–432), which was taken up by A. Harnack, *Sitz. der K. Preussischen Akad. der Wissenschaften zu Berlin*, 27 (1900), pp. 538–556. P. Ladeuze, *Rev. Histoire ecclésiastique*, 4 (1903), pp. 623–644, thinks that the *Magnificat* is a hymn which came into being in the primitive community. These opinions in their turn have been refuted, notably by: A. Durand, S.J.,

"L'origine du Magnificat," *Rev. Bibl.*, 7 (1898), pp. 74–77. — M. Lepin, "Le Magnificat doit-il être attribué à Marie ou à Élisabeth?", *Université Catholique* (Lyon), 39 (1902), pp. 213–242. — J. Van der Meersch, "A propos de l'origine du Magnificat," *Collationes Brugenses*, 9 (1904), pp. 522–529, against Ladeuze.

See also: U. Holzmeister, "Que penser de l'opinion qui attribue le Magnificat à sainte Élisabeth," *Ami du Clergé*, 46 (1929), pp. 65–67. — A. Brassac, "L'origine du Magnificat," *Rev. Apol.*, 33 (1921–1922), pp. 251–254. — L. Pirot, "Commission Biblique et Magnificat," *Dictionnaire de la Bible, Suppl.*, 2 (1934), 1270–1272. *Ami du Clergé*, 46 (1929), pp. 956–962.

[3] M.-J. Lagrange, *Évangile selon saint Luc,* Coll. *Etudes Bibliques*, 3rd ed. (Paris, 1927), p. 54. Here as elsewhere we have the application of St. Bernard's famous principle: " 'The honor of the queen loves justice.' The Virgin has many true titles to honor, many real marks of dignity, and does not need any that are false" — PL 182, 333B, *The Letters of St. Bernard of Clairvaux*, translated by Bruno Scott James (Chicago: Henry Regnery Co., 1953), Letter 215, p. 290 (This is St. Bernard's letter to the canons of Lyons, against the institution of the feast of the Immaculate Conception. It is ironically amusing to note how badly St. Bernard on this occasion was applying the principle that he was expressing so well.)

Chapter 10

A SONG OF VICTORY

My soul magnifies the Lord,
and my spirit rejoices in God my Savior"
(Luke 1:46-47).

A. THE CANTICLE OF ANNA

The text most closely allied to the *Magnificat* is the Canticle of Anna, the wife of Elcana, whose womb had been shut up by the Lord (1 Kings 1:6). "O Lord of hosts," she prayed, "if thou wilt look down on the affliction of thy servant, and wilt be mindful of me, and not forget thy handmaid, and wilt give to thy servant a man child . . ." (1 Kings 1:11). Yahweh was mindful of Anna; she gave birth to Samuel, and when she came to the Temple to offer him and consecrate him to Yahweh, she fashioned this prayer:

My heart hath rejoiced in the Lord,
    and my horn is exalted in my God;
My mouth is enlarged over my enemies,
    because I have joyed in thy salvation.
There is none holy as the Lord is;
    for there is no other besides thee,
    and there is none strong like our God.

Do not multiply to speak lofty things, boasting.
    let old matters depart from your mouth;
For the Lord is a God of all knowledge,
    and to him are thoughts prepared.

The bow of the mighty is overcome,
    and the weak are girt with strength.
They that were full before have hired out themselves for bread:
    and the hungry are filled,

106

So that the barren hath borne many;
  and she that had many children is weakened.

The Lord killeth and maketh alive,
  he bringeth down to hell and bringeth back again.
The Lord maketh poor and maketh rich,
  he humbleth and he exalteth.

He raiseth up the needy from the dust,
  and lifteth up the poor from the dunghill,
That he may sit with princes,
  and hold the throne of glory.
For the poles of the earth are the Lord's,
  and upon them he hath set the world.

He will keep the feet of his saints,
  and the wicked shall be silent in darkness,
  because no man shall prevail by his own strength.
The adversaries of the Lord shall fear him:
  and upon them shall he thunder in the heavens.

The Lord shall judge the ends of the earth,
  and he shall give empire to his king,
  and shall exalt the horn of his Anointed * (1 Kings 2:1-10).

It is amazing that the Virgin Mary should have drawn her inspiration from a song of such warlike and rugged character. Nevertheless, the parallels which it shares with the *Magnificat* are undeniable:

The Canticle of Anna	*The Canticle of Mary*
My heart hath rejoiced in the Lord, I have joyed in thy salvation.	My soul magnifies the Lord, and my spirit rejoices in God my Savior.
There is none holy as the Lord is;	holy is his name.
The bow of the mighty is overcome,	He has shown might with his arm,
and the weak are girt with strength.	he has scattered the proud in the conceit of their heart.
They that were full before have hired themselves out for bread;	He has filled the hungry with good things
and the hungry are filled,	and the rich he has sent away empty.
The Lord . . . humbleth and he exalteth.	He has put down the mighty from their thrones, and has exalted the lowly.

The canticle thus could be called the first *Magnificat*. But at

---

* *Translator's note*: We have here followed the reading "Anointed," which is the meaning of the original Hebrew and is rendered as such in both the French and the English *Jerusalem Bible*.

the same time that we make a further discovery of the continuity
between the two Testaments, we also sense once again the superiority of the one in comparison to the other. Anna is triumphant;
her canticle is much more a battle song than a thanksgiving: "My
mouth is enlarged over my enemies!" She draws herself up to her
full stature against the mighty, upon whom she haughtily looks
down: "The bow of the mighty is overcome. . . . The adversaries
of the Lord shall fear him: and upon them shall he thunder in
the heavens." With what spiteful and ironic glee over those who
had despised her for her barrenness: ". . . the barren hath borne
many; and she that had many children is weakened."

But Mary is all humility and adoration. She makes a selection
of lines from the Canticle of Anna, leaving aside all that breathes
of scorn and disdain, and goes to the opposite length to bring its
themes of humility and poverty to the fore:

Luke 1:48, 54	*1 Kings 1:11*
He has regarded the lowliness	if thou wilt look down on the
ὅτι ἐπέβλεψεν ἐπὶ τὴν	affliction
ταπείνωσιν	ἐάν ἐπιβλέπων ἐπιβλέψῃς
	ἐπὶ τὴν ταπείνωσιν
of his handmaid	of thy servant
τῆς δούλης αὐτοῦ	τῆς δούλης σου
mindful of his mercy	and wilt be mindful of me
μνησθῆναι ἐλέους	καὶ μνησθῇς μου

In Mary, the triumph of the humble lies not in domination over
their despoiled enemies, but in the song of praise that the poor
send up to their God.

From this selection of passages we can see how deeply Mary's
piety was rooted in the themes of the Old Testament. The Canticle
of Anna is centered around these two themes: that of enemies,
whom Yahweh crushes through the exploits of the battlefield; that
of the mighty, the sated, the wicked, who are despoiled to the
profit of the lowly and the poor. These two themes are juxtaposed.
In the *Magnificat*, however, the first theme is relinquished to bring
out the beauty of the second; the enemies of God's people have
been spiritualized to the point of having become simply those who
stand in opposition to God. Thus does Mary eliminate from her
canticle all the shadows of the Old Testament. What had been
only a melodic if wavering alternation between two themes becomes
in her song one single melody, with its clear and luminous song
of the God of the poor.

B. The Canticle of Habacuc

The second passage in which we meet up with the first verse of the *Magnificat* is contained in the Canticle of Habacuc:

God comes from Theman,
    the Holy One from Mount Pharan.
Covered are the heavens with his glory,
    and with his praise the earth is filled.
His splendor spreads like the light;
    rays shine forth from beside him,
    where his power is concealed.
Before him goes pestilence,
    and the plague follows in his steps.
He pauses to survey the earth;
    his look makes the nations tremble.
The eternal mountains are shattered,
    the age-old hills bow low along his ancient ways.

I see the tents of Chusan collapse;
    trembling are the pavilions of the land of Madian.

Bared and ready is your bow,
    filled with arrows is your quiver.

In wrath you bestride the earth,
    in fury you trample the nations.
You come forth to save your people,
    to save your anointed one.
You crush the heads of the wicked,
    you lay bare their bases at the neck.

You tread the sea with your steeds
    amid the churning of the deep waters.

Yet will I rejoice in the Lord
    and exult in my saving God.
God, my Lord, is my strength;
    he makes my feet swift as those of hinds
    and enables me to go upon the heights (Hab. 3:3-7, 9, 12-13, 15, 18-19).

The canticle is divided into three parts: the triumphant advance of Yahweh (vv. 3-7), his warrior's display of might "to save his people" (vv. 8-15), and the thanksgiving of the redeemed (vv. 18-19).

In accordance with a schema that became classical in the post-exilic period, the announcement of deliverance is clothed in imagery reminiscent of the Exodus: Yahweh will work anew the marvels of Sinai,[1] of the land of Madian,[2] and of the Red Sea.[3]

The only point of contact between the *Magnificat* and the Canticle of Habacuc, with its vast and flashing panorama of imagery, is found in verse 18:

Habacuc 3:18	The Magnificat
Yet will I rejoice in the Lord	My soul magnifies the Lord,
and exult in my saving God.	and my spirit rejoices in God
	my Savior.[4]

This parallelism should be pointed up because of its reference to the Exodus. We have already met with this reference in description of the glory of Yahweh;[5] and we shall find a fresh instance of it in the Virgin's song: ". . . he who is mighty has done great things for me!" In the language of the Old Testament, these "great things" denote precisely the glorious story of the Exodus, the marvelous feat of the divine mercy.[6]

The story of our Lady's own life thus presents itself to us as a replica of the history of the people of God; or better, we might say that in Mary the marvels of the Exodus are wrought anew.

C. THE POEM OF ISAIAS

In the poem of Isaias 61, this aspect portraying the mystery of the Church comes even more strongly to the fore:

> *I rejoice heartily in the Lord,*
> *in my God is the joy of my soul;*
> For he has clothed me with a robe of salvation,
>   and wrapped me in a mantle of justice (Is. 61:10).

Here it is Israel herself, personified as the betrothed of Yahweh, who sings the *Magnificat*, and her song is a response to the tidings of salvation that Yahweh's prophet has proclaimed:

> The spirit of the Lord God is upon me,
>   because the Lord has anointed me;
> he has sent me to bring glad tidings to the lowly,
>   to heal the brokenhearted,
> To proclaim liberty to the captives
>   and release to the prisoners [7] (Is. 61:1).

The messianic character of this text is clear. When Christ preached for the first time in his home village of Nazareth, it was this passage that he read; and as "the eyes of all in the synagogue were gazing on him, . . . he began to say to them, 'Today this Scripture has been fulfilled in your hearing' " (Luke 4:20-21).

To sum up, we find the first verse of the *Magnificat* in the Canticle of Anna, in that of Habacuc, and finally in the song of the betrothed of Yahweh in Isaias 61. It is hardly possible to know to exactly which of these three texts the Virgin is referring, but this matters little. What is of real importance is the distinction of the leitmotif that consistently appears in each of these *Magnificats*, the special spiritual approach of each, and the figures who have fashioned its expression, from Anna, Habacuc, and Isaias down to the New Testament:

— this leitmotif is always a song of victory and deliverance;

— this victory is that of God-the-Savior, of God's saving help;

— it is won either over enemies (Anna, Habacuc), over the powerful for the cause of the lowly and the poor (Anna, Isaias), or over sin; it is a victory of holiness and of justice (Isaias); it has the character of a new Exodus (Habacuc).

These conclusions lead us back to a theme whose sound is growing ever more familiar: just as at the Annunciation and at the Visitation, so also in the *Magnificat* does Mary appear as the Daughter of Sion, realizing in her own person the most intensive fulfillment of the mystery of the Church. The very opening verse of the *Magnificat* leads us directly into the victory song of the Church redeemed: as our Lady exults in the Lord, her joy rises as the voice of all his people, as their song of the marvels of salvation, of Jesus-the-Savior.

---

[1] Cf. v. 3; Theman is the northern district of the land of Edom; Mount Pharan is likewise situated in Edom, to the south of Cades; Yahweh therefore is coming from Sinai and marching toward Canaan.

[2] Cf. v. 7; see Exod. 15:13-16.

[3] Cf. v. 15; see Exod. 15–16.

[4] The parallelism will be sensed more vividly if the *Magnificat* is compared with the Septuagint text. The Canticle of Habacuc literally reads: "I will thrill with joy . . . in God, my Savior, $\dot{\alpha}\gamma\alpha\lambda\lambda\iota\dot{\alpha}\sigma\rho\mu\alpha\iota$ . . . $\dot{\epsilon}\pi\dot{\iota}$ $\tau\tilde{\omega}$ $\Theta\epsilon\tilde{\omega}$ $\tau\tilde{\omega}$ $\sigma\omega\tau\tilde{\eta}\rho\dot{\iota}$ $\mu\omega$"; and the *Magnificat*: "My spirit has leapt for joy . . . in God, my Savior, $\dot{\eta}\gamma\alpha\lambda$-$\lambda\dot{\iota}\alpha\sigma\epsilon\nu$ . . . $\dot{\epsilon}\pi\dot{\iota}$ $\tau\tilde{\omega}$ $\Theta\epsilon\tilde{\omega}$ $\tau\tilde{\omega}$ $\sigma\omega\tau\tilde{\eta}\rho\dot{\iota}$ $\mu\omega$."

[5] See pp. 78–81.

[6] See Deut. 10:21; 11:7; Ps. 105:21; 135:4. We can sense the affinity of the *Magnificat* to this latter psalm, which sings of the marvels ($\mu\epsilon\gamma\dot{\alpha}\lambda\alpha$) that God wrought for his people in the name of his mercy ($\ddot{\epsilon}\lambda\epsilon\omega\varsigma$), which endures forever (v. 4).

[7] These lines should be cited in their full context, which treats of the return from captivity (v. 4), the restoration of the covenant ("a lasting covenant I will make with them," v. 8), and the formation of a holy people (vv. 3, 8, 11).

Chapter 11

THE SONG OF THE POOR
OF YAHWEH

A. INTRODUCTION

Along the road which leads us through the Old Testament to the Virgin, the Daughter of Sion, we have already met, at many stages in our journey, the poor, the lowly, and the weak. As a general group, they have appeared as Yahweh's faithful ones, who in their suffering and their love were awaiting the fulfillment of the covenant. The rich, the powerful, and the proud, on the other hand, were classed among the sinning and the unfaithful. This classification may seem a bit rash and over-simplified; to one accustomed to theological concepts and clear distinctions, it may seem hazardous and indeed even scandalous.[1] The *Magnificat* will, in fact, express these same ideas, untempered by any nuances we might wish to find:

> He has shown might with his arm,
>> he has scattered the proud in the conceit of their heart.
> He has put down the mighty from their thrones,
>> and has exalted the lowly.
> He has filled the hungry with good things,
>> and the rich he has sent away empty (Luke 1:51-53).

It will be perceived, however, that these texts are the product of a biblical milieu in which nuances of thought are lived rather than given expression in very clear concepts. This milieu, moreover, is reminiscent of the setting of the Annunciation. At that moment Mary had already summed up her entire attitude of soul in these words: "Behold the handmaid of the Lord; be it done to me according to thy word" (Luke 1:38). It is not mere coincidence that in the

Magnificat she again speaks of herself as "the handmaid" of the Lord, and even sings of her "lowliness": ". . . he has regarded the lowliness of his handmaid" (Luke 1:48).

From other evidence we know that this spiritual poverty and humility were accompanied by real material poverty. Mary was of humble station. Her Child, the "King of kings and Lord of lords" (Apoc. 19:16), will be born in actual destitution. When he came into this world, his Mother could offer him only an animals' feeding trough for his cradle (Luke 2:7); and when she redeemed him in the Temple, it was with a pair of turtledoves, the offering of the poor (Luke 2:24; cf. Lev. 12:8).

These facts pose a problem that is one of the fundamental themes of revelation — that of the *'anawim*, the poor of Yahweh.

B. The Poor of Yahweh in Revelation

In the earliest theology of the covenant, hardly any room was made for a spiritual evaluation of poverty; it was riches, far rather, that were the sign of Yahweh's blessing, the reward that he bestowed on his faithful. The ideal of the ancient patriarchs was a life filled with happiness and riches, reaching a ripe old age in the midst of one's children to the third and fourth generations. To be prosperous in life, to "see the bounty of the Lord in the land of the living" (Ps. 26:13), such was the badge of righteousness that God awarded to those who loved him; and the land of the living was, to be sure, the good land of Palestine, the native land one felt beneath one's feet.

God was to take this ideal, in which the riches of this world were so inseparably bound up with those of the spirit, and modify it little by little, spiritualizing it and bringing it to perfection in the dispensation of the New Testament. He was to teach his people not only by his Word but also by the events of history, events that were often disasters that befell them as a nation. How pointedly this lesson had to be driven home! Israel was not the richest of peoples, it did not enjoy possession of the Land; the impious man often won the upper hand while the faithful man grubbed along in misery and anxiety for the morrow. Each defeat in battle, and each personal reversal as well, took on the features of a new theophany in which Yahweh was revealing the implications of his promises and explaining the meaning of his Word.

In these "divine commentaries," Sophonias occupies a special place (about 630–625). Under Manasses (691–638), the religious situation had deteriorated into an absolutely lamentable state; never had matters sunk to such depths of impiety. It is at this time that Sophonias foretells the Day of Yahweh, a day of fury and terror. But at the same time that God was judging his people he was also purifying them; they were to be set up as the tiny "remnant" whom he would make the heir of his promises:

> . . . then will I remove from your midst the proud braggarts. . . . But I will leave as a remnant in your midst a people humble and lowly, who shall take refuge in the name of the Lord: the remnant of Irael. They shall do no wrong and speak no lies; nor shall there be found in their mouths a deceitful tongue (Soph. 3:11-13).

The poverty of which Sophonias is speaking has a deeply religious significance. It is not simply the wretchedness that is prevailing in these straitened times, but involves far more: it is above all an attitude of soul, a poverty that seeks refuge in the name of Yahweh. The people of God will be, in the future, a people of the poor and the holy: "Seek the Lord, all you humble (*anawim*) of the earth, who have observed his law; seek justice, seek humility (*anawah*)" (Soph. 2:3).

It is this tiny remnant, brought forth in poverty, whom Yahweh is going to crown with the fulfillment of his promises; in Sophonias 3:11-17 it is identified with the Daughter of Sion whom Yahweh will renew in his love and by his presence "in her womb."

Sophonias' message is of capital importance in revelation-history.[2] It has made Yahweh's covenant with all his people his covenant with the poor and lowly; it has opened up the way for the *anawim*; for them has been reserved the first place in the kingdom that is to come.

Jeremias will give definitive confirmation to this promise. It could even be said that the major significance of Jeremias' message lies, not in his oracles, but in his very life. It is he, the most sensitive and gentle of all the prophets, whom Yahweh chooses as "the prophet of suffering." It is not hard to understand how he groaned under the weight of the special loneliness of his mission — "I cannot": ". . . a prophet to the nations I appointed you. 'Ah, Lord God!' I said, 'I know not how to speak; I am too young'" (Jer. 1:5-6). And yet he cannot hold back this word that is in his heart: "My breast! my breast! how I suffer! The walls of my heart! My heart beats wildly, I cannot be still. . ." (Jer. 4:19). He knew the hour of doubt and dereliction, when he cried out to Yahweh: "You have indeed become for me a treacherous brook, whose waters do not abide!" (Jer. 15:18). He uttered these terrible words, which are as close to blasphemy as they are to love: "You duped me, O Lord, and I let myself be duped!" (Jer. 20:7). There even came to him the day when he wished that he had never been born:

> Cursed be the day on which I was born! May the day my mother gave me birth never be blessed! Cursed be the man who brought the news to my father, saying, "A child, a son, has been born to you!" filling him with great joy. Let that man be like the cities which the Lord relentlessly overthrew; let him hear war cries in the morning, battle alarms at noonday, because he did not dispatch me in the womb! Then my mother would have been my grave, her womb confining me forever. Why did I come forth from the womb, to see sorrow and pain, to end my days in shame? (Jer. 20:14-18).

Man of contradiction that he is, Jeremias is himself torn between his love for his kindred who have turned away from God and his love for God who has turned away from his kindred. He is a prisoner in his solitude, a wasteland of enmity and vicious tongues. Because God has demanded his life as a sign, he remains without wife and children (16:1-4). He sees the day of Yahweh's wrath, the day when Jerusalem falls in a welter of fire and blood. And while the captives are deported to the banks of Babylon, where their thoughts finally turn to Sion (Ps. 136), he himself is led away by force into Egypt, that hated land that had been cursed a thousandfold; he will be stripped of everything. But his life will stand as the symbol of all the poor of Yahweh who are steadfast in hope and love: "Sing to the Lord, praise the Lord, for he has rescued the life of the poor from the power of the wicked!" (Jer 20:13).

"Without this extraordinary man, the religious history of mankind would have taken a different course." [3] The very life and message of Jeremias are the definitive stage in the development of the theology and mystique of the 'anawim. They will have "a religious psychology modeled on that of the prophet. Their sufferings (persecution, mockery, sickness, prison, exile) will be a replica of his own. Their scandal at the good fortune of the wicked will be a re-echo of his own. Under the same impulsion as he, they will cast themselves into the divine arms, taking their refuge in 'conversation with Yahweh' and the ever-nearness of God." [4] The tiny remnant of the poor will form "the Israel of God," the true holy people: "Sing out, O heavens, and rejoice, O earth, break forth into song, you mountains. For the Lord comforts his people and shows mercy to his poor * (Is. 49:13).

From Sophonias down to the New Testament, the vocabulary of the poor will continue to widen, all the while rising to a higher spiritual plane. The *'anawim* will recruit in the army of the living God all those afflicted in this world of pain — the imprisoned, the hungry, the sick, the lowly, the meek, all those whose hope is in Yahweh alone. The Spirit of the Lord will send the prophet to bring the glad tidings to the Church of the poor, the captive, and the broken in heart (Is. 61:1).

But without the New Testament, without Jesus, the new Poor Man of Israel, the *'anawim* in their dispossession would have been without hope; the Old Testament would have been a Good Friday without a Pasch and Resurrection. But with the Prophet who is "meek and humble of heart" (Matthew 11:29), the poor enter into possession of the kingdom: "Blessed are you poor, for yours is the kingdom of God" (Luke 6:20). Do we need to add that the heart of Jesus was fashioned by the heart of our Lady, and that the *Magnificat* is thus the herald of the Beatitudes?

These few remarks on the *'anawim* afford us a deeper appreciation of the truly astonishing richness of the spiritual context of the *Magnificat*. When the Virgin proclaims that God has regarded her lowliness, that he has exalted the humble and scattered the proud of heart, that he has filled the hungry and sent the rich away empty, she is not selecting these themes at random and pouring them forth in an unrestrained outburst of emotional fervor. Mary has about her nothing of the elation and undisciplined feeling of a young girl; rather, throughout the entire Gospel she appears to us as a soul of recollection, resting in the deep tranquility of her meditation. Her *Magnificat*, the fruit of this meditation, reveals to us the secret of her heart. And this meditation, as it finds expression here, is a song that the poor are singing in praise of their God. Such is the vista that opens out before us, to which the various texts that served as sources for the *Magnificat* have led us.

C. The Poor of Yahweh in the Magnificat

Let us turn first to Psalm 102. Like the *Magnificat*, it opens with a song of praise:

Psalm 102	*The Magnificat*
Bless the Lord, O my soul;	My soul magnifies the Lord
and all my being, bless his	(Luke 1:46),
holy name (v. 1).	holy is his name (Luke 1:49);

The psalmist goes on to enumerate the benefits that the Lord has bestowed upon him: forgiveness of his sins, the cure of an illness, deliverance from a death that seemed close at hand, an abundance of all kinds of good things; in short, God has truly crowned him with kindness and compassion (vv. 3-5). Clearly such a listing is not contained in our Lady's canticle; its tone is more impersonal, marked by a singular and truly feminine reserve that prefers to veil itself in generalities. But in both these cases, what the theme celebrates is the unfailing mercy of the God of the poor:

Psalm 102	*The Magnificat*
the kindness of the Lord	his mercy
is from eternity to eternity	is from generation to generation
toward those who fear him	on those who fear him
(v. 17)	(Luke 1:50).

The psalm goes on to recall the revelation made by Yahweh to Moses and the love that he continues to show toward "those who keep his covenant" (vv. 17-18). This same idea will be taken up by the Virgin: "He has [been] mindful of his mercy — even as he spoke to our fathers. . ." (Luke 1:54-55).

Going beyond a mere verbal parallelism, we find a real similitude of ideas, the theology of the *'anawim*. This is the way in which the psalm speaks of the God of the poor:

> He redeems your life from destruction,
>   he crowns you with kindness and compassion.
> The Lord secures justice
>   and the rights of all the oppressed.
> Merciful and gracious is the Lord,
>   slow to anger and abounding in kindness.
> As a father has compassion on his children,
>   so the Lord has compassion on those who fear him,
> For he knows how we are formed;
>   he remembers that we are dust.
> But the kindness of the Lord is from eternity
>   to eternity toward those who fear him,
> And his justice toward children's children
>   among those who keep his covenant
>   and remember to fulfill his precepts [5] (Ps. 102:4, 6, 8, 13-14, 17-18).

Of equal significance here is Psalm 33, whose spirituality is such a close foreshadowing of that of the *Magnificat*. Here the thought-pattern is marked by a sturdy simplicity: an *'anaw*, finding himself in distress, turns to the Lord and cries out to him, and his prayer is heard; he then sings his thanks to the God of the poor. In the course of a composition at times hesitant and filled with repetitions (it is one of the alphabetical psalms), we meet the entire retinue of the poor. It is composed of the lowly (v. 3), those who fear Yahweh (vv. 8, 10), who take refuge in him (v. 11), the brokenhearted and crushed in spirit (v. 19); the holy and just (vv. 10, 20, 22). As in the *Magnificat*, these *anawim* bless and magnify the Lord [6] who saves them [7] and fills them with his good things, while the rich and the wicked perish of hunger:[8]

> I will bless the Lord at all times;
> > his praise shall be ever in my mouth.
> Let my soul glory in the Lord;
> > the lowly will hear me and be glad.
> Glorify the Lord with me,
> > let us together extol his name.
>
> I sought the Lord, and he answered me
> > and delivered me from all my fears.
> Look to him that you may be radiant with joy,
> > and your faces may not blush with shame.
> When the afflicted man called out, the Lord heard,
> > and from all his distress he saved him.
> The angel of the Lord encamps
> > around those who fear him, and delivers them.
> Taste and see how good the Lord is;
> > happy the man who takes refuge in him.
> Fear the Lord, you his holy ones,
> > for naught is lacking to those who fear him.
> The great grow poor and hungry;
> > but those who seek the Lord want for no good thing.
>
> The Lord has eyes for the just,
> > and ears for their cry.
>
> When the just cry out, the Lord hears them,
> > and from all their distress he rescues them.
> The Lord is close to the brokenhearted;
> > and those who are crushed in spirit he saves (Ps. 33:2-11, 16, 18-19).

In its essential lines, Psalm 112 is a similar foreshadowing of the *Magnificat*. There we find both the theme of the praise of Yahweh and the theme of the *anawim*; the last verse, which sings of the fruitfulness that God bestows on the barren woman, is reminiscent of the Canticle of Anna: [9]

> Praise, you servants of the Lord,
> > praise the name of the Lord.
> Blessed be the name of the Lord,
> > both now and forever.

From the rising to the setting of the sun
  is the name of the Lord to be praised.

He raises up the lowly from the dust;
  from the dunghill he lifts up the poor
To seat them with princes,
  with the princes of his own people.
He establishes in her home the barren wife
  as the joyful mother of children (Ps. 112:1-3, 7-9).

In Psalm 146 we find again the brokenhearted of the poem of
Isaias 61, in company with the lowly, who are exalted while the
wicked are cast to the ground:

Praise the Lord, for he is good;
  sing praise to our God, for he is gracious;
  it is fitting to praise him.
The Lord rebuilds Jerusalem;
  the dispersed of Israel he gathers.
He heals the brokenhearted
  and binds up their wounds.
He tells the number of the stars;
  he calls each by name.
Great is our Lord and mighty in power;
  to his wisdom there is no limit.
The Lord sustains the lowly;
  the wicked he casts to the ground [10] (Ps. 146:1-6).

The lesson is always the same: Yahweh reveals himself as the
King of glory and the God of mercy. He is the King of glory in that
he is the universal Lord of the cosmos — he knows each star by
its name! — and the Lord of Israel, whose dispersed he gathers;[11]
he is the God of mercy, the Lord of the poor, because he lifts
up the lowly and heals the brokenhearted.

We can only wonder and delight as we listen to the melody
of the Virgin's song, which harmonizes so purely with this Old
Testament symphony of themes. In the light that these texts shed
on the *Magnificat*, we can see in Mary a soul who lived the theology
of the 'anawim to its depths, and who so assimilated the formulas
shaped by the piety of the Old Testament that they became in
truth her very own.

The *Magnificat* is truly "traditional," so to speak; it makes no
pretension to originality, neither in its ideas nor still less in its
form. But what is new is the reality of Jesus, whom Mary is carrying
within herself. In the Old Testament the poor were truly weeping
in the night (cf. Ps. 87:2); they did not know the answer that God

would make to their tears; they had no idea that their deliverance
would be God himself, coming to dwell in their very midst, making
himself poor that by his poverty they might be made rich (2 Cor.
8:9); their own prayer is a prophecy of Christ. And their prayer
is heard, the prophecy is fulfilled, when Mary becomes the Mother
of Jesus. The Savior-God of Mary (Luke 1:47) is also the Savior-God
of all the Church of the poor.

D. The Spiritual Meaning of Biblical Poverty

What is the divine economy of God's special love for the disinher-
ited of this world? Why, in issuing his invitation to the eschatological
banquet, does the Lord single out "the poor, and the crippled,
and the blind, and the lame" (Luke 14:21), running through the
entire pitiful litany of the unfortunate ones of this world, and pass
over the rich, the powerful, and the proud? How could the Apostle
make this astonishing affirmation: "But the foolish things of the world
has God chosen to put to shame the 'wise,' and the weak things
of the world has God chosen to put to shame the strong, and the
base things of the world and the despised has God chosen, and
the things that are not, to bring to naught the things that are"
(1 Cor. 1:27-28)?

1. *Poverty, the Power to Receive*

Christ, to be sure, never proclaimed poverty as such to be blessed
any more than he did riches. He never canonized suffering for
its own sake, nor did he give his blessing to destitution, or his
encouragement to folly. For entrance into his kingdom, Jesus
requires more than simply the possession of a broken heart. This
statement must immediately be qualified, however, by attention
to the truth that distress under all its forms, the most tragic as
well as the most commonplace, is the fertile soil in which spiritual
poverty of soul takes root and blossoms. This is the thought behind
the Greek redaction of Matthew, which, while taking up Luke's
formula: "Blessed are you poor, for yours is the kingdom of God"
(Luke 6:20), adds this further dimension to it: "Blessed are the
poor in spirit, for theirs is the kingdom of heaven" (Matthew 5:3).

And why are they blessed? Because poverty of spirit is *the primary
condition for reception of the divine riches.* The seed of God's Word
cannot bear fruit if it falls on ground covered with thistles and
thorns: "And those who are sown among the thorns are they who

listen to the word; but the cares of the world, and the deceitfulness of riches, and the desires about other things, entering in, choke the word, and it is made fruitless" (Mark 4:18-19).

He whose soul is preoccupied with its concern for the good things of this earth, or even simply wrapped up in the joys of love, is incapable of responding to the Lord's invitation: "The first said to him, 'I have bought a farm, and I must go out and see it; I pray thee hold me excused.' And another said, 'I have bought five yoke of oxen, and I am on my way to try them; I pray thee hold me excused.' And another said, 'I have married a wife, and therefore I cannot come' " (Luke 14:18-20).

In his foolishness the rich man has lost his life to bind himself to things that perish. He was completely absorbed in building new storehouses for his wheat so that afterwards he could rest, eat, drink, and be merry, when God said to him: " 'Thou fool, this night do they demand thy soul of thee; and the things that thou hast provided, whose will they be?' So is he who lays up treasure for himself, and is not rich as regards God" (Luke 12:20-21).

The weakness of the poor man, on the other hand, is an unceasing appeal to the divine mercy. The distress of his torn heart is a continual cry for the favor of the divine love; and because his soul in its pitiable state is stripped of all comfort, it is readied for God's touch:

> Whom else have I in heaven?
> And when I am with you, the earth delights me not.
> Though my flesh and my heart waste away,
>   God is the rock of my heart and my portion forever (Ps. 72:25-26).

The intimate wounding of heart caused by distress, suffering, and failure is the door through which God can enter into the poor man's soul. Poverty of spirit thus becomes the power to receive God's waiting love; it is the complete surrender that opens itself to the inflow of his goodness, the utterly trusting abandonment that makes no account of either consolation or of sorrow:

> O Lord, my heart is not proud,
>   nor are my eyes haughty;
> I busy not myself with great things,
>   nor with things too sublime for me.
> Nay rather, I have stilled and quieted
>   my soul like a weaned child on its mother's lap (Ps. 130:1-2).

Now we see why Yahweh detests the vain self-sufficiency of the proud, the rich, that entire clique of foolish men who stand before him with such confidence in their own strength; why he so loves the bruised of heart, the lowly, the poor, all the "little ones" of heaven's kingdom to come, the stargazers of the Paradise of the future who are waiting for the hour when their misery will end and they will be raised up to their seats at the eschatological banquet. These are the ones whom Yahweh loves and who love Yahweh — the *'anawim* who dwell in the very heart of the people of God because they dwell within God's heart.

To affirm that the *Magnificat* is a song of poverty is to affirm in the same breath that it is a song of love. To say that the Virgin places herself in the ranks of the *'anawim* is equally to say that she is one of God's elite.

But there is more. The mystery of Mary lies within the greater mystery of the Church. Mary is the Daughter of Sion, the fulfillment of Israel. Within her own soul she encompasses the infinite longing of the poor of this world, that longing which forms the spiritual treasure of the people of God and is the milieu of its full flowering in the supernatural order. In looking upon the poverty (τὴν ταπεί-νωσιν) of his handmaid,[12] God has lowered his gaze to rest upon the poverty of the people of the Exodus on their march toward the Promised Land:

> . . . we cried to the Lord, the God of our fathers, and he heard our cry and saw our affliction (τὴν ταπείνωσιν), our toil and our oppression. He brought us out of Egypt . . . (Deut. 26:7-8).
>
> [The Lord] remembered us in our abjection (ἐν τῇ ταπεινώσει), for his mercy endures forever (Ps. 135:23).

In Mary, all the poverty and all the love of the past generations reach out to meet God, and to receive him in the Person of Jesus Christ. In her, the poor of Yahweh reach the end of their spiritual journey and enter directly into the kingdom of Christ-the-*Anaw*. All generations proclaim her blessed because she stands at the center of the salvation history of the Chosen People, at the very point where the Old Covenant becomes the New Covenant, where the suffering of the Old Testament meets and enters into communion with the poverty of Christ who became poor for our sake, that by his poverty we might become rich (2 Cor. 8:9).

2. Poverty, Power of Redemption

Biblical poverty is a power of receptivity, disposing the soul to open itself to God. We must add that it is also a power of redemption. The distress of the *'anawim* not only disposes them to open their starving hearts to God, but also orients them toward the redemption wrought through the Cross, the triumph won through failure. The suffering of the people of the promise is already an anticipation of the suffering of the promised Messias. There is no end to the procession of the poor which moves through the entire history of the Chosen People: Abel the just, immolated by his brother; Abraham the friend of God, who immolates his own son; David the persecuted, climbing with covered head the Mount of Olives (2 Kings 15:30); Jeremias, duped and exposed to ridicule by his God (Jer. 20:7); Job, who in the extremity of his affliction cried out to God to annihilate his very existence and take him from this world:

> Oh, that I might have my request,
>> and that God would grant what I long for:
> Even that God would decide to crush me,
>> that he would put forth his hand and cut me off! (Job 6:8-9).

Also among them are all those nameless souls of sorrow whose plaintive cry rises in a constant monotone of supplication from almost every page of the psalms:

> O Lord, my God, by day I cry out;
>> at night I clamor in your presence.
> Let my prayer come before you;
>> incline your ear to my call for help (Ps. 87:2-3).

This entire cortege, in all its darkling beauty, was unknowingly climbing the way leading to the Cross of Christ, where at long last it could understand, in the anguish of the Lord — "My God, My God, why hast thou forsaken me?" (Ps. 21:2) — the meaning, together with the redemptive value, of their own suffering. Christ's Cross, which stands at the center of human history, which unites the Old Dispensation with the New Covenant, thus becomes the point at which all the sacrifices of the *'anawim* of the Old Testament converge in a common fulfillment, and the point of departure for all the faithful of the New Covenant. The "passion" of the human race thus becomes a "com-passion" with Christ — both the heralding of the sacrifice of the Lord and also its extension.

Viewed from this last angle, the *Magnificat* is an annunciation of the mystery of the Cross. If it is, as we have said above, the song of victory, it is also the song of the Cross. But is it not therein that the entire mystery of Christ lies — the mystery of poverty

and suffering, the mystery of exaltation and glorification? In his
superb fashion, Paul points out the indestructible bond between
Christ's poverty and his glorification:

> [He] emptied himself, taking the nature of a slave and being made
> like unto men. . . . he humbled himself, becoming obedient to
> death, even to death on a cross. That is why (διό καί) God also
> has exalted him and has bestowed upon him the name that is above
> every name, so that . . . every tongue should proclaim that Jesus
> Christ is Lord, to the glory of the Father * (Phil. 2:7-11).

There is a forceful parallel between the victory hymn of Christ,
who became poor (ἐταπείνωσεν, 2:8) in taking on the nature of
a slave (δούλου, 2:7) and is glorified by "every tongue," and the
Magnificat, in which the Virgin sings of her poverty (τὴν ταπεί-
νωσιν) as a slave before God (τῆς δούλης αὐτοῦ, Luke 1:48)
and will be proclaimed blessed by all nations.

Paul begins this hymn with an exhortation to the Philippians
to have in their own hearts (φρονεῖν) the same mind that was in
Christ Jesus (2:5). Could not he, who was not especially gifted with
a Mariological sense, have perhaps been unaware that he was providing a perfect description of the soul of the Virgin? [13]

E. Conclusion

To know the heart of Mary, to penetrate the most secret recesses
of her thoughts, to comprehend the meditative depths of this heart
at once so poor and yet so royal — who among us has never longed
to know what the prayer of the Mother of Jesus was really like?
The *Magnificat* affords us a remarkable insight on this point.

Mary's heart is first of all a heart that sings the praise of God;
and her song is not so much the song of the story of a soul as
it is of the story of the salvation of all the people of God.

Mary's heart is also a heart that sings of the deliverance of the
poor of Yahweh; her voice is that of all the "beggars of God," who,
in her, acclaim the Lord of glory and of mercy. We may wonder
at our Lady's utter self-abasement; did she not know herself to
be the royal Mother of the Lord (Luke 1:43)? Surely she knew
it; but the greater a soul is, the greater is its sense of its own
littleness before God.

Because of its meaning within the mystery of the Church, the
Magnificat will be the song of thanksgiving *par excellence* in the
New Testament liturgy and in Christian piety. All the faithful, to

magnify him who never ceases to work his marvels, will take the words of the Virgin's canticle and make them their own. And this is only just; for as their voices join with our Lady's, they in turn bring about the fulfillment of her prophecy: ". . . behold, henceforth all generations shall call me blessed" (Luke 1:48).

In taking up the great themes of the Exodus and the deliverance of the Daughter of Sion, Mary is already anticipating the song of the heavenly liturgy of the Apocalypse; in heaven, the song of the redeemed who have passed through their great trial is the very "song of Moses, the servant of God, and the song of the Lamb" (Apoc. 15:3).

Blessed be the Virgin, for her gift to us of the *Magnificat*! And blessed be Luke, the careful secretary (cf. Luke 1:3), for having handed it on to us!

---

[1] On the distinction and the relationship between affective and effective poverty, see pp. 120–124.

[2] On Sophonias' place in the development of the poverty literature, see K. Thieme, *Die christliche Demut*, 1. Hälfte, *Wortgeschichte und Demut bei Jesus* (Giessen, 1906), pp. 14–43.

[3] E. Renan, *Histoire du Peuple d'Israël*, III, 153; cited by A. Gelin, *The Key Concepts of the Old Testament*, translated by George Lamb (New York: Sheed and Ward, 1955), pp. 91–93.

* *Translator's note*: We have here reproduced the author's translation of '*anawim*.

[4] A. Gelin, *op. cit.*, p. 73.

[5] This entire passage seems inspired by the theophany of Yahweh to Moses (Exod. 34:6-7): "The Lord, the Lord, a merciful and gracious God, slow to anger and rich in kindness and fidelity, continuing his kindness for a thousand generations, and forgiving wickedness and crime and sin. . . ." The connection can readily be seen in view of verse 7 of the psalm: "He has made known his ways to Moses."

[6] "Magnify the Lord, $\mu\epsilon\gamma\alpha\lambda\acute{u}\nu\alpha\tau\epsilon$ . . . $\tau\grave{o}\nu\,\kappa\acute{u}\rho\iota o\nu$" (v. 4) is perhaps matched by the "My soul magnifies the Lord, $\mu\epsilon\gamma\alpha\lambda\acute{u}\nu\epsilon\iota$ . . . $\tau\grave{o}\nu\,\kappa\acute{u}\rho\iota o\nu$" of Luke 1:47.

[7] The verb "to save", $\acute{\epsilon}\sigma\omega\sigma\epsilon\nu$, in verse 7, and $\sigma\acute{\omega}\sigma\epsilon\iota$ in verse 19, is reminiscent of the "God my Savior," $\tau\tilde{\omega}\,\Theta\epsilon\tilde{\omega}\,\tau\tilde{\omega}\,\Sigma\omega\tau\tilde{\eta}\rho\iota$, of Luke 1:47.

[8] Verse 11 is taken up in this sense in Luke 1:53.

[9] See pp. 106–108; verses 7 and 9 are an approximation to 1 Kings 2:5, 8.

[10] This psalm in reality is composed of three distinct poems: the first, which we have just cited; the second, which runs from verses 7 to 11; these two poems form Psalm 146 in the Septuagint and the Vulgate; the last (verses 12-20) is Psalm 147 in the Septuagint and the Vulgate.

[11] These verses give the psalm its date — the period of Nehemias or Esdras, the time of the return of the captives and the rebuilding of Jerusalem.

[12] The word $\tau\alpha\pi\epsilon\acute{\iota}\nu\omega\sigma\iota\varsigma$ admits of several interpretations. It can mean:

— littleness, weakness (cf. Sir. 11:1, 11-13); but this interpretation does not fit in with the spiritual mood that prevails in the opening lines of the *Magnificat*, in which Mary sings of God-the-Savior;

— humiliation (Gaechter), the sense in which it is most commonly to be found in the Septuagint;

— the humiliation of a wife, suffered by reason of her barrenness (Lyonnet); this is the sense in which it is employed in the Canticle of Anna (see pp. 107–108), the prototype of the *Magnificat*, and squares with Luke 1:25;

— the humility and the humiliation of the people of the Exodus, liberated by Yahweh. This last interpretation harmonizes with the typology of Mary, Daughter of Sion, already presented to us by Luke. To say that it is Mary's motherhood that effects the liberation of the people is hence to unite the third and fourth interpretations of ταπείνωσις.

* *Translator's note*: We here have followed the wording of the French text in order to bring out the force of the author's commentary.

13 If we may be permitted here to make a comparison between Paul and Luke, it might be said that Paul envisages Mary simply as the woman necessary for the Incarnation; she is placed on the side of the Law (to which, moreover, his attachment has ceased, but which was nevertheless the tutor "unto" Christ — Gal. 3:24): "But when the fullness of time came, God sent his Son, born of a woman, born under the Law, that he might redeem those who were under the Law, that we might receive the adoption of sons" (Gal. 4:4-5). Luke, on the contrary, envisages Mary as the fulfillment of this Law, that is to say, the spiritual plenitude which the Virgin herself received from this Incarnation.

Part VI

THE WOMAN CLOTHED
WITH THE SUN

> *A great sign appeared in heaven:*
> *a woman clothed with the sun,*
> *and the moon was under her feet,*
> *and upon her head a crown of twelve stars.*
> (Apoc. 12:1)

INTRODUCTION TO PART VI

Some thirty years separate the redaction of the Apocalypse (about the year 95) from that of Luke's Gospel [1] (about the year 60). During this period, Christian piety had the opportunity to meditate upon and deepen its understanding of the mystery of the Daughter of Sion. This meditation had borne fruit, evidently, in the last half of the second century with the typology of Mary as the new Eve, such as set forth by St. Justin and above all by St. Irenaeus [2] in what was thus the first springtime, as it were, of Marian theology. The witness of John, which completes that of Luke and heralds that of the earliest of the Fathers, marks a special stage in this meditation.

John was singled out in a special way to speak to us of Mary. After the Lord's death he in fact "took her into his home" (John 19:27) and hence knew her as no other apostle or evangelist could have known her; he lived in the intimacy of her presence, sharing with her the humblest joys of daily life and loving her as a son loves his mother. It could, therefore, be expected that he would have presented us with a portrait of the Virgin with features more clearly delineated than they are in Luke's, and in which the historical and psychological details of her life would stand out in all their richness. But his Gospel gives us nothing of the kind.

Luke had not hesitated to speak of Mary's intimate thoughts; he shows her troubled at the angel's greeting, exultant with joy at the Visitation, anxiously searching for Jesus in the Temple, marveling at the words that were spoken of her Child while not always understanding them — details which hold such an appeal for us, because they show us that the "Daughter of Sion," the "Mother of the Lord," withal remained a very simple woman, completely devoted to the welfare of her Child.

John, on the contrary, never speaks to us of these intimate feelings. He was the immediate confidant of her thoughts; yet it could almost be said that, no doubt by way of reaction against what he had seen day in and day out with his own eyes, he devotes none of his attention to Mary's human qualities. His faith, soaring above the horizon of historical fact, is searching for the spiritual meaning of the "sign." In his Gospel, both at Cana and at Calvary, Mary is called "Woman," a title which embodies nothing of human tenderness. Likewise in the Apocalypse she appears as a wondrous sign in heaven, but still under the image of Woman. Futhermore, while in the Annunciation narrative Mary, as is entirely natural, occupies the central place, in his prologue John succeeds in speaking to us of the Incarnation without so much as mentioning her in whom Jesus took on human flesh.

This particular orientation of John's thought must dictate the procedure of the exegete; a too "fleshly" admiration of the mystery of Mary must give way to the spiritual contemplation of her mystery. We thus come full circle and rejoin the fundamental Mariological theme of the Synoptics: Mary is more blessed for having heard the Word of God than for having given birth to Christ according to the flesh.

We shall begin our study with the text of the Apocalypse. Generally speaking, the text of the Gospels presents fewer exegetical difficulties than does that of the Apocalypse. In the present case, however, we shall find that analysis of the Apocalypse will shed light on certain points in the Gospel that require a special delicacy of interpretation.

The Woman of The Apocalypse

And a great sign appeared in heaven: a woman clothed with the sun, and the moon was under her feet, and upon her head a crown of twelve stars. And being with child, she cried out in her travail and was in the anguish of delivery. And another sign was seen in heaven, and behold, a great red dragon having seven heads and ten horns, and upon his heads seven diadems. And his tail was dragging along the third part of the stars of heaven, and it dashed them to the earth; and the dragon stood before the woman who was about to bring forth, that when she had brought forth he might devour her son. And she brought forth a male child, who is to shepherd * all nations with a rod of iron; and her child was caught up to God and to his throne. And the woman fled into the wilderness, where she has a place prepared by God, that there they may nourish her a thousand two hundred and sixty days.

And there was a battle in heaven; Michael and his angels battled with the dragon, and the dragon fought and his angels. And they did not prevail, neither was their place found any more in heaven. And the great dragon was cast down, the ancient serpent, he who is called the devil and Satan, who leads astray the whole world; and he was cast down to the earth and with him his angels were cast down.

And I heard a loud voice in heaven saying, "Now has come the salvation, and the power and the kingdom of our God, and the authority of his Christ; for the accuser of our brethren has been cast down, he who accused them before our God day and night. And they overcame him through the blood of the Lamb and through the word of their witness, for they did not love their lives even in face of death. Therefore rejoice, O heavens, and you who dwell therein. Woe to the earth and to the sea, because the devil has gone down to you in great wrath, knowing that he has but a short time."

And when the dragon saw that he was cast down to the earth, he pursued the woman who had brought forth the male child. And there were given to the woman the two wings of the great eagle, that she might fly into the wilderness unto her place, where she is nourished for a time and times and a half time, away from the serpent. And the serpent cast out of his mouth after the woman water like a river, that he might cause her to be carried away by the river. And the earth helped the woman, and the earth opened her mouth and swallowed up the river that the dragon had cast out of his mouth. And the dragon was angered at the woman, and went away to wage war with the rest of her offspring, who keep the commandments of God, and hold fast the testimony of Jesus. And he stood upon the sand of the sea [3] (Apoc. 12:1-18).

---

[1] Despite the endeavors of criticism, these dates are still only approximate. For the Apocalypse the problem is a special one, owing to the hypothesis of a twofold redaction, the first going back to before the year 70, and the second to around the year 95. In any circumstances, the fusion of the two texts could have taken place only after the year 95. We shall not touch here upon the problem of authenticity, apart from pointing out that it has no bearing upon the fact of its canonicity. In other words, even if the Apocalypse had been committed to writing, either totally or in part, by someone who was an immediate disciple of John's and the inheritor of his thought, the writing for all this remains an inspired writing, and a part of the canon of Scripture as fixed by the Council of Trent (cf. Denz. 783–784). In attributing the Apocalypse to John, we are not thereby committing ourselves to a position on the problem of its authenticity.

[2] See Excursus I, pp. 199–208.

* *Translator's note*: We have here preserved the wording of the author, who is rendering the verb ποιμαίνειν of the original Greek in its full literal sense.

[3] The hypothesis of a twofold version, of which we have just been speaking, (see n. 1, above), here seems to be verified:

— Verses 1-12 in effect form a coherent ensemble which terminates in a song of victory; but from verse 13 on the scene of all-out war is resumed and we meet with a certain number of doublets which lead us back to what has gone before.

— Thus in verse 14 the woman flees into the wilderness to a place which is prepared for her; but in verse 6 she had already been shown to us as in the wilderness, in her place of refuge.

— In the same way, in verse 14 the dragon wages war with "the rest of her offspring"; but in verse 11 this offspring has already overcome the dragon.

It is therefore possible that verses 13-18 may be evidence of another redaction which has been reworked to provide a link with verses 1-12.

This hypothesis allows of the organization of the entire chapter into a view of the whole:

1) in which the two accounts are fused into one;

2) one account is seen in the light of the other.

Chapter 12

THE DRAMA AS A WHOLE

A. THE CHARACTERS

The characters on stage are: (1) on one side, the Dragon and his angels; (2) on the other, all those who fight against the Dragon and overcome him. They are: the Woman, her Child, the rest of her offspring, Michael and his angels, and those who are dwelling in heaven and singing the song of victory. These personages have joined forces and formed a coalition against the Dragon.

B. THE ACTION

The battle takes place simultaneously on earth and in heaven:

1. *On Earth*

The Dragon wages war first of all against the Child; but the Child is caught up to God and to his throne.

The Dragon then turns against the Woman; but she escapes his fury and takes refuge in the wilderness. The earth likewise comes to her aid by swallowing up the river that the Dragon had cast after her.

The Dragon finally attacks "the rest of her offspring," which have already overcome him "through the blood of the Lamb."

2. *In Heaven*

We are witnesses, first of all, to the battle waged by Michael and his angels against the Dragon and his legions. Michael triumphs and the Dragon is cast down to the earth.

We next hear the song of victory which celebrates the kingdom of God (the Father), the sovereignty of Christ, and the victory of the "brethren." We are thus told that the battle fought in heaven is superimposed on the battle fought on earth: the triumph of Michael is also the triumph of the Child, of the Woman, and of the "brethren."

133

Chapter 13

THE FIGURES OF THE DRAMA

A. THE DRAGON

Here John's terminology of the "sign" enters into such detail as to embrace a host of varying meanings: he is "the ancient serpent, he who is called the devil and Satan" (v. 9, cf. 22:2). He leads all the inhabited world astray.[1] In his Gospel, John had called him "the prince of this world;"[2] here he shows him to us crowned with seven diadems, the insignia of his royal power (v. 3). He always is standing in opposition to God, and God always is triumphant over him.[3]

This warfare is pictured as a gigantic struggle with Michael and his angels. Michael is in effect the champion and protector of the Israel of God;[4] he inflicts a spectacular defeat upon him, ejects him from heaven, and casts him down to earth (vv. 9, 13). We are reminded of the words our Lord had spoken before the final Passover: "Now is the judgment of the world; now will the prince of the world be cast out" (John 12:31; cf. Luke 10:18).

B. THE CHILD

The identity of the Child can be established from these two expressions: (1) he is to shepherd the nations with a rod of iron; (2) he is caught up to God's throne.

1. *He is to shepherd the nations with a rod of iron*

This metaphor is meant to signify the irresistible power of kingship over the nations, and has been taken from Psalm 2:

> "I myself have set up my king
>   on Son, my holy mountain."

The Lord said to me, "You are my son;
  this day I have begotten you.
Ask of me and I will give you
  the nations for an inheritance
  and the ends of the earth for you possession.
You are to shepherd them with an iron rod;
  you shall shatter them like an earthen dish" (Ps. 2:6-9).[5]

In its primitive literal sense, the oracle applied first of all to a king of Israel. In the post-exilic period, this royal psalm took on an eschatological perspective, in which the figure of the Davidic king expands to include that of the Servant of Yahweh, who as the light of the nations is to send forth the rays of salvation to the uttermost ends of the earth.[6]

The widening of the dimensions of this early Scriptural motif should not be cause for surprise. The Bible is not a collection of desiccated texts but the living Word of God, lived from day to day by the people of God. And so the New Testament, with the light of the Holy Spirit, will recognize Christ Jesus himself in the Davidic king of Psalm 2: ". . . the promise made to our fathers, God has fulfilled to our children, in raising up Jesus, as also it is written in the second Psalm, *Thou art my son, this day have I begotten thee*" (Acts 13:32-33; cf. 4:24-30). The Epistle to the Hebrews will use this same passage to establish the superiority of the Son over the angelic world: "For to which of the angels has he ever said, *Thou art my son, I this day have begotten thee?*" (Heb. 1:5; cf. 5:5).

The history of Psalm 2 reaches its culminating point in these texts. They show us, in the ancient king of Israel, the figure of the Lord Jesus. They also show us, in this same Jesus, the full realization of royal lordship; in Jesus Christ the Davidic king has become God's Son. It is thus that John contemplates him: he is the Word of God, escorted by heavenly armies, exercising dominion over all the peoples of the earth:

> And I saw heaven standing open; and behold, a white horse, and he who sat upon it is called Faithful and True, and with justice he judges and wages war. And his eyes are as a flame of fire, and on his head are many diadems; he has a name written which no man knows except himself. And he is clothed in a garment sprinkled with blood, and his name is called The Word of God. And the armies of heaven, clothed in fine linen, white and pure, were following him on white horses. And from his mouth goes forth a sharp sword with which to smite the nations. And he will shepherd them with a rod of iron (Apoc. 19:11-15).

If, accordingly, we consider the messianic context in which Acts and the Epistle to the Hebrews have placed Psalm 2, and moreover the exegesis which is given by John himself in chapter 19 of the Apocalypse, we can draw the conclusion that the Child who is to shepherd the nations with a rod of iron is Christ Jesus.

It must immediately be added, however, that this conclusion is but a partial one. The expression, in fact, possesses a twofold meaning, for it can also designate the faithful themselves. Insofar as they participate in the mystery of Christ, they too have a share in his royalty: [7]

> And to him who overcomes, and who keeps my works unto the end, I will give authority over the nations. And he shall shepherd them with a rod of iron, and like the potter's vessel they shall be dashed to pieces, as I also have received from my Father; and I will give him the morning star (Apoc. 2:26-28).

As we were saying, the history of Psalm 2 reaches its culminating point in Christ; but it can equally be said that this history has Christ for its point of departure. It is in effect through him, the King of kings and Lord of lords (Apoc. 19:16), that the faithful themselves become kings and lords, thus forming a living extension of his royalty: "He who overcomes, I will permit him to sit with me upon my throne; as I also have overcome and have sat with my Father on his throne. . . . and they shall reign forever and ever" (Apoc. 3:21; 22:5).

Are we obliged to make an exclusive choice between these two exegeses? It does not seem so, for the mystery of Jesus is also the mystery of those who belong to him; he has written down the spiritual history of each of the individual faithful in the unfolding mystery of his own life. Here again we encounter a central aspect of the Johannine message: the real, albeit most mysterious unity that exists between Christ and the faithful. It is precisely this unity with Jesus that is the foundation of the unity of the faithful among themselves. To borrow one of John's own expressions, we are all each other's "brother and partner in the tribulation and kingdom and patience that are in Jesus" (Apoc. 1:9).

Here too it can be pointed out that the context of Psalm 2 — the struggle and triumph of Yahweh's Anointed — is taken up in nearly all these citations. In Acts 13:27-33, Jesus triumphs through his resurrection, but only after having passed through the mystery of his death; in Hebrews 1:3-5, Jesus is seated in the highest heaven, "at the right hand of the majesty," but after having effected the purgation from sin; likewise in Apocalypse 19:11ff., the fanciful picturing of the Word of God mounted on horseback closes with the portrayal of his universal victory, but the apparel in which Jesus is clothed is sprinkled with the blood of his Passion; finally, in Apocalypse 12, Jesus is caught up to God's throne, where he is welcomed with the hymn of his sovereignty, but this victory is preceded by his combat with the Dragon. Here we are at the very heart of John's message — the struggle and the triumph of Jesus, and his death which ends in victory.

And this mystery of Christ's is also that of his faithful: "They overcame [the Dragon] through the blood of the Lamb" (Apoc. 12:11). In 7:13-14, John had already shown us the white-clad cortege of the elect, who have passed through the great trial: "These who are clothed in white robes, who are they? and whence have they come?" And I said to him, "My lord, thou knowest." And he said to me, "These are they who have come out of the great tribulation, and have washed their robes and made them white in the blood of the Lamb" (Apoc. 7:13-14).

2. *And her Child was caught up to God and to his throne*

Here John is speaking of the mystery of Christ's glorification, namely, his resurrection and ascension to his Father. The birth of the royal Child is directed precisely at the destruction of the Devil's empire: "To this end the Son of God appeared, that he might destroy the works of the devil" (1 John 3:8). The Devil seeks to devour the Child as soon as he is born, but he is powerless against him: ". . . the prince of the world is coming, [but] in me he has nothing" (John 14:30). His very death marks the inauguration of his triumph: "I am the First and the Last, and he who lives; I was dead, and behold, I am living forevermore; and I have the keys of death and of hell" (Apoc. 1:17-18).

This personal history of Jesus in turn continues in the lives of all the rest of the offspring. He is "the First and the Last." If John presents him to us as a newborn Child enthroned at the side of the Father, it is precisely, it seems to us, because his birth, his struggle with the Dragon, his resurrection and his ascension constitute the initial phase of the birth of the Church, its struggle and its triumph. This is why the heavenly canticle of chapters 5 and 12 sings simultaneously of both the victory of Christ and the triumph of the redeemed: ". . . the lion of the tribe of Juda, the root of David, has overcome. . . . and has made them for our

God a kingdom and priests, and they shall reign over the earth" (Apoc. 5:5, 10).

We are now ready to identify the Child "who is to shepherd all nations with a rod of iron," and who is "caught up to God and to his throne." He is first of all Jesus, the Son of Mary, the royal Messias. John is contemplating him in the mystery of his birth, his death, and his ascension. In addition to this first sense, it is also possible to see a collective meaning in the sign. It is intimated that the destiny of the disciples is bound up with that of the Master, that they share in his combat and his triumph. These two sign-meanings do not appear to be mutually exclusive; rather they are complementary. We should be ready to maintain that here we are presented with Christ as containing all the faithful within himself. John will, in fact, present the disciples to us in terms that are more explicit.

C. THE WOMAN

Our identification of the Woman clothed with the sun and crowned with stars will hinge on our exegesis of the Child "who is to shepherd all nations with a rod of iron." If this Child is Christ, his mother is the Virgin Mary. But if this Child represents the totality of the faithful, then his mother is none other than the Church, represented under the traditional allegorical figure of the Woman.[8]

Mary or the Church? Each of these exegeses has the advantage of illuminating one of the two sets of features of the sorrowful yet glorious Woman, the Mother of the individual Messias and the Mother of the rest of the offspring. But this is precisely where their weakness lies — neither can explain the entire assemblage of features under which the Woman appears: the birth of the individual and the collective Messias, the sorrows of the delivery, the sojourn in the wilderness. They are partial explanations which fragment the unity of the "sign in heaven." For if we interpret this "sign" as applying to the Virgin Mary, we cannot take due account of the sorrows of the delivery and the sojourn in the wilderness. But if we opt, on the other hand, for a broader exegesis, how can we still explain how this Church, the assembly of the redeemed, has given birth to the individual Messias?[9]

In our opinion, the problem of "Mary or the Church" is a false issue; and as we know, every false issue remains unresolved. We must isolate a single reality which embraces the entire ensemble of truths relating both to Mary and to the Church, a reality which can explain how the Woman is crowned with stars and clothed with the sun, cries out in the anguish of her delivery, and gives birth to the individual Messias, while yet remaining the mother of the rest of the offspring and, finally, passing a period of time in the wilderness.

1. Mary, Archetype of the Church

This reality is not Mary or the Church, nor even Mary and the Church. It is Mary understood as the archetype of the Church, insofar as in her person the mystery of the Church achieves its most intense point of fulfillment. As A. Müller has so finely observed: [10]

> It is insufficient to say: the Woman is Mary; for she is presented also as the type of the Church. It is insufficient to say: the Woman is the Church; for her features have been borrowed from Mary's portrait; she is the image of Mary. In these two cases the Woman would be playing two different roles: in one she is herself; in the other, she plays the role of another. But this does not represent the truth of the matter, for there is only one role that is played, the bringing forth of Christ: both in its pristine historical reality and its ultimate full-flowering in the history of the world. And this is why the Woman is only one Woman: the Mother of Christ in his primary historical reality and in his ultimate completion in the history of the world.

He goes on to conclude: "Mary is the perfect (realization of the) Church; the mystery of the Church is, in essence, the mystery of Mary." [11] John himself orients us toward this conclusion with the double meaning he assigns to the expression "who is to shepherd all nations." This Child, as we have seen above, is at the same time both the individual Messias and the entire assembly of the redeemed; he is Christ considered as containing within himself all those who belong to him. Hence the Mother of the Child is at the same time both Mary and the Church, Mary considered as the archetype of the Church.

2. The New Eve

Within this same ecclesial perspective, Luke, as we shall recall, had presented Mary as the personification of the Daughter of Sion. John will make the same association of ideas, but will clothe them in different imagery; the Woman is linked with her who was the Woman *par excellence*, Eve.

The reference to Genesis is explicit; it is seen in the mention of the Dragon — he is the ancient Serpent (v. 9). It is recalled that he is the seducer of the whole world (*ibid.*), reminding us of Eve's words: "The serpent deceived me" (Gen. 3:13). The anguish of her delivery could equally be reminiscent of Genesis 3:16: ". . . in pain shall you bring forth children. . . ." Above all, and of central importance, there is the Woman's waging of war with the Serpent and her victory over him, paralleled by the struggle of her offspring with the Serpent's legions. This warfare, inaugurated in Genesis, is going to continue down through the entire history of God's people, finally to end with the total yet pain-marked victory of the Woman and her offspring: "I will put enmity between you and the woman, between your seed and her seed; he shall crush your head, and you shall lie in wait for his heel" (Gen. 3:15).

In translating this text, the Septuagint editors had already accentuated the messianic character of the prophecy. They attributed the victory, not to the Woman's descendants in general, but to one of her sons. With John, the meaning of the text takes on, so to speak, a world-wide dimension; the victory is simultaneously that of the Child, that of the Woman, and that of her offspring.

These different points of contact might be schematized as follows:

Genesis 3	*Apocalypse 12*
The serpent deceived me	the ancient serpent, . . . who leads astray the whole world
I will put enmity between you and the woman	the dragon . . . pursued the woman
between your seed and her seed	and [he] went away to wage war with the rest of her offspring
in pain shall you bring forth children	she cried out in her travail and was in the anguish of delivery

Over and above the part played by this parallelism, beyond the tallying of words and images, the identity and the continuity of the message are to be plainly seen: the prophecy of Genesis heralds that of the Apocalypse; that of the Apocalypse takes up that of Genesis and brings it to fulfillment. In her struggle against the Dragon, the ancient Serpent, the victorious Woman clothed with the sun and crowned with stars takes the place of the first Eve; in Mary, God is mindful of Eve.[12]

3. *The Mother of the Rest of the Offspring* [13]

The very reference to Eve seems implicitly to introduce the question of spiritual motherhood. "[Adam] called his wife Eve because she was the mother of all the living" (Gen. 3:20). Can it be said that Mary, the new Eve, is equally Mother of the living, namely, of "the rest of the offspring"? We think that several points should be made in this connection.

a) Mary is the Mother of Jesus

These words contain the entire story of her life. But this story, at once so intimate and so personal, leads her straight across the threshold of the history of the Church. Her motherhood places her at the very fountainhead of the Mystical Body. With the totality of her being, her soul and her body, she participates in the very act by which the Body is constituted. If Christ is born of her, it is not exclusively in order that she may be his Mother; it is also in order that we may become brothers of Christ, that we may all be reestablished in him (Eph. 1:10). Thus, in becoming the Mother of Jesus, she becomes, and in a wholly natural way, the spiritual Mother of the rest of the offspring, of all those whom Christ himself calls his brothers (cf. John 20:17; Heb 2:11, 17).

John does not follow this line of reasoning to its conclusion, but he does, at least, furnish us with the premises for it in the doctrine of the Mystical Body. In the present text, taking another line of approach, he supplies us with other clues which merit special attention:

— The Child who is to shepherd all nations with a rod of iron is, first of all, as we have said above, Christ Jesus himself, and following upon this, all the faithful who participate in his kingship. Hence motherhood, considered in terms of its relation to the royal Child, can also signify motherhood in relation to all the brothers of Jesus;

— In verse 17, it is a question of "the rest of the Woman's offspring." In its literal sense, the word $\sigma\pi\acute{\epsilon}\rho\mu\alpha$ signifies seed or germ, and in a wider sense, descendants, posterity, lineage. John is familiar with both these senses, as evidenced in his first Epistle, where he will write in language of extraordinary forcefulness and realism: "Whoever is born of God does not commit sin, because his seed abides in him and he cannot sin, because he is born of God" (1 John 3:9). In his Gospel he will say, moreover, that Christ is to come from the seed, namely, that he is of the offspring of David (7:42).

But this descent is prolonged and continues in the New Testament. When he speaks of the "rest" of the offspring, John in his own mind clearly is speaking of the continuity between the Church of the Old Testament and the Church of the New.

More than this, Christ appears as constituting in himself, in a unique and transcendent manner, all the offspring of the promise:

> The promises were made to Abraham and to his offspring. He does not say, "And to his offsprings," as of many; but as of one, "And to thy offspring," who is Christ. . . . For you are all the children of God through faith in Christ Jesus. . . . For you are all one in Christ Jesus. And if you are Christ's, then you are the offspring of Abraham, heirs according to promise (Gal 3:16, 26, 28-29).

In virtue of the very fact that she is the Mother of Christ Jesus, Mary is the Mother of him in whom we are all "one." We truly cannot separate these two maternities, any more than we can separate Christ the First-born from the rest of his brethren.

b) The Church is the Mother of all the faithful

The texts of the post-exilic period already were celebrating the new Sion possessed of innumerable sons, the Mother whose tent was to become too small to shelter all her children:

> Raise a glad cry, you barren one who did not bear,
>   break forth in jubilant song, you who were not in labor,
> For more numerous are the children of the deserted wife
>   than the children of her who has a husband, says the Lord.
> Enlarge the space for your tent,
>   spread out your tent cloths unsparingly;
>   lengthen your ropes and make firm your stakes.
> For you shall spread abroad
>   to the right and to the left [14] (Is. 54:1-3).

Paul, citing this text, will write with complete simplicity, "Jerusalem is our mother." [15]

Now Mary is the archetype of the Church. Hence the universal motherhood which embraces all the faithful must first of all exist in Mary before its subsequent existence in the Church, since the Church does no more than to reproduce the mystery of Mary.

John thus furnishes theological reflection with the premises which permit it to conclude that the Mother of Jesus is also the Mother of the rest of the offspring. He does not teach this explicitly — and we must never do violence to the texts, seeking to wrest from them an avowal that they would never make; but neither may we underestimate the value of the theological reasoning which bases

Mary's spiritual motherhood on one of the most essential truths of Scripture, the unity of Christ and the faithful.

[1] Cf. Wis. 2:24.

[2] Cf. John 12:31; 14:30; 16:11. This does not mean that the devil reigns over this world, but only over its followers, over sinners. When he says to Christ: "To thee will I give all this power and their glory; for to me they have been delivered, and to whomever I will I give them," he is revealing himself as he really is; he might be called a liar by profession: "When he tells a lie he speaks from his very nature, for he is a liar and the father of lies" (John 8:44).

[3] Cf. Is. 27:1; 51:9.

[4] Cf. Dan. 10:21.

[5] We have touched up verse 9a, following the Septuagint translation: "Thou shalt shepherd them ($\pi o\iota\mu\alpha\nu\epsilon\hat{\iota}\varsigma$) with a rod of iron.

[6] Cf. Is. 42:6; Luke 2:32.

[7] It is because of this text of Apocalypse 2:26-28 that we feel we cannot follow here the exegesis (which is in other respects excellent) of P. Braun. Also, when he writes (*Le Mère des Fidèles, op. cit.*, p. 134): "This reference to Psalm 2:9 is decisive. Mighty and king of peoples, the Child cannot be other then the Messias Jesus, the Son of Mary," the expression "cannot be" seems rather strongly weighted to us. The exegesis of P. Allo (*Saint Jean, Apocalypse*, Coll. *Études bibliques*, pp. 160–161), who centers his interpretation on Christ, although not to the exclusion of the faithful, is more finely nuanced.

[8] Hippolytus was already expounding that the Woman clothed with the sun is most certainly being presented by John as a sign of the Church: for she is clothed with the Logos, the Only-begotten of the Father, who shines more brilliantly than the sun. . . . She is with child and cries out in the sorrows and the travail of her delivery, because the Church begets the Logos in her heart all the while that she suffers persecution in the world at the hands of the unfaithful. And she brought forth, it was said, a male Child, who is to shepherd all nations: this is Christ in all his manhood and perfection, the Child of God, God and Man, he who was announced by the prophets; in bringing him forth, the Church teaches the peoples (*De Anti-Christo*, 61; *G.C.S. Hip.* 1–2, p. 41). Hippolytus does not intend, however, to exclude Mary from his exegesis; see, on this subject, the fine points which A. Müller (*Ecclesia-Maria* [Freiburg, 1951], p. 82, n. 84) brings to bear on the exegesis of Rahner (*Our Lady and the Church*, translated by Sebastian Bullough, O.P. [New York: Pantheon Books, 1961], pp. 105–107).

[9] As E. Tobac has in fact pointed out: "If the prophets do speak from time to time of Sion as giving birth to a holy people (Is. 66:7ff.), never do they present her as bringing the individual Messias into the world" (*Les Prophètes d'Israël*, 1 [Lierre, 1919], p. 267).

[10] A. Müller, *Ecclesia-Maria* (2nd edition, 1955), p. 234.

[11] *Ibid.*, p. 239: "Maria ist die vollkommene (Verwirklichung der) Kirche. Das Wesengeheimnis der Kirche ist das Mariengeheimnis" (the parentheses are the author's). P. Allo (*Saint Jean, L'Apocalypse* [Paris, 1933], p. 193) explains from his point of view: "All difficulties vanish if we keep in mind: (1) the multiple virtuality of the symbols of our Apocalypse; (2) the mystical sense that the word $\kappa\rho\iota\sigma$-$\tau\acute{o}\varsigma$ = Messias had taken on in the apostolic communities well before the composition of this book. Christ is at the head of the Church; but the Church is the Body

of Christ. The mystical Christ, the total Christ, takes in head and body. . . . This virtuality explains the fact why there are certain features which at once belong both to the personal and to the mystical Christ, while at the same time there are others which can be referred only to the personal or only to the mystical Christ."

12 On the traditions of the patristic period and the theological significance of Mary, the new Eve, see Excursus I, pp. 199–208.

13 Mary's spiritual motherhood in regard to Christians is one of the truths most deeply cherished by contemporary Marian devotion. It should be borne in mind, however, that this teaching made its appearance in patristic thought at a rather late date. This is as much as to affirm that it is not in evidence in the data of Scripture. Prudence and discretion, therefore, must characterize exegesis on this theme.

14 Cf. Is. 60:4.

15 Gal. 4:26; cf. Ps. 86:5.

Chapter 14

ANALYSIS OF THE TEXT

A. Clothed with the Sun, Crowned with Twelve Stars

> And a great sign appeared in heaven: a woman clothed with the sun, and the moon was under her feet, and upon her head a crown of twelve stars (Apoc. 12:1).

There is something suggestive of liturgical ritual in the manner in which this presentation of the Woman clothed with the sun and crowned with twelve stars unfolds. Her sudden appearance is reminiscent of that of the High Priest coming forth from the Holy of Holies: "Like a star shining among the clouds, like the full moon at the holyday season; like the sun shining upon the temple, like the rainbow appearing in the cloudy sky" (Sir. 50:6-7).

These stars with which she is arrayed place the Virgin in the sphere of the divine; she who thus appears belongs to the super-celestial world. The stars in effect compose, together with the angelic myriads, the court of Yahweh-Sabaoth; it was in their presence that the Creator, at the dawn of creation, laid the cornerstone of the world: "While the morning stars sang in chorus and all the sons of God shouted for joy" [1] (Job 38:7). In union with the angelic host they sing his glory (Ps. 148:3-4; cf. Dan. 3:63); they form the floor of the heavenly Temple: "Does not God, in the heights of the heavens, behold the stars, high though they are?" (Job 22:12). Yahweh pitches his tent in the sun (Ps. 18:5-6); he robes himself with light as with a cloak: "O Lord, my God, you are great indeed! You are clothed with majesty and glory, robed in light as with a cloak" (Ps. 103:1-2).

Clothed with the sun, Mary thus appears truly as a great sign "in heaven," belonging already to the heavenly world; in her starry crown she is Queen of the cosmos; resting upon the moon, she holds dominion over time while dwelling in eternity. The first fruits of earth's redeemed, the image of the risen Church, she stands in the vanguard of the pilgrim Church as in her it enters into the kingdom, her own fulfillment heralding the consummation of the mystery of the rest of her offspring — their dwelling with the Father and the Lamb in splendor and in glory.

Mary's personal vocation also heralds the state of the entire Church, for the faithful, too, will one day be clothed with the sun. Daniel, in his apocalypse, foretells in effect that when the archangel Michael, the angel of the Apocalypse, rises up to fight for the cause of the children of Israel, the just will shine brightly like the splendor of the firmament, like the stars forever, for all eternity (Dan. 12:1-3). Nor should we forget the All-Beautiful One of the Canticle of Canticles, ascending from the desert: " [Coming] forth like the dawn, as beautiful as the moon, as resplendent as the sun" (Cant. 6:10).

More beautiful still will the new Jerusalem be, radiant with the very glory of Yahweh (Is. 60:1ff.). John will take up these images in the final vision of the new Jerusalem, in chapters 21 and 22 of the Apocalypse. A comparison of these with chapter 12 is particularly suggestive:

— In Apocalypse 12, the Woman is a sign in heaven; in Apocalypse 21, she is the new Jerusalem that comes down out of heaven from God, "made ready as a bride adorned for her husband" (Apoc. 21:2).

— Here, she is clothed with the sun and crowned with stars; there, the Bride of the Lamb is resplendent, "having the glory of God" (Apoc. 21:11). The sun itself has disappeared: "And the city has no need of the sun or the moon to shine upon it. For the glory of God lights it up, and the Lamb is the lamp thereof" (Apoc. 21:23).

— Here, she is crowned with twelve stars; there, we are shown the twelve gates upon which are inscribed the names of the twelve tribes of Israel and the twelve foundation-stones representing the twelve apostles of the Lamb (Apoc. 21:12-14).

— Here, the Woman cries out in the anguish of her delivery; there, God "will wipe away every tear from their eyes. And death shall be no more; neither shall there be mourning, nor crying, nor pain any more" (Apoc. 21:4).

— Here, the Child is to shepherd the nations with a rod of iron; there, we witness to the triumph of the Child: "And the nations shall walk by the light thereof; and the kings of the earth shall bring their glory and honor into it" (Apoc. 21:24).

The Woman clothed with the sun and crowned with stars is, then, also the Church triumphant of Apocalypse 21; if in its splendor this last vision surpasses that of Apocalypse 12, it is because there John is contemplating the Church at the hour of her final triumph, when her period of strife has come to its end. The sorrows of her bringing-forth have reached their term; the devil-seducer and his worshippers are cast into the pool of fire and brimstone, where "they will be tormented day and night forever and ever" (Apoc. 20:10). It is the hour when God will make all things new (cf. Apoc. 21:5) and give himself to him who has overcome as his inheritance: "I will be his God, and he shall be my son" (Apoc. 21:7). The sorrows of the delivery will have come to an end, for the Woman will have brought forth the full number of those whose names are written in the book of life.

The sign in heaven thus conceals a twofold reality. It is at the same time both the Virgin Mary, the Mother of Jesus, and the Church as the Bride, the Mother of all who belong to Jesus, two aspects which compenetrate each other to form one ordered whole — the Virgin Mary, the archetype of the Church. Reset in this perspective, certain aspects of John's vision which at first sight seemed contradictory are now seen to complement and to explain each other. In Mary, the Church has already attained her final state; she is "in heaven"; but in her children, she remains in the course of her pilgrimage; she is still in the desert. In Mary, she brings forth Christ in the joy of Bethlehem; but in her children, she is still crying out in the throes of her delivery.

The real problem here is not so much that of setting the mystery of Mary against that of "the rest of her offspring" as it is that of grasping the essential continuity that binds these two mysteries to each other. The mystery of Mary is also, insofar as it can be communicated, the mystery of her children. The Virgin clothed with the sun and crowned with stars prefigures, in a very exact manner, the future glory of the faithful, who "will shine forth like the sun in the kingdom of their Father" (Matthew 13:43). The children will follow the Mother; if Mary is the first, this means, to be sure, that she goes before us, but it also means that we shall follow her. For there is but one Church, that of Jesus Christ; Mary, its most eminent member, is the archetype.

In Mary, the Church is already shining resplendent in heaven; in her children, she is still struggling along in the wilderness. But precisely because the Church is one, it must be added that its mystery is not realized only according to its glorious mode in Mary and its sorrowful mode in her children; it simultaneously attains a further dimension in all her children, who share, at the same time, in both her glory and her suffering. John is envisaging the Church not simply in its state of becoming, its progressive realization that is measured by time, as if today it is in the wilderness, but at the Parousia will enter into God's light; he is envisaging it rather as it exists in its essential reality, as it is in the eternity of the divine vision, not only as it appears to the eyes of men — the Church at once heavenly and earthly, the Church illumined by the light of the Lamb while yet sojourning in the wilderness, the Church ever victorious yet ever subject to the assaults of the demon.

Here we are touching on a point of capital importance in the mystery of the Church, or better, in the mystery of the Church's participation in the very life of Jesus. Because this life comes from Christ, the individual member of the faithful somehow is drawn out of the world of sin and set in the world of God: "The Father . . . has made us worthy to share the lot of the saints in light. He has rescued us from the power of darkness and transferred us into the kingdom of his beloved Son" (Col. 1:12-13). But because this divine life is brought to fulfillment in a human freedom that is frail and wounded, in men of flesh and blood, the Christian remains bound to the earthly world: "But our citizenship is in heaven from which also we eagerly await a Savior, our Lord Jesus Christ, who will refashion the body of our lowliness, conforming it to the body of his glory" (Phil. 3:20-21).

Herein lies the real paradox of Christianity, a paradox of misery and glory, of light and shadow, of victory and struggle. Through Jesus our humanity is already raised up and seated in heaven (Eph. 2:6), and yet we are saved only in hope (Rom. 8:24); through Jesus, henceforth we are sons of God — *nunc filii Dei sumus* — yet meanwhile we are still awaiting the glorious manifestation of the *similes ei erimus*, when "we shall be like to [God], for we shall see him just as he is" (1 John 3:2). We already possess eternal life (John 6:40), but at the same time we love Christ without seeing him (1 Peter 1:8); we have already vanquished the powers of darkness in dying with Christ on the Cross (Col. 2:15), but we must still continue unceasingly to "stand against the wiles of the devil" (Eph.

6:11). This is the key to the mystery of the Woman, who though crowned with glory is racked with anguish.[2]

B. THE ANGUISH OF HER DELIVERY

. . . she cried out in her travail and was in the anguish of delivery (Apoc. 12:2).

The pangs of childbirth are the image habitually used by Scripture to denote violent and sudden suffering. The metaphor occurs ordinarily in a context of war, distress, and oppression;[3] the force and violence of its symbolism made it a particularly apt literary expression of the tribulations which were to accompany the Day of Yahweh. Thus runs Isaias' announcement to Babylon:

> Howl, for the day of the Lord is near; as destruction from the Almighty it comes. Therefore all hands fall helpless, every man's heart melts in terror. Pangs and sorrows take hold of them, like a woman in labor they writhe; they look aghast at each other, their faces aflame. Lo, the day of the Lord comes cruel, with wrath and burning anger[4] (Is. 13:6-9).

In its application to the Daughter of Sion, the image of the sorrows of childbirth can be seen to connote, with complete naturalness, a twofold reality: one of suffering and anguish, and one of joy and deliverance. The moans of a woman in labor are not, in effect, an expression of agony, but of the birth of new life. Micheas utilizes this twofold meaning when he prophesies: ". . . you are seized with pains like a woman in travail. . . . Writhe in pain, grow faint, O daughter Sion, like a woman in travail; for now shall you go forth from the city and dwell in the fields; to Babylon shall you go, there shall you be rescued. There shall the Lord redeem you from the hand of your enemies" (Mich. 4:9-10). The sorrows of childbirth are the anguish of deportation; the joy of deliverance is the redemption wrought by Yahweh.

The image will be taken up again by Jeremias. The context in which we find it (Jer. 4:5-31) recalls that in which it occurs in Isaias — a context of war and trial. We see a hurricane of chariots, the piercing thrust of swords, the tottering of mountains. It is the Day of Yahweh, when the Daughter of Sion, of old betrothed to Yahweh but now an adulteress, undergoes the expiation demanded for her infidelities: "Yes, I hear the moaning, as of a woman in travail, like the anguish of a mother with her first child — the cry of daughter Sion gasping, as she stretches forth her hands: 'Ah, woe is me! I sink exhausted before the slayers!' " (Jer. 4:31).

The text which most closely approximates Apocalypse 12 occurs in Isaias 66, in which we see the Daugher of Sion bring forth a male child and at the same time become the mother of an entire nation, the mother of innumerable sons whom she fills with peace and glory:

> Before she comes to labor, she gives birth; before the pains come upon her, she safely delivers a male child. Who ever heard of such a thing, or saw the like? Can a country be brought forth in one day, or a nation be born in a single moment?
>
> Rejoice with Jerusalem and be glad because of her, all you who love her; exult, exult with her, all you who were mourning over her! . . . As nurslings, you shall be carried in her arms, and fondled in her lap; as a mother comforts her son, so will I comfort you; in Jerusalem you shall find your comfort. When you see this, your heart shall rejoice, and your bodies flourish like the grass; the Lord's power shall be known to his servants, but to his enemies, his wrath. Lo, the Lord shall come in fire, his chariots like the whirlwind . . . (Is. 66:7-8, 10-15).

The following points of contact with John's text will have been evident:

— The Woman brings forth a male Child; this Woman is Jerusalem;

— She gives birth to a child, but she becomes at the same time the mother of an entire people, an entire nation;

— Yahweh is engaged in combat with his enemies; this divine warfare is also waged by Michael together with his angels;

— As in the Apocalypse, we hear the song of the victory and joy of the redeemed;

— The entire scene is unfolded as a marvelous event, a prodigy such as man has never seen; in the Apocalypse, we are given a great sign in heaven.

Historically speaking, the text relates to the period following the return from exile in Babylon. We know that in cold fact this return was anything but an overflowing of glory and peace; the straggling little caravans of survivors of the deportation that arrived in Jerusalem, painfully to begin over again, hardly convey the impression of an entire nation brought forth in joy and caressed on its mother's lap. But the fulfillment of this prophecy was to lie not in the immediate future, but in the domain of the eschatological.

These different points of contact with the Old Testament open the way for the following reflections:

In showing us the Woman in the anguish of delivery, John thereby is teaching us that the Church is to undergo violent and mysterious sufferings. This teaching ties in with a theme that is constant in the gospel message: to enter the kingdom, we must pass through many tribulations (Acts 14:21); in order to partake of the paschal life of Christ we must share the communion in his sufferings and death. It is precisely in her sufferings that the Church gives birth to Christ, or better, that she gives birth to Christ in her faithful.

This point established, it must immediately be added that the Woman who has given birth to the flesh and blood Christ is not the Church, the assembly of the redeemed, but a woman of flesh and bone, who bore Christ within her womb and brought him forth — the Virgin Mary. The birth at Bethlehem, to be sure, shone with the purity of her virginal joy; but Bethlehem is oriented toward the Cross. Her child is given to her only because he is to die, because it is according to this plan that he is to be Israel's redeemer. And it was at the hour of this redemption that a sword of sorrow was to pierce her soul, it was then that her motherhood, until then seen only in relation to Christ himself, was to be revealed in all its sorrows as a universal motherhood.

There is, then, in Mary a twofold motherhood. One is virginal and filled with joy, and finds its fulfillment with the birth of Christ at Bethlehem. The other is sorrowful and filled with agony, and finds its fulfillment with the death of Christ upon the Cross. In the first, she gives birth to Christ; in the second, she gives birth to the faithful. Yet, we must add, it is a single motherhood, for Mary never ceases to be the Mother of Jesus, whether she gives birth to him in the flesh or in the souls of the faithful.

It is precisely in this way that Mary fulfills her role as the Daughter of Sion, the archetype of the Church. For it is through her that Christ is born of the blood of ancient Israel, as she is herself the Daughter of David according to the flesh and the Mother of the new David according to her faith. Equally through her is the continuance of the mystery of the new Daughter of Sion, the Church, who never ceases to give birth to Christ in the hearts of the faithful and thereby to prolong the mystery of Mary.

So do we see that our own vocation attains to fulfillment through her. Our sufferings and our victories are the continuance of the mystery of the Church, and thus in turn the prolongation of the mystery of Mary. Every suffering and every victory leaves its own living record inscribed in this perspective that is both Marian and ecclesial, and which thus contains them all in the living context of the total Christ.

What is the relationship between this victory and this warfare, between the pains of childbirth and the joy of deliverance? It could be said that these pains are natural to the wayfaring state of the Church, as natural as those suffered by a woman as she brings forth her child. John had already given us his account of these words of Christ in his Gospel: "Amen, amen, I say to you, that you shall weep and lament, but the world shall rejoice; and you shall be sorrowful, but your sorrow shall be turned into joy. A woman about to give birth has sorrow, because her hour has come. But when she has brought forth the child, she no longer remembers the anguish for her joy that a man is born into the world" (John 16:20-21).

In Apocalypse 12, this successive pattern of sadness and joy is, as it were, removed and placed outside of time. For John is contemplating the mystery of the Church in its totality, the Church that is at once both glorious and sorrowful. This is why the Woman is a wondrous sign in heaven, even though she seeks refuge in the wilderness; why she is clothed with the sun and crowned with stars, and yet cries out in the anguish of her delivery.

By the use of this imagery, John is only pointing out that the Church is glorious in Christ and his Mother, but persecuted in the rest of her offspring; he no longer is dwelling solely on the fact that it is persecuted today, but also on the truth that it will be victorious tomorrow, at the time of the Parousia; it is, at one and the same time, both persecuted and victorious, weeping and glorious, the Mother of sorrows and the Mother triumphant. Is it not the very nature of all the realities of Christian life to participate, at the same time, in both the life of this world and the life of the world to come, to bring us into communion with Christ in the mystery of his death and resurrection?[5] It is for this reason, as we were saying, that the Woman's cries are not those of agony, but much rather those accompanying the bringing of new life into the world, the sorrowful and yet triumphant delivery of all the rest of her offspring.

C. THE SOJOURN IN THE WILDERNESS

And the woman fled into the wilderness. . . . And there were given to the woman the two wings of the great eagle, that she might fly into the wilderness . . . (Apoc. 12:6, 14).

The theme of the wilderness — together with that of the Exodus, to which it is allied — represents one of the favorite themes of the Old Testament, and it has arrived at this latest context charged with such a weight of historical associations that the mere mention of it is enough to awaken a whole world of memories in the heart of Israel.[6] For it was in the desert that Moses, the man of the covenant, had his first personal encounter with Yahweh, experiencing the reality of his presence in the blinding flame of the burning bush. It was there, also, during those forty years of tenderness and patience, that God formed his people, guiding them by the luminous cloud, feeding them with heavenly manna, quenching their thirst with the water from the rock, revealing his Law to them in the shattering solitude of Sinai; it was there, finally, that he received his first sacrifices from his people.

This sacred character of the desert is such that the Elias cycle will be in some way a renewal of the marvel of the Exodus. For Elias, this will be literally "a return to the sources," an inverse retracing of the path taken by the Israel of older days; like Israel, he is fed by a miraculous bread, and "walked in the strength of that food forty days and forty nights, unto the mount of God" (3 Kings 19:8), where he encountered anew the God of the people of the Exodus.

To signify the conversion of Israel, the prophets will instinctively turn to the imagery of that epoch of miracles. Israel's conversion will be a new Exodus, when Yahweh will renew the love of his espousals:

So I will allure her; I will lead her into the desert and speak to her heart. From there I will give her the vineyards she had, and the valley of Achor as a door of hope. She shall respond there as in the days of her youth, when she came up from the land of Egypt. On that day, says the Lord, she shall call me, "My husband," and never again "My baal" [7] (Osee 2:16-18).

The desert will continue to be the scene of God's revelation of himself to his people. Habacuc, in announcing the theophany and warlike advance of Yahweh, recalls to mind the marvels of the Exodus period,[8] the battles of Pharan (cf. Hab. 3:3), Chusan, and Madian (cf. *ibid*. 3:7).

This desert theme is such a forceful one that we find it recurring in the post-exilic writings to describe the return to Jerusalem. The desert which separates Babylon from Jerusalem is not the same as that of the Sinai peninsula, but that matters little; the desert stands as the symbol of return, as the rallying-point of God's people, the wide road of promise over which Yahweh leads Israel into the Promised Land: "A voice cries out: In the desert prepare the way of the Lord! Make straight in the wasteland a highway for our God!" (Is. 40:3).

It is in a desert whose solitude will one day break into new flower that Israel is returning "home," to Jerusalem, and the divine glory will again shield her march with its luminous protection: "The desert and the parched land will exult; the steppe will rejoice and bloom. They will bloom with abudant flowers, and rejoice with joyful song . . . they will see the glory of the Lord, the splendor of our God" (Is. 35:1-2).

Finally, let us remember that the All-Beautiful One of the Canticle of Canticles, the bridal Church, is coming up from the desert, leaning on her Beloved (Cant. 8:5).

All these texts are too important not to find them again coming to the fore in the New Testament. Beginning with the announcement of the "good news" by John the Baptist, the three Synoptics take zealous care to cite the prophecy from the Book of Isaias: "The voice of one crying in the desert, 'Make ready the way of the Lord, make straight his paths' " (Luke 3:4; Mark 1:3; Matthew 3:3).

The New Testament is thus prefaced by the Old. St. Paul will affirm that the Exodus events were the prefiguration of Christian realities; he will say very plainly and simply: These were "types," that is, images of what with us is coming to pass (cf. 1 Cor. 10:6, 11). Luke, in relating the discourse of Stephen, will speak without any further explanation of the Church of the desert (cf. Acts 7:38). Christ's own life is marked with this typology; we are referring not only to the forty days' temptation in the wilderness, which is an obvious reference to the forty years of the Exodus, and where he mysteriously relived the same testing to which his people had been subjected; we are above all thinking of the mystery of his death, which is called "his Exodus," ἡ ἔξοδος (Luke 9:31); it is through this agony which is in truth a liberation that he becomes our passover (1 Cor. 5:7), that is, the passage from this world to the Father, from the desert of the Exodus to the Promised Land.

Having seen the importance of this theme, we shall not be astonished to find this mention of the wilderness recurring in John. The text bears the mark of his customary reserve, proceeding rather by way of simple allusion. The evangelist takes it for granted that his reader is sufficiently familiar with the Bible to render a more emphatic treatment unnecessary. For those of us who do not possess this same familiarity, some explanation will not be without profit.

1. Under the Divine Wings

> And there were given to the woman the two wings of the great eagle, that she might fly into the wilderness (Apoc. 12:14).

The sojourn in the wilderness is the time above all times that witnesses to the manifestation of the divine power. It is that privileged period of history in which the unflagging tenderness of Yahweh never fails to come to succor Israel in her time of need. John is alluding to this divine protection when he writes: "And there were given to the woman the two wings of the great eagle, that she might fly into the wilderness" (Apoc. 12:14).

Before the theophany at Sinai, Yahweh, with Moses as his spokesman, issued the following message to the people: "I bore you up on eagle wings and brought you here to myself" (Exod. 19:4). The Deuteronomist, from his meditation on this text, could write:

> He found them in a wilderness, a wasteland of howling desert. He shielded them and cared for them, guarding them as the apple of his eye. As an eagle incites its nestlings forth by hovering over its brood, so he spread his wings to receive them and bore them up on his pinions. The Lord alone was their leader (Deut. 32:10-12).

The image will be taken up in the psalms, which will detach it from its historical context and concentrate upon its spiritual meaning — the Lord overshadows and protects the faithful man in time of trial:

> Keep me as the apple of your eye;
>   hide me in the shadow of your wings (Ps. 16:8).
>
> How precious is your kindness, O God!
>   The children of men take refuge in the shadow of your wings (Ps. 35:8).
>
> Have pity on me, O God; have pity on me,
>   for in you I take refuge.
> In the shadow of your wings I take refuge,
>   till harm pass by (Ps. 56:2).

. . . you are my refuge,
    a tower of strength against the enemy,
Oh, that I might lodge in your tent forever,
    take refuge in the shelter of your wings (Ps. 60:4-5).

You who dwell in the shelter of the Most High,
    who abide in the shadow of the Almighty,
Say to the Lord, "My refuge and my fortress,
    my God, in whom I trust."
With his pinions he will cover you,
    and under his wings you shall take refuge [9] (Ps. 90:1-2, 4).

The atmosphere surrounding these images is formed of two invariable elements. On the one hand, there is constant reference to oppression and the threatening approach of war, to the difficulties which assail the man of faith: to enemies who, like beasts panting after their prey, circle about him (Ps. 16:9-12); to the impious and proud men who are intent on trampling and crushing him (Ps. 35:12), with teeth like spears and arrows, and tongues like sharp swords (Ps. 56:5). His soul lies prostrate in the midst of lions ready to devour him (Ps. 56:5); he looks on at the battles of giants where a thousand fall at his right and ten thousand at his left (Ps. 90:7). But on the other hand, he is always assured of the efficacious protection of his God: he calls; Yahweh answers, shows his favor to him, and saves him (Ps. 16:6-7); he keeps him in his love and his justice, and is a fountain of life for him (Ps. 35:10-11); he sends him his love and his truth (Ps. 56:4) and is with him in his distress to deliver him (Ps. 90:15).

The man of faith who takes refuge in the shadow of the divine wings is thus at once threatened by his enemies and persecuted by the wicked, and yet also protected by God and defended by the all-powerful strength of his love. Key words which unceasingly occur — to take refuge, to seek shelter, to entrust oneself — are all attempts to convey the spiritual depth of this imagery: the man of faith lives under God's protection; he dwells "in the shadow of his wings."

In showing us the Woman in the wilderness, John is giving us a picture of the wayfaring Church. In her march toward the Promised Land, the Church is dwelling under the divine protection; the wings of the great eagle which are given to her are a figure of the efficacy of this help and the suddenness with which it comes.

It is to be clearly seen that in these figures the Marian perspective gives way to the ecclesial. This can be explained very naturally by the fact that at the time of John's redaction of his text, Mary had already arrived at the term of her Exodus and entered into heavenly glory. The evangelist who upon the death of Jesus had received her into his home could not have been unaware of this event. What must have been for him a mystery deeply to be pondered exists for us today under the title of her Assumption; with her entrance into the holy eternity of God, Mary attained to the fulfillment, with a transcendent title, of what the pilgrim Church possesses only in an inchoate manner. The protection with which God had always surrounded her was the sign of the assistance with which God would ceaselessly continue to protect the Church. In theological terms, this protection is called the absence of all sin; God protects the Church by preserving it in holiness. "Holy and without blemish in his sight in love" (Eph. 1:4), Mary thus is the archetype of the Church" in all her glory, not having spot or wrinkle or any such thing, but . . . holy and without blemish" (Eph. 5:27). The Immaculate One is thus a prefiguration of the immaculate Church.[10]

For the entire Church will follow the way taken by Jesus the First-born (Apoc. 1:5). While the people of the first Exodus wandered for forty years in their journey across the desert because their heart was itself wandering — *populus errans corde!* (Ps. 94:10) — the Church of the Apocalypse takes possession of the refuge that God has prepared for her. The Dragon who is her persecutor is powerless against her, for she takes her refuge in Jesus. In the Johannine text there is a lively opposition between the devil and his accomplices who are cast out of heaven, whose place was not found any more in heaven (Apoc. 12:8), and the Woman who takes refuge in the *place* that God has prepared for her.

2. The Place That God Has Prepared for Her

And the woman fled into the wilderness, where she has a place prepared by God. . . . [She flies] into the wilderness unto her place (Apoc. 12:6, 14).

There can be no doubt that this same idea — that of the divine protection — is what John is evoking when he writes that the Woman flees into the wilderness "unto her place." In her flight away from the serpent, the Woman does not wander about at random, but on the contrary seeks refuge in a safe haven, in the place that God has prepared for her.

It is interesting to note that the verb ἐτοιμάζω (a *prepared* place) is the one usually found in those texts which refer to the eschatological realities that God is making ready for the faithful. So does the Father prepare for seating at the Lord's right and left hand (Matthew 20:23; Mark 10:40). In like manner he is preparing the kingdom for those whom he has blessed (Matthew 25:34). It is still a matter of the salvation that has been prepared, which is to be revealed in the last time (1 Peter 1:5). Paul will be speaking of all the "things God has prepared for those who love him" (1 Cor. 2:9). With these texts the use of the verb "to prepare" is anchored firmly in an eschatological perspective.

As a matter of fact, the expression "to prepare a place" will, in the only other instance that it does occur in John, be found in a similar context: "In my Father's house there are many mansions. Were it not so, I should have told you, because I go to prepare a place for you. And if I go and prepare a place for you, I am coming again, and I will take you to myself; that where I am, there you also may be" (John 14:2-3).

These ideas manifestly recall what we read in the Apocalypse: Christ is returning to his Father, a reference, most certainly, to the mystery of his Passion, resurrection, and ascension, namely, the very mystery of his own Exodus, his passage from this world to the Father.

Here again Mary is a prefiguration of the Church. The place in the wilderness that is prepared for the Church conjures up the image of the eternal dwelling-place into which she enters on the morning of her Assumption. "In reascending to his Father, the Child was preparing a place for the disciples who make up Mary's second posterity. . . . Without waiting for the Day of the general resurrection, his mother is awarded her share in his destiny. At the same time she is also the prefiguration of what in the normal course of events has been reserved for the end of the world, when the pilgrim Church will be assumed into the glory of the new Jerusalem."[11] Mary stands in the vanguard of the Church on its march toward the kingdom; in her, the desert Church that is still battling against the Dragon has already reached the shore of eternity; in her, she already contemplates, in joy and peace, the eternal face of God.

3. The Feeding of the Church

And there were given to the woman the two wings of the great eagle, that she might fly into the wilderness into her place, where she is nourished (Apoc. 12:14).

One of the miracles that is richest in expression and most typical of the Exodus is uncontestably that of the manna (Exod. 16). For forty years Yahweh miraculously fed his people with the "bread from heaven." Each time that Israel will sing of this period in its history, it will relate this marvel with pride:

> He rained manna upon them for food
>   and gave them heavenly bread.
> The bread of the mighty was eaten by men (Ps. 77:24-25).
> . . . with bread from heaven he satisfied them (Ps. 104:40).

Beyond the material fact lies the spiritual meaning. Down through the entire course of its history, the mind of Israel sought to penetrate the ultimate mystery that was expressed through the gift of this heavenly food. In the thought of Deuteronomy these considerations will reach this conclusion: "The Lord, your God . . . fed you with manna, a food unknown to you and your fathers, in order to show you that not by bread alone does man live, but by every word that comes forth from the mouth of the Lord. . . . Therefore, keep the commandments of the Lord, your God, by walking in his ways and fearing him" (Deut. 8:2-3, 6).

This manna therefore was not only food, but a parable as well; while satisfying the body, it also nourished the soul. God was feeding his people, but they were also to live by "every word that comes forth from the mouth of the Lord," that is to say, his Word. The keeping of this word will be life; disobedience to it will be death:

> I, the Lord, am your God
>   who led you forth from the land of Egypt;
>   open wide your mouth, and I will fill it.
> If only my people would hear me,
>   and Israel walk in my ways.
> . . . Israel I would feed with the best of wheat,
>   and with honey from the rock I would fill them (Ps. 80:11, 14, 17).

After the entry into Canaan, the milk and honey of the Promised Land took the place of the manna, but the principle on which this food was to be obtained remained the same — the keeping of the Word. When Israel is faithful, God nourishes her. Her crops become heavy and rich, her flocks multiply, her vines and fig trees flourish. But as soon as Israel is unfaithful, God leaves her to the ravages of hunger and the scourge of her enemies. God could be said to feed his people in the measure that this people nourished themselves on his Word.

In the Book of Wisdom a new meaning of the manna is revealed to us: that of the tenderness and sweetness of God:

> . . . you nourished your people with food of angels and furnished them with bread from heaven, ready to hand, untoiled-for, endowed with all delights and conforming to every taste. For this substance of yours revealed your sweetness toward your children, and serving the desire of him who received it, was blended to whatever flavor each one wished. . . . that your sons whom you loved might learn, O Lord, that it is not the various kinds of fruits that nourish man, but it is your word that preserves those who believe you! (Wis. 16:20-21, 26).

Thus on the threshold of the New Testament, barely fifty years before Christ's own epiphany, Israel's scrutiny of its sacred history sees revealed in that history Yahweh's tenderness toward his children; and this meditative gaze is prepared to recognize in Jesus the sweetness of the food that is God's gift to his faithful.

The theme is, in effect, brought to its culminating perfection in Jesus.

1) He is the true heavenly Bread, both living and life-giving, that replaces — and with what fullness — the manna of the Exodus:

> I am the bread of life. Your fathers ate the manna in the desert, and have died. This is the bread that comes down from heaven, so that if anyone eats of it he will not die. I am the living bread that has come down from heaven. If anyone eat of this bread he shall live forever; and the bread that I will give is my flesh for the life of the world. . . . This is the bread that has come down from heaven; not as your fathers ate the manna, and died. He who eats this bread shall live forever (John 6:48-52, 59).

The history of the Exodus thus continues in the New Testament. God is still nourishing his people on their march toward the Promised Land, but with the Flesh and the Blood of his Son Jesus. The divine reality now takes the place of the figure, at the same time going beyond it. The manna was truly the day-by-day sustenance of the pilgrims of Canaan; it appeased the daily hunger of this world, but not the hunger of eternity; it could almost be said that it kept that hunger alive from one day to the next. But this new Manna fills to the fullness of eternity; it is living, it is life-giving; and its life-giving power reaches out not only to souls but even to bodies, rendering passible mortality both glorious and immortal.

2) Christ is also the living and life-giving Word that the Father

speaks to men. In the Old Testament, God had already spoken
at sundry times and in diverse manners (Heb. 1:1-2); now he speaks
to us by his Son. Christ is, as it were, the flesh in which the Father
clothes his teaching; more than that, he is himself the living and
life-giving Incarnation of the Word of the Father, in the body that
the Apostles saw with their eyes and handled with their hands
(1 John 1:1). In other terms, no longer does the Father beget his
Word (*Verbe*) simply within the family-life of the Trinity; he now
begets it also in a human nature, prolonging in creation the mystery
of his eternal Word (*Parole*). To listen to this Word, to keep it,
to believe in it, is nourishment and life. "He who believes in him"
("comes" to him, as John writes, to bring out all the dynamic meaning
of faith) has life everlasting: "Do not labor for the food that perishes,
but for that which endures unto life everlasting, which the Son of
Man will give you. For upon him the Father, God himself, has set
his seal." They said therefore to him, "What are we to do that we
may perform the works of God?" In answer Jesus said to them, "This
is the work of God, that you believe in him whom he has sent." . . .
"For this is the will of my Father who sent me, that whoever be-
holds the Son, and believes in him, shall have everlasting life . . ."
(John 6:27-29, 40).

In recalling the Lord's rule of life: "My food is to do the will
of him who sent me" (John 4:34), we could establish the following
parallel. Just as what sustained Christ in the course of his earthly
life was the accomplishment of his Father's will, so too the food
of the man of faith, namely, that which sustains him in the course
of his Exodus, is in like manner to do the Father's will; and this
will is to believe in Jesus, who is the Word of the Father and
the Food of our souls in the mystery of the Eucharist.

To sum up:
— Under the old dispensation, Yahweh nourished his people:
1) by his Word;
2) by the manna in the desert.
— Under the new dispensation, the Father nourishes his Church:
1) by Christ, the Word-made-flesh;
2) by Christ, the Eucharist.

Here again, Mary precedes the Church. Her faith had always
been exemplary; it was precisely because of her faith that she had
been blessed: "Blessed is she who has believed" (Luke 1:45). She
had always listened to the Word; it was in listening to the Word
that she had become the Mother of Jesus: "My mother and my

brethren are they who hear the word of God, and act upon it"
(Luke 8:21).

In equal measure, the food with which God sustains his Church
conjures up the vision of the heavenly banquet of which she was
already partaking, for at the Parousia faith will be replaced by vision
unveiled, when "we shall see him just as he is" (1 John 3:2). Obedience to the Word will be replaced by total liberty of love, a liberty
so full that it will indefectibly be drawn by God. This eschatological
condition of the Church is already the actual condition of our Lady.

Hence Mary never ceases to be present to the desert Church.
She is present as archetype to type, or rather, if we prefer, as
a mother to her children. Her life in glory at the side of the risen
Christ is thus an annunciation of the mystery of her children, who
one day are to rejoin her at the side of Jesus.

D. Mary's Spiritual Children

In bringing our analysis to a close, we should like once again
to draw some conclusions of both practical and immediate value.
John is actually portraying the disciples of the Woman with differing
sets of features; and these sets of features are not only the mark
of belonging to Jesus and Mary, but also rules of life. What we
have here is the setting-forth of a genuine spirituality, if we may
venture to use the expression, of children of Mary, in the most
beautiful sense of the word. This spirituality, it hardly needs repeating, is moreover completely Christocentric. Mary's children, who
comprise the rest of her offspring, are those who have overcome
the Dragon through the blood of the Lamb, who keep the testimony
of Jesus, who offer him their lives and who keep his commandments.

1. *They overcame the Dragon through the blood of the Lamb (Apoc. 12:11)*

As we recall, the Dragon delivered his assault in three successive
attacks. He first seeks to devour the Child, but the latter is caught
up to God's throne. He next attacks the Woman, but she flees
into the wilderness, to the place that God has prepared for her.
Thwarted, he seeks to take revenge by waging war against "the
rest of her offspring" (v. 17); but these overcome him "through the
blood of the Lamb" (v. 11). All the devil's efforts — both his warfar-
ing schemes and his outbursts of hatred — are seen to come to

nothing. All his attacks end in his being routed; his rages are power-less.

It will also be noted that the victory of the faithful is really the victory of Christ in them; if they do overcome, it is "through the blood of the Lamb." In his first Epistle, John had already spoken of the extraordinary strength of the children of God: "We know that no one who is born of God commits sin; but the Begotten of God preserves him and the evil one does not touch him" (1 John 5:18). Here the devil unites into the same object of hatred both the Only-begotten Son of God and the Woman and her off-spring; but God unites the Child, the Woman, and the offspring in the same victory.

The spirituality of the children of Mary will thus be a spirituality of combat and victory.[12] Their membership in the Church will always be marked by the attacks of the demon. Always emerging victorious through Christ, they belong to the Beloved who is as beautiful as the moon, as resplendent as the sun, but also as terrible as troops in battle array (Cant. 6:10).

2. *They hold fast the testimony of Jesus*

To the blood of the Lamb the faithful add the blood of their own witness.[13] John is saying that they overcome through the word of their witness (v. 11), that they "hold fast the testimony of Jesus" (v. 17). This witness-theme occupies a very important position in Johannine theology.[14] Jesus himself is described as "the witness," "the faithful one;"[15] he proclaims the Word of the Father, and this Word is Truth: "This is why I was born, and why I have come into the world, to bear witness to the truth" (John 18:37).

The faithful of Jesus share in the mission of their Master. They bear witness not simply to the historical events of Christ's life (cf. 1 John 1:1-3) but also, and even more, to the divine glory that dwells in Jesus, and which they discover with their eyes of faith (John 1:14). They bear this witness without faltering, even to a martyrdom of blood.[16] This witness-theme is of such importance that it is identified with faith itself: to bear witness to Jesus is to believe in him, to possess life.

> . . . this is the testimony of God which is greater, that he has borne witness concerning his Son. He who believes in the Son of God has the testimony of God in himself. He who does not believe the Son, makes him a liar; because he does not believe the witness that God has borne concerning his Son. And this is the testimony, that

God has given us eternal life; and this life is in his Son. He who
has the Son has the life. He who has not the Son has not the life
(1 John 5:9-12).

The spiritual doctrine concerning the children of Mary and of
the Church is thus completely Christocentric. Those comprising
the rest of the offspring are those who believe in Jesus and who
possess his life. And it is this faith in Jesus, in which their witness
is rooted, which constitutes the essential character of their victory.
In the struggle against the dragon it is the most redoubtable of
weapons, the weapon that snatches the victory: ". . . this is the
victory that overcomes the world, our faith" (1 John 5:4).

3. *They did not love their lives even in face of death*

Another mark of the disciples of Jesus and the children of Mary
is the tie of absolute preference which binds them to their Master.
In the struggle that they carry on against the dragon, they are
prepared "not to love their lives even in face of death" (v. 11).
This turn of phrase, which is very Semitic, appears somewhat cumbersome;[17] the sense, however, presents no difficulty, especially
if we compare it with the primitive *logia* as John has kept them
in his Gospel:

> Amen, amen, I say to you, unless the grain of wheat falls into the
> ground and dies, it remains alone. But if it dies, it brings forth much
> fruit. He who loves his life, loses it; and he who hates his life in
> this world, keeps it unto life everlasting. If anyone serves me, let
> him follow me; and where I am there also shall my servant be [18]
> (John 12:24-26).

To lose one's life in this world is hence to save it for eternal
life; to save one's life in this world is to lose it for eternal life.
Astounding, paradoxical words that forcefully convey the limitless-
ness of the demand Jesus exacts on his disciples. To serve him,
one must follow him, must be his "acolyte" (John 12:26), follow
him even as in the mystery of the grain that dies and consequently
bears much fruit, that dies in order to bear much fruit. He is a
true disciple of Jesus who observes this paradoxical equation (to
lose his life = to save his soul) as the rule of the love he bears
his Master.

4. *They keep the commandments of God (Apoc. 12:17)*

John has been called the evangelist of charity. This is true, but
he can with equal reason be called the evangelist of obedience,

of the practice of the Word. No one has so forcefully insisted on the absolute necessity of keeping the commandments. For this obedience is the mark of love; it opens the way to love; it lives on love, and finds in it its fullest mode of expression:

If you love me, keep my commandments (John 14:15).

He who has my commandments and keeps them, he it is who loves me (John 14:21).

If anyone love me, he will keep my word (John 14:23).

And by this we can be sure that we know him, if we keep his commandments (1 John 2:3).

For this is the love of God, that we keep his commandments (1 John 5:3).

With John, the practice of the Word thus leads us to the very heart of the mystery of Christ; it is to abide in Jesus, that mutual inhabitation through faith and love. John brings out this truth in the allegory of the Vine [19] (John 15:1ff.) in a series of propositions that are admirably linked together:

— In order to be the branches of this Vine that is Christ, we must abide in him: "Abide in me, and I in you" (John 15:4).

— For it is by abiding in Christ's love that we abide in him: "As the Father has loved me, I also have loved you. Abide in my love" (John 15:9).

— But this abiding in love is effected by the practice of the Word: "If you keep my commandments you will abide in my love, as I also have kept my Father's commandments, and abide in his love" (John 15:10).

We can now understand John's attraction for characterizing the disciples of the Woman by this distinctive mark: "They keep the commandments of God." This practice grafts them into Christ as branches into the Vine, in a discipleship so intimate that they abide in him as he himself abides in the Father.

It will be seen that this spirituality of the children of Mary is eminently practical. There is no suggestion here of any sugary or languishing sentimentality. In direct opposition to this, it is to combat with the dragon that John is summoning the faithful! And this combat is, moreover, an entirely spiritual one; it is waged with the weapons of faith and the observance of the commandments. The faithful, it is true, enjoy a sure protection, but this protection is a shield to be worn on the battlefield. It is a call to total commitment, a commitment that does not hesitate before the sacrifice of the

most sublime consolations this world can offer, to ensure for itself
the joy of eternal life.

This spirituality is entirely Christocentric. It is impossible to be
children of Mary without first belonging to Christ. But this is the
very operation of the mystery of the divine maternity. Mary has
but one son — Christ. The faithful are her children only in the
measure in which they are a living reproduction of the mystery
of her Son.

Conclusion

The text of the Apocalypse is of such density that it discourages
all attempts to reduce it to a set of formulas. St. John is not to
be summed up in one phrase, any more than a symphony can be
summed up in a single note. We can, however, attempt to isolate
its fundamental theme. This theme is the very one that runs throughout the entire Apocalypse and which constitutes its essential message: the battle and the victory of Christ, victory in battle.

This theme is drawn out in a twofold perspective: on one plane
we encounter the mystery of Mary; on the other, the mystery of
the Church. Mary, the Mother of Jesus, is associated with the victory
of her Child. Her victory consists precisely in the triumph of her
royal motherhood; she is crowned with stars and clothed with the
sun because she has brought forth "him who is to shepherd all
nations." The faithful, who form the rest of her offspring, are likewise
associates in the victory of Christ, according to the measure in
which they belong to Christ, the measure, it could be said, in
which they are living members of the rest of the offspring.

The mystery of Mary thus opens out on a twofold perspective:
— *the Christological perspective*: Mary cannot be separated from
Christ. Since the prophecy of Genesis, and its prophetic transmission
through Isaias and Micheas, "she who is to bring forth" is linked
with the combat of the Messias and shares his condition and destiny.
Because the Messias is a suffering Messias, she undergoes an agony
of sorrow; because he is glorious and triumphant, she is resplendent
in the radiance of his glory;

— *the ecclesial perspective*: Just as Christ cannot be separated
from his Mother, so the faithful cannot be separated from their
Lord. And it is precisely for this reason that they also cannot be
separated from his Mother: they comprise the rest of her offspring.
Thus it might be said that the relationship between Mary and the
faithful is not a direct one, as if Mary were their Mother indepen-

dently of Christ, or even in addition to being the Mother of Christ. There is only one relationship here, that of Mary to Christ, and through Christ, to the faithful. Mary has but one motherhood, but the vastness of its embrace extends to include the dimensions of the Mystical Body.

Need it be added that these facts of Scripture must be recognized as the commanding principles by which a true Marian and a true Christian piety must be directed? It is only too clear that we cannot love Mary without first loving her Son and all her other children as well; and neither, with equal impossibility, can we love Christ and his brothers without a love for his Mother, who is our Mother also.

[1] Cf. Is. 40:26. The "sons of God" are the angels, who together with the stars form the army of Yahweh-Sabaoth.

[2] From the standpoint of its theological structure, the Christian paradox will more easily be understood if we distinguish:

1) redemption *in actu primo* — the acquisition of merits through the sacrifice of the Cross; perfect redemption, to which nothing can be added and from which nothing can be taken away;

2) redemption *in actu secondo* — the application of Christ's merits to the faithful; this redemption is continually in process of further realization, being accomplished in the faithful to the degree of their participation in the life of the Lord. In this connection, it may be said that the life of the Church is eschatological in the sense that it is already being realized in the present, never ceases to develop, and finally will reach its ultimate fullness at the Parousia. We could speak of the "transitional incompleteness of Christian realities, which at once participate in both this present world-in-time and the future world-to-come" (L. Cerfaux, *Le Christ dans la théologie de saint Paul*, Coll. *Lectio divina*, 6 (Paris, 1951), pp. 53–54. *Translator's note*: cf. also the published English translation, *Christ in the Theology of St. Paul, op. cit.*, pp. 64–68). Here we have the very mystery of the incarnate Logos, who is at once of heaven, because he is born of the Father, and of earth, because he is born of the Woman.

[3] Cf. Is. 21:3; Jer 6:24-26; 13:21; 48:41; Ps. 47:7; Sir. 48:19.

[4] Christ will make use of this comparison in a similar context in his foretelling of the Parousia: Matthew 24:8; cf. 1 Thess. 5:3.

[5] Thus in Apocalypse 5:5-6, the Lamb "standing as if slain" is also "the lion of the tribe of Juda, [who] has overcome."

[6] "The Exodus is the decisive event in Israel's history. In the popular consciousness, the desert march between the two miracle-events, the one at the Red Sea and the one at the Jordan, holds the place occupied in Christian consciousness by the life of Jesus" (J. Guillet, *Thèmes bibliques*, Coll. *Théologie*, 18 [Paris, 1951], p. 9).

[7] There can be no doubt that it was through the Valley of Achor that the Israelites had formerly penetrated into Canaan. This valley with its mournful title ("valley of misfortune") will become a gateway of hope through which Israel will enter into the Promised Land.

8 Cf. the text of the Canticle of Habacuc, p. 109 *supra*.

9 To the texts cited from the psalms the following can be added: Ps. 62:8; Is. 30:2; Ruth 2:12.

10 Theology has given expression to this truth in the dogma of the Immaculate Conception. On the relationship which unites this mystery with that of Mary, see H. Rahner, *Our Lady and the Church*, translated by Sebastian Bullough, O.P. (New York: Pantheon Books, 1961), pp. 18–21.

11 Braun, *La Mère des Fidèles, op cit.*, p. 167.

12 May we point out here that this aspect corresponds rather closely to what we know from other contexts about John's psychology? By temperament John was inclined to place virtue in strength; it was not for nothing that Jesus had surnamed him "son of thunder" (Marx 3:17; cf. Luke 9:54).

13 The word μαρτυρία has the double meaning of "witness" and "martyr."

14 With him alone, the verb μαρτυρεῖν, "to bear witness," recurs about thirty-two times in the Gospel, nine times in the Epistles, and four times in the Apocalypse.

15 Apoc. 1:15; cf. 3:14; the expression seems to have been borrowed from the Septuagint, Ps. 88:38.

16 Cf. Apoc. 6:9; 11:7; 20:4. In Apocalypse 17:6, John shows us the Great Harlot drunk "with the blood of the saints and with the blood of the martyrs of Jesus." For an over-all treatment of this theme, Strathmann's article "μάρτυς," *Theological Dictionary of the New Testament*, 4 may be consulted, in particular pp. 489–495.

17 The fact that this formulation is so cumbersome will explain the diversity of its translations. "And they had not love for their souls, even to dying" (P. Allo); "they scorned their life even to (suffering) death"; "they scorned their life even to dying" (Boismard, Gelin).

18 See the parallel texts in the synoptics: Luke 9:22-25; Matthew 16:21-26; Mark 8:31-36. All these texts (John, Luke, Matthew, Mark) are introduced by the announcement of the Passion. Christian renunciation thereby is written into Christ's own death sentence: in this death it finds its own *raison d'être*, and is at the same time the prolongation, in the disciple, of the mystery of the Passion of the Master.

19 See C. Hauret, *Les adieux du Seigneur* (Paris, 1951), pp. 126–133.

THE SIGN AT CANA

> *. . . and the mother of Jesus was there.*
> (John 2:1)

INTRODUCTION TO PART VII

Of all the Gospel miracles, the miracle at Cana is one of those having the most popular appeal. The Christian imagination is captivated by the sight of Jesus, "the only-begotten of the Father, full of grace and of truth," accepting an invitation to a wedding feast, and even further — what scandal to the piety of the Pharisees! — providing a miraculous wine for the guests.[1] John himself is not insensitive to the picturesque side of the event and brings out its highlights with delicate skill. In essence, however, the import of the narrative lies elsewhere.

Of all the numerous miracles of the public life John has taken only seven, and each has been purposely chosen with an eye to its spiritual meaning:

1) the cure of the royal official's son, a manifestation of the power of faith (John 4:46-54);

2) that of the paralytic at Bethsaida, on the Sabbath, a sign that the Son of God is master of the Sabbath (John 5:1-18);

3) the multiplication of the loaves, which introduces the discourse on the Bread of life (John 6:1-71);

4) the walking on the water, a foreshadowing of the glory of Christ's risen body (John 6:16-21);

5) the cure of the man born blind, which affirms that he is the Light of the world (John 9:1-41);

6) the raising of Lazarus, a proclamation that he himself is the Resurrection and the Life (John 11:1-44).

It is this spiritual meaning of the miracle at Cana that analysis must endeavor to disengage; it also governs the interpretation of Mary's presence and intervention.

The Narrative

And on the third day a marriage took place at Cana of Galilee, and the mother of Jesus was there. Now Jesus too was invited to the marriage, and also his disciples. And the wine having run short, the mother of Jesus said to him, "They have no wine." And Jesus said to her, "Woman, what is that to me and to thee? My hour

171

has not yet come." His mother said to the attendants, "Do whatever he tells you."

Now six stone water-jars were placed there, after the Jewish manner of purification, each holding two or three measures. Jesus said to them, "Fill the jars with water." And they filled them to the brim. And Jesus said to them, "Draw out now, and take to the chief steward." And they took it to him.

Now when the chief steward had tasted the water after it had become wine, not knowing whence it was (though the attendants who had drawn the water knew), the chief steward called the bridegroom, and said to him, "Every man at first sets forth the good wine, and when they have drunk freely, then that which is poorer. But thou hast kept the good wine until now." This first of his signs Jesus worked at Cana of Galilee; and he manifested his glory, and his disciples believed in him (John 2:1-11).

Jesus was about to begin his public life; just a few weeks earlier he had left his holy Mother, with whom he had shared an intimacy of thirty years, and already his life had been oriented into a clearly messianic perspective by these first events that had come to pass:

— John the Baptist had designated him as he who would baptize with the Holy Spirit and with fire (Luke 3:16; cf. Mark 1:8; Matthew 3:11; John 1:33);

— at his baptism a voice from heaven had designated him as the beloved Son in whom the Father was well pleased (Mark 1:11; Matthew 3:17; Luke 3:22);

— the devil himself had indirectly borne witness to him when he tempted him: "If thou art the Son of God . . ." (Matthew 4:6; Luke 4:9);

— and finally Nathanael had designated him: "Rabbi, thou art the Son of God, thou art King of Israel" (John 1:49).

All these events were pregnant with meaning: the humble son of Mary and Joseph the carpenter was now being revealed as Messias and Son of God, titles of which the reality and significance were to become progressively established.

The miracle at Cana is ordered within this same perspective. Hence, from the very outset there can be no question that it is just a simple happening, a village wedding feast at which all the wine had been drunk, and to which the Lord came to rescue from embarrassment. Neither is it a miracle, however marvelous it may have been, that John is proposing for the admiration of the faithful.[2] Rather, it is the first time that the glory of Jesus is manifested to his Apostles, the very manifestation-event that will elicit the response of their faith. John is emphatic on this point: "This first of his signs Jesus worked at Cana of Galilee; and he manifested his glory, and his disciples believed in him" (John 2:11). The role of the Johannine sign [3] is precisely the awakening of faith, that life-giving faith which makes us children of God (cf. John 1:12). If the evangelist gives us an account of the sign at Cana, it is with this end in view: "Many other signs also Jesus worked in the sight of his disciples, which are not written in this book. But these are written that you may believe that Jesus is the Christ, the Son of God, and that believing you may have life in his name" (John 20:30-31)

---

[1] We know that the Pharisees will dare to bring against Jesus the monstrous charge of gluttony and drunkenness; cf. Matthew 11:19.

[2] There can be no doubt that of all the evangelists, John is the one who least stresses the prodigious character of Jesus' miracles and concentrates rather on their spiritual meaning. On this subject P. Huby writes: "It is not paradoxical to say that in the Fourth Gospel they [the miracles] appear as signs which are better adapted to a crowd whose awareness of spiritual realities is still feeble, to a mass of Jews whose minds were still centered on the carnal. This is why we have with Jesus the constant practice of performing only signs which join to this prodigious character some other related notion which has positive value in its own right — sometimes of justice (as in the example of the barren fig tree), most frequently of beneficence (the Lord will change water into wine, but not bread into stone) — as if this prodigious character is not, in the New Testament, in itself sufficient reason for a physical miracle" ("La Connaissance de foi chez saint Jean," in *Le Discours après la Cène*, Coll. *Verbum salutis* (Paris, 1932), p. 179; this entire study is indeed excellent. The reader may also consult R. Aubert, *Le problème de l'acte de foi* (Universitas catholica Lovaniensis, Series II, 36 [Louvain, 1945], pp. 11–13).

[3] On the sense of the Johannine sign and its relation to faith, see O. Cullmann, *Les Sacrements dans l'Évangile Johannique* (Paris, 1951), pp. 9ff.

Chapter 15

COMMENTARY

A. The Mother of Jesus Was There and the Wine Having Run Short

Jesus, together with his disciples, was also invited to the wedding. Since Joseph's death it is Jesus, not Mary, who has been the head of the Holy Family. The very fact of her presence at the festivities indicates that Jesus had been invited.

Jesus had brought his disciples with him.[1] They were for the most part fishermen, who not long ago had left their boats and their nets, and we can readily imagine that they would not pass up a glass of wine. Then, too, Nathanael was himself from Cana (cf. John 21:2). He who had confessed the Messias in no uncertain terms must have spread a little "propaganda" on his own; in a small town where every wall had ears and every door a tongue, the least little urchin knew in short order that Jesus, the new Rabbi, had come. A most likely picture, even though we shall not find it in the text. Everyone had plenty of time during the celebration (it lasted a whole week!) to come to congratulate the new couple and also to pay their respects to the new Rabbi. But while everyone was making merry, those in charge of the refreshments received terrible news — the wine was almost gone.

In biblical lands wine had always had an important place. In announcing the approach of the general desolation and the divine chastisement, the prophets used to say that there would be no more wine in the land: "Stilled are the cheerful timbrels, ended the shouts of the jubilant, stilled is the cheerful harp. . . . In the streets they cry out for lack of wine; all joy has disappeared and cheer has left the land" (Is. 24:8, 11). By the same token, a promise of wine would always find a ready throng of listeners (Mich. 2:11).

174

A shortage of wine, when it did happen, would assume almost the dimensions of a household catastrophe. Humiliation was lying in store for the bridal couple, who as yet suspected nothing.

B. THE MOTHER OF JESUS SAID TO HIM: "THEY HAVE NO MORE WINE."

In the East, as it still is with us — for human nature has not changed — women's great joy is in looking after the thousand little details of a celebration. Thus it was that Mary realized what was happening. She may have felt that she herself was partially responsible, for her Son's arrival with his disciples had not made matters any easier, and a mother will always take her son's side of an affair. And so she says to Jesus: "They have no more wine." A communication simple in itself, in its context it is the most delicately phrased of requests, barely a suggestion. Jesus was to keep all freedom of action for himself, but his filial love would also set the example of bowing to the humble request of his Mother.

C. JESUS SAID TO HER: "WOMAN, WHAT IS THAT TO ME AND TO THEE?"

The reply that Jesus makes has always seemed strange to us. At first sight it sounds like a refusal. All things considered, it might be thought that what we have here is a manner of speaking with nuances that cannot be conveyed by a literal translation, and that the majority of its translations are paraphrase. Osty translates it as "Woman, leave it to me," and comments: "and not: 'What is there between me and thee?'; and still less: 'What is there in common between me and thee?' " [2] P. Lagrange proposes: "What does that matter to me and to thee, Woman?" and explains: "The import of this reply lies entirely in the accentuation it is given. Sometimes it means 'Go about your business,' and sometimes, when said with a smile, 'Leave it to me, all will be well.' " [3] We are left with the impression that these translations are trying to soften the sharp tone of the original text — a laudable intention, but one that runs the risk, albeit in the very name of the love that Jesus had for his holy Mother, of masking the spiritual quality of this love.

The word "Woman" presents the first difficulty. Granted, there can be no doubt that the expression has a certain solemnity about it, but not so excessively as to be out of place on the lips of a

Semite who is addressing himself to his mother. Yet there is in fact no other passage in the Bible that would confirm this sense of the word. It is really only a very simple form of address, and when all is said and done, one that is quite commonplace, which Jesus uses in addressing any woman, whether it be the Samaritan woman, the woman taken in adultery, or Mary Magdalene.[4] Besides these three instances in John's Gospel, we also find the expression in Matthew 15:28, where Jesus addresses the Canaanite woman, and in Luke 13:12, where he cures the bent woman. If we are to believe John and the Synoptics, the appellation "Woman" thus implies neither special affection, solemnity, aloofness, nor disdain; it is a neutral term; Jesus is addressing an ordinary woman.

But would Jesus have addressed his Mother in the same terms as he would address any other woman? Here again, we do not have, either in the rabbinic writings or in the Bible, any other instance in which a son so addresses his mother. There is thus room to suppose, until proved to the contrary, that Jesus is, so to speak, abstracting from his sonhood and treating Mary as any other woman. Any other hypothesis, as P. Braun writes, is "entirely gratuitous," and has no other example in the Bible to rest upon.[5]

The expression "What is that to me and to thee?" presents the same difficulty. What was there between Jesus and Mary? But she was his beloved Mother, the most loving of all mothers; he was her Son, and "he was subject to them" (Luke 2:51). Nevertheless, turning to the literal translation: "What to me and to thee?" according to Scriptural usage the expression signifies that there was nothing in common between Jesus and Mary. "It is always an instance of a refusal, motivated by a certain absence of common interest between the persons involved."[6] The instance of this usage in the New Testament is of particular significance, and we shall find two episodes in which this expression will recur:

— first, at the time of Jesus' cure of the possessed man at the synagogue in Capharnaum. The unclean spirit cried out, saying, "What is there between us and thee, Jesus of Nazareth? Hast thou come to destroy us? I know who thou art, the Holy One of God" (Mark 1:24; cf. Luke 4:34);

— a second time, when Jesus expels a demon in the country of the Gerasenes: "What is there between me and thee, Jesus, Son of the most high God? I adjure thee by God, do not torment me!" (Mark 5:7; cf. Matthew 8:29; Luke 8:28).

Hence, if we replace the expression "Woman, what is there

between me and thee?" in its Scriptural context, Jesus is seemingly treating his Mother like any other woman; and his deliberate lack of compliance with her request is based on the fact that they have nothing in common. Any other interpretation is extraneous to the use that Scripture makes of these expressions, and because of this usage as we find it in Scripture, this interpretation alone can prevail.

D. My Hour Has Not Yet Come

This "hour" of Jesus has likewise been given diverse interpretations. In the present case, the context quite clearly indicates it to be the time at which his Mother's wish will be fulfilled, namely, that he work a miracle.[7] In one sense this is true, but it is incomplete. If once again we turn to John himself for an interpretation of his Gospel, we in fact will discover that each time Jesus speaks of his "hour," he is alluding to his Passion and glorification. Thus on the Feast of Tabernacles, Jesus reveals himself as the Messias; the Jews "wanted therefore to seize him, but no one laid hands on him because his hour had not yet come." And further in the text: "Jesus had not yet been glorified" (John 7:30, 39). The day after the feast, Jesus reveals his divine origin and proclaims the truth of his testimony. John writes: "Jesus spoke these words in the treasury, while teaching in the temple. And no one seized him, because his hour had not yet come."[8]

As it draws ever closer, this Hour seems to have left such a deep mark on the soul of Jesus that it troubles him to the point of anguish. He fears it because it is the Hour of his Passion; he desires it because it is the Hour of his glorification. In John's report we hear these words which reveal the dismay of his human nature in the face of death, and at the same time his humble submission to the will of his Father. These words, uttered on Palm Sunday, are already a prelude to the scene in Gethsemani: "The hour has come for the Son of Man to be glorified. Amen, amen, I say to you, unless the grain of wheat falls into the ground and dies, it remains alone. But if it dies, it brings forth much fruit. . . . Now my soul is troubled. And what shall I say? Father, save me from this hour! No, this is why I came to this hour" (Jn 12:23-25; 27).

John himself has been struck by the insistence with which Jesus was wont to speak of this solemn hour, and accordingly he begins his account of the Last Supper as follows: "Before the feast of the Passover, Jesus, knowing that the hour had come for him to pass out of this world to the Father, having loved his own who were in the world, loved them to the end" (John 13:1). And further on, he recounts this prayer of our Lord: ". . . raising his eyes to heaven, [Jesus] said : Father, the hour has come! Glorify thy Son, that thy Son may glorify thee" (John 17:1).

Taken all together, these texts function as a constant theme. Each time that Jesus speaks of his "hour," he is alluding to his Passion and his glorification. It is therefore reasonable to conclude that in John 2:4: "My hour has not yet come," Jesus is speaking equally of his Passion and of his glorification. There are all the more grounds for this inference in that John is presenting the miracle at Cana to us as the manifestation of Jesus' glory (2:11). But the Passion is precisely the hour of his exaltation (John 12:32).

E. His Mother said to the Attendants: "Do Whatever He Tells You."

Mary does not appear to be at all disconcerted by Jesus' refusal; on the contrary, her order to the attendants indicates that she knew her plea would be answered. How could she know this?

We can presume that John has given a summary account of the essentials of the dialogue, omitting those elements and explanations that he judged unnecessary to include in the Gospel. This is not the only time that he has proceeded along these lines. We have, for example, the discourse on the Bread of life (John 6), a discourse of capital importance since it will determine the adherence or the defection of many of his disciples, and one that is, relatively speaking, rather short. But we know from other sections of the Gospels that the sermons Jesus preached were of considerable length.

We must also bear in mind that the tone of voice or even a simple glance can charge speech with a nuance that cannot be conveyed by the text. But Mary, with the intuition of a woman — and a mother — would instinctively have divined the meaning of the words that had been spoken. A mother has her own secret way of understanding her child. It was not for nothing that Mary had spent thirty years in the intimate company of her Son; every word that she is speaking now is still an expression of this atmosphere of tenderness and love, the same tenderness that binds the Son in a oneness with the Mother.

Where the letter of the text may convey only a refusal, she can discern consent. On one hand, she understood that Jesus was claiming complete freedom for his messianic ministry, that he would brook no interference in that ministry, even on the part of his Mother. On the other hand, she also understood that he was inclining to her plea, not out of submission but with a sovereign liberty. This is no half-hearted miracle, wrested from him by a mother's love. He was no longer subject to Mary as he had been in the days at Nazareth; it is now rather Mary who is placing herself in subjection to the messianic vocation of her Son.

Finally, notice how the words she speaks to the attendants: "Do whatever he tells you," are again a manifestation of the inner dispositions of her heart, dispositions of confidence, abandonment, of perfect openness to whatever God might ask of her. We know already from Luke that her fundamental attitude was that of the handmaid of the Lord: ". . . be it done to me according to thy word" (Luke 1:38). She is now asking this same openness of the attendants: "Do whatever he tells you." Only a simple detail, to be sure, but it is such details that reveal the secrets of a heart.

F. The Miracle

Now six stone water-jars were placed there, after the Jewish manner of purification, each holding two or three measures. Jesus said to them, "Fill the jars with water." And they filled them to the brim. And Jesus said to them, "Draw out now, and take to the chief steward." And they took it to him. Now when the chief steward had tasted the water after it had become wine, not knowing whence it was (though the attendants who had drawn the water knew), the chief steward called the bridegroom, and said to him, "Every man at first sets forth the good wine, and when they have drunk freely, then that which is poorer. But thou hast kept the good wine until now" (John 2:6-10).

Our imaginations could not wish for a more captivating scene. John knows how to give his narrative both sparkle and color in a way that is out of the ordinary. First we see the attendants filling the jars; the process took some time, for to get one hundred fifty gallons of water [9] they would have had to make many trips to the cistern or fountain. This task will be accomplished conscientiously: "they filled them to the brim." Upon the command of Jesus, they then will carry some of it to the chief steward of the feast; they will have already succumbed to Mary's persuasion ("Do whatever he tells you"), for otherwise they would have looked twice before bringing the water to their employer.

The chief steward of the feast (*architriclinus*) was the one officially charged with the material supervision of banquets; to him fell the special task of spicing the wine and regulating its consumption. We see him dipping his goblet into one of the pitchers that is brought to him . . . a few moments of silence and reflection . . . and he calls the bridegroom. The little speech that he makes to him is typically Eastern — a hint of reproach, clothed in a semblance of congratulations: "Thou hast kept the good wine until now." In virtue of his office of *architriclinus* he was responsible for seeing that all ran smoothly: first the good wine, and then the poorer. But this rule had just been violated because the entire supply of wine had not been put at his disposal; he did not know where it had come from.

The bridegroom, we can imagine, protests vigorously; the attendants, who had drawn the water and knew what had happened, intervene in the discussion. There are explanations, and everything is straightened out. The bridegroom had proved his "innocence," the *architriclinus* had demonstrated that his professional competence was not wanting, and further that, having produced such wine, he really knew his business.

---

¹ These were the first five disciples whose calling John has just related (John 1:35-51).

² *Le Nouveau Testament* (Ed. Siloé), p. 198, n. 4.

³ *Évangile selon saint Jean*, Coll. *Études Bibliques*, *op cit.*, pp. 57 and 56; Braun (*op cit.*, p. 51) still cites: "What do you want of me?" (Lesêtre); "What do you expect of me?" (Durand); "What dost thou want of me?" (Bible du Cent.); "What is that for me and for thee?" (Cadoux).

⁴ John 4:21; 8:10; 20:13, 15.

⁵ Braun, *op cit.*, p. 50. Jesus will use the word "Woman" one more time, when he commends John to his mother: "Woman, behold, thy son" (John 19:26). This last instance of its use does not resolve the present problem but on the contrary accentuates it. See pp. 241–244.

⁶ Braun, *op cit.*, pp. 53–54.

⁷ *Évangile selon saint Jean*, *op. cit.*, p. 57. P. Lagrange, while he is familiar with the interpretation that we are proposing, does not hold to it.

⁸ John 8:20. The "treasury" refers to the treasury rooms that were located in the Court of the Women.

⁹ A "measure" was equivalent to about nine or ten gallons; therefore, each jar contained from twenty to thirty gallons, all adding up to a total of 120 to 180 gallons. As P. Lagrange writes (*op. cit.*, p. 58): "The miracle will not be stingy."

Chapter 16

THE MIRACLE AS "SIGN"

What remains to be explained is the meaning of the miracle:

1) The first angle from which it should be considered concerns the most obvious: the immediate aim of Jesus is to provide wine for a marriage feast where it was about to run out.[1] In doing this, Jesus thereby manifests his kindheartedness and delicacy of feeling; he knows how to be attentive to the humble "little things" that bring joy to a family gathering. He who will exact of his disciples a love of absolute preference, a preference over the love of wife and children (cf. Luke 14:26), is for all that no "kill-joy." Quite the contrary. Multiplying the wine, he multiplies joy as well: "Wine to gladden men's hearts" (Ps. 103:15).

2) As it concerns his disciples, Jesus is manifesting his glory and thereby stirring up their faith. This is the very purpose of the Johannine sign, and John dwells on this aspect with particular emphasis: "This first of his signs Jesus worked in Cana of Galilee; and he manifested his glory, and his disciples believed in him" (John 2:11).

3) Now what is the more particular meaning of this sign? As P. Braun points out,[2] this entire section is dominated by the theme of renewal, of the passage from the old to the new order. In the prologue John had written: ". . . the Law was given through Moses; grace and truth came through Jesus Christ" (John 1:17). John will return to this central theme:

— In the meeting with Nicodemus: the birth according to the flesh, whereby Nicodemus had become a member of God's people, was about to be replaced by a new birth, a birth which comes from heaven and is according to the Spirit (John 3:1ff.);

— In the conversation with the Samaritan woman: the worship on Mount Garizim and even on Mount Sion, in the Temple at

181

Jerusalem, was about to be replaced by an adoration "in spirit and in truth," namely, an adoration that will be wholly spiritual and embracing all truth (John 4:1ff.);

— In the cure of the sick man at Bethsaida: the Sabbath rest was about to be replaced by God's work (John 5:1ff., particularly v. 17);

— In the discourse on the Bread of life: for the bread of the Exodus, God was now substituting the true Bread of life, the very Flesh and Blood of the Son, to be received in faith (John 6:1ff.).

By studying these events in the light of the Cana narrative, we can conclude that the miraculous changing of the water into wine likewise is a sign of the replacing of the old order by the messianic.

4) Perhaps this can be elaborated further. The allusion to the Jewish ablution ritual — there were six urns there, intended for the Jewish ablution ritual — is in point of fact completely gratuitous. It does not, in itself, add anything to our understanding of the narrative and has no bearing, properly speaking, on the working of the miracle. But as John has given us this fact, we can have no doubt that in his eyes it possesses a symbolic value, evoking a spontaneous association with the Old Law and its purification rites. But under the messianic covenant there are no longer, as formerly, rites for our purification from sin, but the Blood of Christ Jesus (1 John 1:7; Apoc. 1:5; 7:14; 22:14). But the miraculous wine was entirely intended, within the dimensions of the mystery of the Eucharist, to be a sign of the Lord's Blood. In this we have a fresh allusion to the "hour" of Jesus, the "hour" of his Passion; [3] the Blood of Christ thus replaces the water of the Jewish purification rites.

Besides these principal points, it will be worthwhile to turn to the secondary aspects which concern the Mother of Jesus and which in relation to our title have a more direct interest.

1) The manifestation of the glory of Jesus was also, for our Lady, the revelation that her Son had definitively entered upon his messianic ministry. All through the years that he had lived with her in the intimacy of Nazareth, he had belonged to her as a child to his mother; henceforth, he was to belong totally to his heavenly Father. The bonds of human tenderness, so delicately and subtly woven, would now become only fetters, as it were, to the fulfillment of his vocation; the Mother's love would have to yield to the love of the Father's will.

The lesson is not a new one — it links up with the one that Jesus had already given to his parents eighteen years before, when he said to them in the Temple: "How is it that you sought me? Did you not know that I must be about my Father's business?" (Luke 2:49).

Providence had decreed that Jesus' public life would take its course far from his Mother's side, far from her mother's tenderness. A group of women — Mary Magdalene, Joanna the wife of Chuza, Susanna, and many others (Luke 8:2-3) — were to provide for him out of their means, but Mary does not figure among them. And each time that she does appear, Jesus makes use of the occasion to assert the superiority of the bonds of the spiritual world over those of fleshly parenthood:

> My mother and my brethren are they who hear the word of God, and act upon it (Luke 8:21).
>
> Blessed is the womb that bore thee, and the breasts that nursed thee. — Rather, blessed are they who hear the word of God and keep it (Luke 11:27-28).

These words do not mean that in Jesus' heart a mother's affection and solicitude counted for nothing. They are, however, a forceful assertion of the superiority of the spiritual order over the world of the flesh.

2) Mary's vocation is oriented more and more towards the "hour" of Jesus, the Passion. When Jesus states to her that his Hour has not yet come, he is also indicating to her, in veiled terms, that once his Hour has come, she again will be with him. The Hour of the Son's Passion will then be the Hour of the Mother's compassion. The sign-event at Cana and the time of the Passion are the only instances when John does in fact speak of Mary. The sign at Cana thus is, in some way, a prelude to the "sign" of the Cross, when Jesus will be exalted.

3) It can be pointed out, finally, that it is at Mary's petition that Jesus works this miracle. Hence Cana is a revelation, not only of the glory of Jesus, but of the maternal intercession of Mary. From the very abundance of the wine, we can gain some insight into the power of her influence. The evangelist, to be sure, does not state any of this directly, and the affirmation of Mary's mediation which takes the miracle of Cana as its point of departure cannot fail to give the impression of overstepping the bounds of strict exegesis. But popular devotion, and the liturgy as well, will at times overstep

these bounds. For if Mary concerned herself with the supplying of wine for a wedding feast, how much more, indeed, will she not be concerned with the spiritual interests of those who turn to her?

[1] Perhaps the six urns of wine stood as the wedding gift that Jesus was offering for himself and his five disciples. According to the rules of etiquette, the guests were obliged to bring gifts to the bridal pair.

[2] Braun, *La Mère des Fidèles, op. cit.*, p. 69.

[3] Treating together of the discourse on the Bread of life and the allusion to the Jewish purification ritual, Cullmann thinks it possible to write: "The miracle of the loaves, narrated in chapter 6, is the exact counterpart of the miracle at Cana: the latter involves wine, the former, bread; the latter quenches thirst, the former feeds. If, then, we consider the evangelist, as shown by this mention of the hour that has not yet come, to be approaching the miracle at Cana within the framework of his reflection on the death of Christ, and on the other hand, to be connecting the marvelous multiplication of the loaves in chapter 6 with the Bread of the Last Supper, the following explanation seems inescapable: the wine here stands for the Blood of Christ, offered at the Last Supper. . . . Until now the Jews used water for their purification. But henceforth it is the wine of the Last Supper, the Blood of Christ, that will insure the efficacy of these rites" (*Les Sacrements dans l'Évangile Johannique, op cit.*, pp. 38–39). Braun writes from his position (*op cit., ibid.*): "On the contrary the wine, which Jesus declared must be kept from being poured back into the old bottles of Judaism (Matthew 9:17; Mark 2:22; Luke 5:37), stands for the new order of the Spirit." This explanation is perhaps a little further from the text, since in the Johannine texts wine is never a symbol of the Spirit.

Part VIII

MARY AT CALVARY

"Woman, behold, thy son."
(John 19:26)

INTRODUCTION TO PART VIII

Notwithstanding the ministry of the public life which lies between Cana and Calvary and the apparent dissimilarity of these two Gospel events, the marriage feast at Cana, with its joyful miracle of the water changed into wine, is in John's thought connected with his account of the Passion. A whole series of concordances and mysterious harmonies forms an underlying unity in his presentation of these two pericopes: "At Cana, Jesus is inaugurating his messianic ministry: it is there that he works his first miracle: ἀρχὴν τῶν σημείων. At Calvary, he finishes his work: πάντα τετέλεισθαι — All is consummated. In both places, the Mother of Jesus is with her Son. The first time, he is in the company of his disciples; the second, with the disciple whom Jesus loved. At both these times Jesus addresses Mary in the same solemn manner, saying to her: 'Woman.' Again, at Cana he makes her understand that she is not meant to intervene in his public life until his Hour does come. At Calvary, this Hour having come, Mary's entire bearing shows the depth of her union with him in his redemptive sacrifice." [1]

The Text

Now there were standing by the cross of Jesus his mother and his mother's sister, Mary of Cleophas, and Mary Magdalene. When Jesus, therefore, saw his mother and the disciple standing by, whom he loved, he said to his mother, "Woman, behold, thy son." Then he said to the disciple, "Behold, thy mother." And from that hour the disciple took her into his home (John 19:25-27).

The Gospel narrative is sober in the extreme. John's reporting of the facts is completely objective, leaving the reader with a stark and simple picture of the crucified Jesus and his Mother. There can be no doubt that this discretion of John's is also explained by the fact that he himself is an actor on the scene. The disciple whom Jesus loved and who received into his home the Savior's own Mother — the Woman clothed with the sun and crowned with stars — is none other than himself. However, for all its sobriety the text is not thereby divested of rich content; quite the contrary, for John knows that the faith of his reader, taking its natural course, will lead him to the very heart of the mystery. Are not these wonderful words also his:

> . . . you have an anointing from the Holy One and you know all things (1 John 2:20).
>
> . . . let the anointing which you have received from him, dwell in you, and you have no need that anyone teach you . . . his anointing teaches you concerning all things (1 John 2:27).
>
> . . . we know that the Son of God has come and has given us understanding (1 John 5:20).

It can truly be said that John is trusting in the exegetical gifts of the man of faith; the "enlightened eyes of the mind," to use St. Paul's words (Eph. 1:18), were a profound reality in which he placed his confidence.

---

[1] Braun, *La Mère des Fidèles, op. cit.*, p. 77 (Perhaps it would not be necessary to insist on the *solemnity* of the term "Woman;" cf. *supra*, pp. 175–177).

Chapter 17

CONTEXT

In order not to wrest the pericope from its context, we must keep these several points in mind:

1) This supreme hour at which Jesus is suffering and dying on the Cross represents the supreme manifestation of God's love.

— It is the hour of the Father's love for men: "For God so loved the world that he gave his only-begotten Son" (John 3:16).

— It is the hour of Jesus' love for his own: "Before the feast of the Passover, Jesus, knowing that the hour had come for him to pass out of this world to the Father, having loved his own who were in the world, loved them to the end" (John 13:1).

— It is the hour, finally, of Jesus' love for his Father: ". . . the prince of the world is coming, and in me he has nothing. But he comes that the world may know that I love the Father, and that I do as the Father has commanded me" (John 14:30-31). It is particularly noteworthy that Christ, who so often speaks to us of the love his Father bears toward him, speaks to us only once of the love he bears toward his Father, and then in the context of the Passion; Christ's death is indeed the hour of truth and the fullness of love.

2) The Passion is not simply the hour of the Lord's death, but also the hour of his glorification:

> Now is the Son of Man glorified, and God is glorified in him. If God is glorified in him, God will also glorify him in himself, and will glorify him at once (John 13:31-32).

> Father, the hour has come! Glorify thy Son, that thy Son may glorify thee (John 17:1).

Passion and glory, therefore, are inseparable; Christ's being "lifted

189

up" on the Cross is the very sign of his universal kingship (John 12:32).

3) It will also be worthwhile to study this fresh instance of the care with which John notes how the Passion is the realization of the prophecies of Scripture. He has an extremely sensitive feeling for the argument from prophetic tradition, marshaling his evidence to show us that events have not overtaken Christ unawares, that the humiliation and the scandal of the Cross have been foreseen by Scripture. Arriving at that solemn hour, he therefore is doubly painstaking in bringing forward the texts which the Lord has "fulfilled." Accordingly he cites:

— Psalm 21:19: "They divided my garments among them; and for my vesture they cast lots" (John 19:24). The citation is introduced by the solemn formula "that the Scripture might be fulfilled."

— Exodus 12:46 (cited *ad sensum*), with its allusion to the paschal lamb: "Not a bone of him shall you break" (John 19:36). Here again he notes with special emphasis: "these things came to pass that the Scripture might be fulfilled."

— Zacharias 12:10: "They shall look upon him whom they have pierced" (John 19:37). This text is introduced by the formula: "And again another Scripture says. . . ."[1]

— The episode of the sponge soaked in vinegar reflects the same preoccupation: "After this Jesus, knowing that all things were now accomplished, that the Scripture might be fulfilled, said, 'I thirst' " (John 19:28). All things are *accomplished*, that the Scripture may be *fulfilled*. The forceful way in which this verse is structured will better be appreciated if we look at the original Greek, where the verb τελεῖν (to accomplish, fulfill) is emphatically repeated and thereby set in special prominence as forming the conclusion of one statement and the beginning of the one immediately following. * The significance of this wording is heightened by the fact that the citation "I thirst" is not given such a fixed reference and is, in any case, too brief to enable us to locate it definitively in a messianic context.[2]

4) Finally, it must be pointed out that Calvary, in the Johannine tradition, represents the supreme struggle of Jesus with the "adversary." We know that "the Son of God appeared, that he might destroy the works of the devil" (1 John 3:8). This struggle between Christ, the living Light, and the kingdom of darkness is heralded as early as the prologue: "In him was life, and the life was the

light of men. And the light shines in the darkness; and the darkness grasped it not" (John 1:4-5).

With the Passion, the struggle enters into its final phase: "the prince of the world is coming" (John 14:30). He is mobilizing all the forces of his race, his "children," as John calls them; [3] it is "the final struggle" and at the same time the enthronement of Christ the universal King: "Now is the judgment of the world; now will the prince of the world be cast out" (John 12:31).

If we would take this entire assemblage of texts at its full value, it will not be rash to infer that the pericope which shows us Mary standing by the Cross has, in virtue of its context, been given the place of honor. For this is the Hour when God's love stands plainly revealed, when Jesus' glory is made manifest, when the Scriptures are fulfilled, when the devil is vanquished. It can safely be said that John's account, despite the reserve characteristic of his style, cannot be matched for the spiritual richness it contains. If the evangelist has left in shadow many other features of the Passion that the Synoptics have recorded for us, and instead related Mary's presence by the Cross, he has not done so merely as a scrupulous chronicler of objective fact; to treat this episode as a simple anecdote would be, we think, to wrest it from its context. Exegesis must always be governed by prudence, to be sure; but here prudence will consist precisely in placing the facts in their true spiritual dimension.

A. Mother of Sorrows

In showing us the sorrowful Mother at the foot of the Cross, John seems to be calling attention to the intimacy of Mary's communion in the sufferings of her Son; at that supreme hour she is sharing, as only a mother can, in the deepest movements of her Child's soul. John himself and the group of holy women were of course equally present, but Mary is not simply the first of all the disciples of Jesus — she is also his Mother. Here our thoughts turn spontaneously to Simeon's prophecy: "Behold, this child is destined for the fall and for the rise of many in Israel, and for a sign that shall be contradicted. And thy own soul a sword shall pierce" [4] (Luke 2:34-35).

The whole course of Mary's life had unfolded in this perspective of sorrow. We know that she had "kept in mind all these things,

pondering them in her heart" (Luke 2:19, 51). Simeon's prophecy
had been part of the very spiritual atmosphere that she breathed;
it made up, so to speak, the backdrop against which all the years
had passed and left their mark — first the thirty years of the hidden
life, then the three years of the public life, and now the death
of her Child. She had already come to understand, on that day
so long ago when she had found him in the Temple, that he would
have to be completely "about his Father's business"; now more
than ever he belonged totally to his Father: "Father, into thy hands
I commend my spirit" (Luke 23:46).

At Cana, she had likewise come to understand that the bonds
of human tenderness would have to bow before the demands of
the prophetic mission; now the hour had come when it would once
again be permitted her to be close to her Son. For the sorrowful
yet royal "lifting up" of the Cross was to be the triumph of which
the angel had spoken on the day of her Annunciation: ". . . the
Lord God will give him the throne of David his father, and he
shall be king over the house of Jacob forever; and of his kingdom
there shall be no end" (Luke 1:32-33). It was at this very Hour,
when the flood-waves of sorrow were overwhelming her mother's
soul, that Jesus was to reveal himself in fulfillment of Simeon's
prophecy: " [The] salvation prepared before the face of all peoples:
A light of revelation to the Gentiles, and a glory for thy people
Israel" (Luke 2:31-32).

It is beyond all doubt that Mary let herself be drawn, with all
the ardor of her loving soul, into the very depths of the mystery
of the Cross. At Calvary, as at the Annunciation, she remains "the
lowly handmaid of the Lord."

B. THE NEW EVE

The array of Scriptural texts which John selects to frame his narrative of the Passion invites us to broaden the range of our inquiry,
and to see whether Mary's presence was not itself also the fulfillment
of a prophecy.

Notice first of all the reference to the vision of Apocalypse 12;
the similarity of the two texts is self-evident. In both instances
we find:

Christ the King	the Child who is to shepherd all nations
Mary, his Mother	the Woman, the Mother of the Child
the disciples	the rest of her offspring.

We know too from elsewhere that at the hour of the Passion the devil is to be cast out, a truth that Apocalypse 12:9 manifestly recalls: "And that great dragon was cast down, the ancient serpent, he who is called the devil and Satan" (Apoc. 12:9). The author of the Fourth Gospel does not forget to associate the devil, Christ's persecutor, with the devil of Genesis. In this vein he writes that the devil is a murderer "from the beginning" (John 8:44), that he sins "from the beginning" (1 John 3:8).

For the Apocalypse, as we have seen, contains an explicit reference to Genesis. Hence, if we place the scene at Calvary in the perspective of the Apocalypse, we should arrive at the same conclusion: Mary would be present as the new Eve. Dealing with the entire picture that this assemblage of texts presents, P. Braun says: "To pretend that the Fourth Gospel drew no inspiration from the Proto-gospel is possible only if we refuse to look at the evidence." [5] It will be conceded that the text of the Apocalypse is more explicit, but what we have already said on the subject makes it unnecessary to return to it here.

C. THE MOTHER OF THE DISCIPLES

Mary's appearance at the foot of the Cross serves as a kind of introduction to the words of Jesus which follow: "When Jesus, therefore ($o\hat{v}\nu$), saw his mother and the disciple standing by, whom he loved, he said to his mother, 'Woman, behold, thy son.' Then he said to the disciple, 'Behold, thy mother' " (John 19:26-27). What is the exact import of these words?

Early exegesis (that most favorable to Mary [6]) saw them in a rather general way as an expression of a son's devotion: before dying, Jesus confided his Mother to the disciple whom he loved, and the latter was to watch over her as a son would his mother, with his presence by her side to console her in the loneliness left by her Son's death. [7]

This interpretation is perfectly acceptable in what it affirms. John goes on to say: "And from that hour the disciple took her into his home." However, we think that this interpretation would be incomplete if, by minimizing the import of Christ's words, it thereby entailed the exclusion of quite another interpretation. Several considerations do, in fact, lead us to a wider interpretation of the text.

John's Gospel is certainly the one which is the least sensitive to what might be called the "familial dimension" of the life of Jesus.

This is so true that in the prologue of his Gospel, John speaks of the Incarnation without even explicitly mentioning her in whom the Logos took flesh! Can we then be justified in believing that all he meant to tell us was that the Lord, at the very hour when he was accomplishing the supreme act of redemption, was simply setting his family affairs in order? As P. Dubarle points out, "This was an act that concerned the whole world, not simply a manifestation of a son's devotion to alleviate the loneliness of a widowed mother. Jesus is portrayed as lucidly aware of the significance of events (John 13:1-3; 18:4; 19:28). How can we believe that at that solemn moment he, who is from above and who was about to return whence he had come, would have spoken only of the realities of this world (cf. John 3:11), and not of divine mysteries? Without denying the immediate objective of his words, we are compelled to attribute to them a more profound meaning." [8]

This so-called "familial" interpretation would also run counter to the witness of the Synoptics. For we have seen that, during the public life, Jesus utilizes each of Mary's appearances on the scene as an opportunity to assert the superiority of faith and obedience over the bonds of the flesh. Hence it would be surprising if Jesus, at the very hour of his deepest expression of his love for his Father, would have been thinking exclusively of family matters.

This interpretation would also be a departure from the context of the Passion. As we have seen above, John regroups his recollection of events by ordering them around the prophecies of which he sees them to be the fulfillment. All the action unfolds in a manner that is almost liturgical: "that the Scripture might be fulfilled." These continual references place the account in a very solemn setting, a setting of both royal glory and unspeakable suffering, a setting which these words evoke: "And I, if I be lifted up from the earth, will draw all things to myself" (John 12:32). In such an atmosphere there is, we think, little room for a minimizing exegesis. It would be as if a false note were to intrude to mar the structure of an admirable symphony.

Notice, finally, that it is not Mary who is first entrusted to John, but John who is first entrusted to Mary. The accent is placed on the solicitude with which Mary is to surround the disciple, a solicitude to which the disciple is to respond with the tenderness of a son.

Taken in themselves, none of these considerations seems decisive; taken as a unified whole, however, they challenge us to pass beyond the narrow framework of too timid an exegesis, one that is insufficient by reason of its hesitancy and over-modesty of method. The entire text must be placed in the perspective of the great drama of the redemption which is being unfolded before our eyes. Here, it seems to us, is what should be said:

In Apocalypse 12 we have seen the mysterious relationship between Christ and "the rest of the offspring." This relationship between Christ and his "brothers" creates in Mary a new motherhood, one reaching out beyond the person of Jesus alone to embrace all the members of the Mystical Body. It is a motherhood that is real, yet truly mysterious, opening out on the very mystery of the Mystical Body, the identification of Christ with the faithful; a motherhood that takes its beginning at the very moment of the Incarnation when the Woman clothed with the sun and crowned with stars brings forth her male Child; a motherhood that is sorrowful, continuing through the war that the Dragon carries on against the rest of the offspring. Here by the Cross, this motherhood, in its extension to all the members of the Mystical Body, is expressed toward John as toward a favored disciple. It is precisely because John belongs to the rest of the offspring that he receives for his Mother her who has brought forth the First-born.

The words "Son, behold thy mother" should not, in our opinion, be considered as establishing the spiritual motherhood of Mary. From the exegetical standpoint, this assertion seems too difficult to maintain; moreover, from the patristic standpoint, it is manifestly too late in date to be regarded as the authentic interpretation of an early tradition; finally, from the theological standpoint, it would be extremely awkward to establish a sort of adoptive motherhood, as if Mary at that moment were adopting the beloved disciple and receiving him "as" a son (while in reality he would not be her son).

What we do affirm is this: Mary is really our Mother, not because John receives her for a mother, but simply because she is the Mother of Jesus, in whom all the faithful are contained as a unity: "Christ's words, far from creating the motherhood of grace, only presuppose it." [9] And if John does receive her for his mother, it is not precisely because he is the representative of all the disciples, but rather because he is one of them.

We do not conceal the fact that this exegesis owes more to the Johannine data taken as a whole than it does to a strict analysis of the text itself; it presupposes what is inferred from Apocalypse 12. There is a very interesting point of contact between the text of the Apocalypse and the Calvary narrative which it will be profitable to bring forward here:

John is called "the disciple whom Jesus loved" (cf. John 19:26). The relative clause "whom Jesus loved" indicates, it seems to us, not so much a preferential love, a special affection which singled him out from all the others — there is in fact no term of comparison — as a belonging to Christ. Jesus loves all his disciples: "I have called you friends" (John 15:15); but this love is subordinated to the practice of the commandments:

> He who has my commandments and keeps them, he it is who loves me. But he who loves me will be loved by my Father, and I will love him (John 14:21).

> You are my friends if you do the things I command you (John 15:14).

The Fourth Gospel thus equates loving Jesus and being loved by him with the keeping of his commandments. But in Apocalypse 12:17, the practice of the commandments is precisely what characterizes the rest of the offspring.[10] In calling himself "the disciple whom Jesus loved," John thereby is counting himself among the offspring of the Woman crowned with stars and the Mother of the royal Child.

A weighing of the exegetical points in John 19:25-27 may lead some to consider our position over-prudent. However we think that the texts cannot be forced to affirm more than they contain. Moreover, each of us can transcend the confines of this exegesis in the spiritual exploration of his own meditation. In all events, it will be understood why we began our analysis of the Johannine data with the richer and more explicit text of the Apocalypse.

D. CONCLUSION

Of all the disciples of Jesus, John is the one who knew Mary most intimately. He would have been able to give us an "inside story," so to speak, with a captivating wealth of details about "the real Mary," or even "Mary day by day." However, he judged it expedient to disclose to us nothing in this connection; he is even much less specific in detail than Luke. And much later, when the apocrypha set themselves to the task of filling in this "gap," they will fail lamentably; they will pretend to know all, but will have nothing of value to teach us; compared with the well-tempered reserve of the evangelist, their lyric verbosity only leaves us in confusion.

For the mystery of Mary is wholly interior. This extraordinary and absolutely unique event, which made a young daughter of Israel the Mother of God, is before all else an event in the world of the spirit. Doubtless by way of reaction against what he saw every day with his bodily eyes, John as it were transposes his filial devotion to the supernatural plane. He who so intimately knew "the real Mary" shows us the Mary of salvation-history. His meditation gravitates around the poles of these two themes:

— Mary is *par excellence* the Woman associated with the Redeemer. The Cana narrative serves in some way as an introduction to the Calvary narrative; once the Hour of Jesus has come, Mary will be present with her Son, united with him in the communion of his sufferings. The hour of the Passion of the Son will be the hour of the compassion of the Mother;

— As the Mother of Jesus, Mary also appears as the Mother of the rest of the offspring. At that hour of greatest suffering, it would have been so easy for Mary to draw within herself, to keep her suffering for herself alone, to keep her love for Jesus alone, to center her heart inward upon this meditation. But it is precisely at this hour that Christ demands of her that she open her mother's love to the rest of his brothers, thereby reminding her that her motherhood, which had been directed to his own person, is to be widened to the dimensions of the Church, that it is as immense and as universal as the Mystical Body. John's case will be the concrete application of this principle; lesson is clothed in life.

This twofold conclusion leads us to what we already know from the Apocalypse: on one plane, the mystery of Mary is oriented toward Christ; on another, toward the Church. The Mother of Jesus and the new Eve is also the spiritual mother of all the redeemed; and that is why this motherhood, which had its beginnings at Nazareth, continues down through the whole of salvation-history until the Parousia.

It was in loving Jesus that Mary learned to love us; we can now add that it is in loving Jesus and his brothers that we learn to love Mary.

---

[1] This text may have been occasioned by the mention of the living fountain that was to gush forth from Jerusalem in the eschatological times: "On that day there shall be open to the house of David and to the inhabitants of Jerusalem, a fountain

198 Mary at Calvary

to purify from sin and uncleanness" (Zach. 13:1). John may have seen in it an allusion to the water coming out of the heart of Jesus.

* *Translator's note*: The original Greek text reads as follows: Μετὰ τοῦτο εἰδὼς ὁ Ἰησοῦς ὅτι πάντα ἤδη τετέλεσται, ἵνα τελειωθῇ ἡ γπαφή, λέγει, διψῶ. In the French text, both the first and second instances of the Greek verb τελεῖν are rendered by the verb *accomplir*. However as the English "accomplish" cannot convey all the nuances of the French, we have reproduced the Confraternity translation, which renders the first instance of τελεῖν as "accomplish" and the second as "fulfill," and taken the liberty of rewriting this paragraph to adapt it to English readers.

² Our thoughts ordinarily turn back to Psalm 68:22 or to Psalm 21:16.

³ 1 John 3:10. Judas himself is called a devil (John 6:71); it is the devil who inspires him to hand over Jesus (John 13:2) and who subsequently enters into him (John 13:27).

⁴ On the prophecy of Simeon as an announcement of the Passion, the following of the more recent works may be consulted: T. Gallus, "De sensu verborum Lc II, 35 eorumque momento.mariologico," *Bibl.*, 29 (1948), pp. 220–239; the author has a résumé of his study in *Verb. Dom.*, 26 (1948), pp. 234–235. — C. de Coninck, "The Compassion of the Virgin and the Prophecy of Simeon," *Lav. Phil. Theol.*, 6 (1950), pp. 314–324. — A.-M. Dubarle, "Les fondements bibliques du titre de Nouvelle Eve," *Rech. Sc. Rel.*, 39 (1951), pp. 57–61; the author thinks that Luke 2:34-35 admits of a certain parallel with Genesis 3:15. — A. De Groot, "Die schmerzhafte Mutter und Gefährten des göttlichen Erlösers in der Weissagung Simeons, Lk II, 35. Eine biblisch-theologische Studie," *Diss. Gregoriana* (Rome, 1953); this study was subsequently edited at Kaldenkirchen, 1956.

⁵ "Ève et Marie dans les deux Testaments," *Études Mariales, La Nouvelle Ève,* I (1954) (*Bulletin de la Société française d'Études Mariales*), p. 31.

⁶ In patristic exegesis there does in fact exist another current of thought; see pp. 211–212.

⁷ See, for example, St. Augustine, *In Joannis Evangelium*, Tract 119, 1–2; PL 35, 1950–1951. St. Augustine adds that Christ is showing us by his example that we must care for our parents when necessity demands.

⁸ Dubarle, "Du titre marial de Nouvelle Eve," *Mélanges Lebreton*, pp. 62 ff.

⁹ T. Koehler, "Maternité spirituelle de Marie," *Maria, Études sur la Vierge*, I (Paris, 1949), p. 583.

¹⁰ See pp. 164–166.

THE EVE-MARY PARALLEL IN PRIMITIVE TRADITION

Outside of Scripture, the Eve-Mary parallel finds a confirmation in primitive tradition that is of the utmost significance; it is one of the earliest-laid foundation stones in the teaching of the Fathers on the mystery of Mary. We find it in the writings of St. Justin, St. Irenaeus, and Tertullian.

A. ST. JUSTIN

This theme is treated by St. Justin in his *Dialogue with Trypho the Jew*. We quote it here as it appears in its immediate context.

> The words, "But Thou dwellest in the holy place, Thou praise of Israel," signified that He would do something worthy of praise and admiration, which He did when through the Father He arose again from the dead on the third day after the crucifixion. I have indeed pointed out earlier that Christ is called both Jacob and Israel, and that not only in the blessing of Joseph and Juda have things been predicted mysteriously of Him, but also in the Gospel it is written that He said: "All things have been delivered to Me by My Father; and no one knows the Father except the Son; nor does anyone know the Son except the Father, and those to whom the Son will reveal Him."
> He thus revealed to us all that we have learned from the Scriptures by His grace, so that we know Him as the First-begotten of God before all creatures, and as the Son of the patriarchs, since He became incarnate by a virgin of their race, and condescended to become a man without comeliness or honor, and subject to suffering. Hence, He alluded to His imminent passion in this way, "The Son of Man must suffer many things, and be rejected by the Pharisees and Scribes, and be crucified, and rise again on the third day." He called Himself Son of Man, either because of His birth by the

virgin who was, as I said, of the family of David and Jacob and Isaac and Abraham, or because Adam himself was the father of those above-mentioned Patriarchs from whom Mary traces her descent. It is clear that the fathers of girls are also considered the fathers of the children born to their daughters.

And Christ changed the name of one of His disciples from Simon to Peter, when he, enlightened by the Father, recognized Him to be Christ, the Son of God. And since we find it written in the Memoirs of the Apostles that He is the Son of God, and since we call Him by that same title, we have understood that this is really He and that He proceeded before all creatures from the Father by His power and will (for in the prophetic writings He is called Wisdom, the Day, the East, Sword, Stone, Rod, Jacob, and Israel, always in a different way); and that He is born of the Virgin, in order that the disobedience caused by the serpent might be destroyed in the same manner in which it had originated. For Eve, an undefiled virgin, conceived the word of the serpent, and brought forth disobedience and death. But the Virgin Mary (Μαρία ἡ παρϑένος), filled with faith and joy (πίστιν δε καὶ χαρὰν λαβοῦσα), when the angel Gabriel announced to her the good tidings that the Spirit of the Lord would come upon her, and the power of the Highest would overshadow her, and therefore the Holy One born of her would be the Son of God, answered: "Be it done unto me according to Thy word."

And, indeed, she gave birth to Him, concerning whom we have shown so many passages of Scripture were written, and by whom God destroys both the serpent and those angels and men who have become like the serpent, but frees from death those who repent of their sins and believe in Christ (*Dialogue with Trypho*, 100, in *Writings of St. Justin Martyr*, translated by Thomas B. Falls, *The Fathers of the Church* (New York: Christian Heritage, Inc., 1948), pp. 303–305. PG 6, 710A–712A).

It must be admitted that, taken as a whole, this long passage is not particularly conspicuous for its inner logic; it was principally intended as a commentary on Psalm 21:4: "But Thou dwellest in the holy place, Thou praise of Israel." But in its nexus of ideas one reflection leads to another, and we find ourselves embarked on a rather complex affair. It would seem, however, that its shifting thought-patterns gravitate about a twofold affirmation: Christ is at once both Son of God and Son of Man — we understand that he is really the Son of God . . . we understand that he was made man.

It is precisely on this latter affirmation that the Eve-Mary parallel hangs; its attractiveness is enhanced, moreover, by the mention of Mary as "the Virgin:"

Eve	Mary
an undefiled virgin	the Virgin

| conceived the word of the serpent | filled with faith and joy when the angel Gabriel announced to her . . . |
| brought forth disobedience and death | answered: "Be it done unto me according to thy word" |

The parallelism, as has often been pointed out, is not absolutely balanced. Justin counterweights the two sides as he goes along, turns back, and starts off in a new direction. Eve conceives the word of the serpent and brings forth disobedience and death; Mary answers: "Be it done unto me according to thy word." Perhaps this literary imperfection should not be taken too seriously; we must beware of demanding always and everywhere an absolute and almost mathematical balance between the two sides of a comparison. The author happens to be setting forth the first term, leaving the intelligent reader to complete it himself (such an easy and simple thing to do!), and goes on to open up a new perspective. All of us who are familiar with the Bible, where parallelism so often intervenes, know how frequent a procedure this is and how puerile it is to look upon it as a stumbling block.

As for the parallel itself, it will be profitable to call attention to these two particular aspects:

— Mary is placed in correspondence to Eve, and this correspondence itself is based on the fact that she is the Mother of Jesus: it was when she brought forth Christ that God destroyed the empire of the serpent. It can even be pointed out that Justin sets forth this aspect as a truth that is already familiar and requires no proof. From elsewhere in his writings we know that he was concerned only with giving an account of the deposit of "tradition," ὡς ἐδιδάχθημεν, according to his expression, "as we have learned" (I Apol. 13; PG 6, 345). This idea is actually only a taking-up of the Johannine datum of Apocalypse 12; it will be recalled that it was precisely when the Woman clothed with the sun and crowned with twelve stars had brought forth the royal Child that the victory over the serpent began;

— The principle on which Justin bases his parallelism is that of the *recircumlatio*: he is born of the Virgin, in order that the disobedience caused by the serpent might be destroyed in the same manner in which it had originated. Here we have a first attempt at theological reflection on the primitive data of Scripture. This attempt, begun with Justin, will reach its perfect expression with St. Irenaeus.

B. St. Irenaeus

Faced with the increasing encroachments of Gnosticism, St. Irenaeus sought to achieve a first synthesis of Christian theology in explaining, as he himself puts it, "the whole body of truth" (*Epideixis*, 1; cf. *Adv. Haer.*, 1, 9, 4; PG 7, 584). With this he has admirable success, in that he places Christ at the center of his theology and the doctrine of the "re-establishment" at the heart of his Christology. As a result of his endeavors we are given a theology which, while fresh and bold in outlook, is already laid firmly on the foundation of tradition (cf. *Adv. Haer.*, 3, 3, 1; PG 7, 848A), and embraces the full significance of Paul's famous dictum "to re-establish * all things in Christ" (Eph. 1:10):

> There is only one God the Father, and one Christ, Jesus Our Lord, coming through all the universal dispensation that is connected with him, and re-establishing all things in himself (*Adv. Haer.*, 3, 16, 6; PG 7, 925C). *

As can be seen, this perspective is fully Pauline, and one which, considered in itself, has little originality; but by this return to the sources, as we say today, Irenaeus made the end of the second century the springtime of Marian theology.

It is precisely within this perspective of the "re-establishment" that he presents us with the Virgin Mary at the side of Christ, the new Adam. He takes up this theme three times: twice in the *Adversus Haereses* (*Against Heresies*), and once in the *Epideixis* (*Proof of the Apostolic Preaching*):

> Luke shows the genealogy, which goes back from the birth of Our Lord to Adam, to contain seventy-two generations, by which he connects the end with the beginning and thereby emphasizes that it is he who has *re-established in himself* all peoples who have been scattered since the time of Adam, all tongues and generations of men, together with Adam himself. It was hence also that Paul called Adam himself *the figure of him who was to come*; for the Word, the maker of all things, had sketched out beforehand what would be brought to fulfillment in himself, the dispensation of the Incarnation concerning the Son of God — God having first formed the natural man (Adam) with the design of saving him by the spiritual man (Christ). For inasmuch as the Savior had a pre-existence, it was necessary for him to become the very being that he was to save, in order that this salvation should not exist in vain.
>
> But in accordance with this special design we also find the Virgin Mary, obedient and saying: *Behold the handmaid of the Lord; be it done unto me according to thy word!* (. . .)
> If Eve was disobedient and became, both for herself and all the

human race, the cause of death, Mary, betrothed to a man yet still a virgin, through her obedience became, both for herself and all the human race, the cause of salvation.

It is on account of this parallelism that the Old Law calls a woman who has been joined to a man, even though she may still be a virgin, the spouse of him who has betrothed her, manifesting through these similitudes that the meaning of the life which comes through Mary has its back-reference in Eve; for what has been joined can be put asunder only when the bonds of union are undone by an inversion of the process by which they were knotted, so that the former bonds are loosed in the fastening of the second; or in other terms, the second loose the first.

It is for the same reason that Luke begins his genealogy with the Lord while carrying it back to Adam, to indicate clearly that it was not our fathers who gave the Savior life, but on the contrary he who caused them to be born again in the Gospel of life.

Likewise also, the knot that Eve's disobedience had tied was untied by Mary's obedience; for what the virgin Eve had bound by her unbelief, the Virgin Mary unbound by her faith (*Adv. Haer.*, 3, 22, 3–4; PG 7, 958; PG 7, 958A).

The Lord came visibly into his dominion and was carried by the creature whom he himself sustains in being; he accomplished the reparation for the disobedience that had been wrought through the tree (of knowledge) by being himself obedient through the tree (of the cross); as the remedy for that deception by which Eve, who though already betrothed to a man but still a virgin, was seduced, the good news of truth was brought by the angel of truth to Mary, who though already betrothed, was a virgin.

Just as Eve, led astray by the word of an angel, fell away from God and betrayed his word, so Mary heard the good tidings of truth from the angel; she carried God within her womb, having been obedient to his word. Eve had disobeyed God; Mary consented to obey God; thus did the virgin Eve have Mary for her advocate.

Thus the human race, having fallen into bondage through a virgin, is delivered by a virgin, virginal disobedience having been balanced in the opposite scale by virginal obedience. The sin of the first man is remedied by the suffering of the First-Born Son (of God); the prudence of the serpent yields to the simplicity of the dove; the bonds by which we had been held in death are unloosed (*Adv. Haer.*, 5, 19, 1; PG 7, 1175A–1176A). *

And just as it was through a virgin who disobeyed that man was stricken and fell and died, so too it was through the Virgin, who obeyed the word of God, that man resuscitated by life received life. For the Lord came to seek back the lost sheep, and it was man who was lost; and therefore He did not become some other formation, but He likewise, of her that was descended from Adam, preserved the likeness of formation; for Adam had necessarily to be restored in Christ, that mortality be absorbed in immortality, and Eve in Mary, that a virgin, become the advocate of a virgin, should undo and destroy virginal disobedience by virginal obedience (*Epideixis*, 33, *Proof of the Apostolic Preaching*, translated by Joseph P. Smith, S.J., *Ancient Christian Writers*, 16 [Westminster, Md.: Newman Press, 1952], p. 69). *

As for Justin, so too for Irenaeus the Mary-Eve parallel is based on the fact that Mary is the Mother of Jesus; Mary's correspondence to Eve consists in the event of her becoming the Mother of the Lord. It is precisely at this point that Irenaeus links up his teaching with the Johannine tradition; the other aspects which he elaborates upon are only theological developments.

These developments, it must be admitted, mark a considerable progress over the contribution of Justin. The antithetical parallelism which in the former had been only roughly outlined will be taken up by Irenaeus, who will ably weigh both sides with meticulous attention to the smallest details. In the first pertinent text of the *Adversus Haereses* we find the following schema:

Eve	Mary
still a virgin	the virgin
the spouse of Adam	already betrothed
was disobedient	through her obedience
became both for herself	became both for herself
and all the human race	and all the human race
the cause of death	the cause of salvation
what the virgin Eve	the Virgin Mary
had bound	unbound
by her unbelief . . .	by her faith . . .

This parallelism permits Irenaeus to put forth statements that are the boldest yet seen in primitive Mariology. Mary is the cause of salvation both for herself and for all the human race; she sets it at liberty. Through her obedience she counter-balances and liberate what the disobedience of the first woman had placed in bondage: Eve is restored in Mary.

The sureness with which Irenaeus sets forth this typology, the fullness with which he thrusts forward its developments, seem explicable only in the light of the fact that this teaching was already traditional in the Church. In a work as controversial as the *Adversus Haereses*, moreover, it would have been poor strategy to appeal to "new principles"; Irenaeus would not have escaped the accusation of "modernism." But contrary to this, we see the excellent tactic of resting an argument on principles that are already universally recognized. In this connection, we should also take into consideration the strong likelihood that Irenaeus is linking up his teaching with the apostolic catechesis; for he knew St. Polycarp, who was himself the disciple of St. John.

In making use of these texts and working them over (dare it be said) to the best advantage, we must be alert to the danger of overextending their meaning. We know them only through the medium of a series of translations. The passages cited above from the *Adversus Haereses* are in Latin translation; that from the *Epideixis* is in Armenian. Once we are no longer in possession of the original, it is rash to split hairs over terms which to us appear essential but may perhaps already be interpretations. Above all, we must guard against projecting problems and theories of contemporary Mariology into the text, at the risk of committing a gross anachronism. If we would avoid all danger of forcing the text to say more than it does, we must modestly content ourselves with its fundamental content: Mary restores Eve, she is the cause of salvation for all the human race, etc., simply because she is the Mother of Jesus. We will thus link up these considerations with what is surest in the Eve-Mary parallel, that which is based on the comparison between the scenes of the temptation of Eve and the Annunciation of Mary.

C. Tertullian

The last text that we shall cite is from Tertullian. While it will introduce no new elements, it will permit us to formulate an appraisal of the contribution of the first two centuries of the patristic age.

> Eve, while still a virgin, had allowed to penetrate within her the word that works unto death. Hence it was necessary that there penetrate within a virgin the word that works unto life, so that the sex which had brought about ruin would also be the author of salvation. Eve had believed the Serpent; Mary believed Gabriel. The wrong that the former had committed by her believing, the latter, by her believing, had righted.
>
> But then (it will be said) Eve conceived nothing of the Serpent in her womb! Yes, she did conceive. For since from that time onward she brought forth her children in abjection and sorrow, the word of the devil was the seed sown in her, and in due course she brought into the world a devil, one who was the murderer of his brother.
>
> Mary, on the contrary, gave to the world him who was, in his time, to be the Savior of Israel, his brother according to the flesh and the author of his death. Hence God, into Mary's womb, wrought the descent of his Word, the good Brother, to destroy the memory

of the wicked brother. Christ was to go forth to save man from the
very place where man, already condemned, had entered (*De carne
Christi*, c. 17; PL 2, 782BC).

As for Justin and Irenaeus, so also for Tertullian the Mary-Eve
parallelism is based on the comparison between the scene of Eve's
temptation and that of the Annunciation. Mary repairs the wrongdo-
ing of Eve in becoming the Mother of Jesus.

We were saying, in connection with Irenaeus, how imperative
it is that we avoid forcing the texts to say more than they contain.
Tertullian's case confirms us in this position, and with all desirable
clarity. The parallelism that he sets forth here in such a striking
manner has not, in effect, opened the way to any further positive
inferences concerning the mystery of Mary. His opinions relating
to the Mother of Jesus are in this respect so surprising that it may
be wondered whether they represent anything more than the
whimsy of a high-spirited African who has gone off on a tangent,
or whether they are, rather, evidence of a concerted determination
to be singular, even scandalizing if need be, which still leaves them
branded with the mark of a studied individualism. For if he does
hold to the virginal conception of Christ as a dogma belonging to
the faith of the Church (cf. *De praescriptione haereticorum*, cc.
13, 36 and 44; PL 2, 26B, 49B, and 60A; *De carne Christi*, c.
4; PL 2, 760A), he does not however believe in the virgin birth
(cf. *De carne Christi*, c. 23; PL 2, 790B), and feels equally free
to attribute a more or less numerous progeny to Mary (cf. *Adv.
Marcionem*, lib. 3, 11; lib. 4, 19, 26, 36; PL 2, 335BC, 404B–406A,
427BC, 450C; *De carne Christi*, c. 7; PL 2, 766A–769A; *De
monogamia*, c. 8; PL 2, 939B).

Such affirmations are all the more surprising in view of the fact
that elsewhere in his writings Tertullian evidences a very high regard
for virginity and succeeds in finding formulas of captivating beauty
to express this ideal: "Thou hast taken Christ for thy spouse; thou
hast made him the confidence of thy flesh; thou hast vowed to
him the full-flowering of thy life (*De virginibus velandis*, c. 16;
PL 2, 911B). We must be grateful to the impetuous African for
the delicacy of feeling that these formulas reveal, all the while
regretting that he did not apply them to her who was "blessed
among all women" (cf. *De virginibus velandis*, c. 6; PL 2, 898AB).

Tertullian's case does give us the opportunity to see that in these
early days it could be affirmed that Mary had repaired the wrongdo-

ing of Eve without drawing other positive inferences from this truth. But this does not at all mean, far from it, that a true theologian has no freedom to dig down into the primitive data to unearth new riches; but it does demand that his desire to appeal to primitive tradition be implemented with considerable discretion in the interpretation of the texts.

D. Conclusion

We find the Mary-Eve parallelism in the writings of St. Justin, St. Irenaeus and Tertullian, witnesses representative of a quite far-ranging diversity of milieux. Justin, a native of Palestine, came into contact with the climate of religious thought at both Ephesus and Rome; Irenaeus, a native of Asia Minor, the disciple of Polycarp, was a priest of the Church of Lyons, at least from 177 on, becoming bishop of that Church; Tertullian, finally, represents the faith of the African Churches.

It can therefore be seen that the Mary-Eve parallelism enjoyed, in the second half of the second century, a certain universality, which can hardly be explained if one single author — in this case St. Justin — had put it into circulation around 155, the approximate date of the *Dialogue*. The very manner in which these witnesses express this teaching, without proving it but already making use of it as a proof, lets us suppose a previously existing tradition. This universality can substantially be accounted for only if it is a theme which dates back beyond the apostolic Fathers to the teaching of the Apostles themselves; more specifically, to St. John. The exegesis of Apocalypse 12, where John presents the Mother of the royal Child in terminology corresponding to the story of Genesis, therefore receives from patristic tradition a confirmation of the weightiest significance.[1]

---

* *Translator's note*: The literal meaning of the original Greek is "to sum up under one heading."

* *Translator's note*: To date the only available English version of the *Adversus Haereses* is the *Against Heresies*, *The Ante-Nicene Fathers*, Vol. I, Rev. Alexander Roberts and James Donaldson (eds.), revised by A. Cleveland Coxe (New York: Charles Scribners Sons, 1913). The passage cited here will be found on pp. 442–443. Due to the unfortunate shortcomings of this translation, however, we have instead followed

the text as quoted by P. Deiss, who cites the French translation of F. Sagnard, *Irénée de Lyon. Contre les hérésies*, Coll. *Sources chrètiennes* (Paris, 1952), p. 293.
  * *Translator's note:* Again, we are following P. Deiss' citation of F. Sagnard, *op. cit.*, pp. 378–383. Cf. also the French translation of P. d'Alès, in *D.A.F.C.*, 3, 159–160. Cf. Roberts-Donaldson-Coxe, *op. cit.*, p. 455.
  * *Translator's note:* P. Deiss quotes this text according to the French translation of P. d'Alès, *op cit.*, 160. Cf. Roberts-Donaldson-Coxe, *op. cit.*, p. 547.
  * *Translator's note:* Here P. Deiss follows the French translation of J. Barthoulot, in *R.S.R.*, 6 (1916), p. 391.
  [1] In subsequent history the "new Eve" theme met with somewhat varying degrees of success. The research undertaken on this subject by La Societé Française d'Études Mariales (*La Nouvelle Ève*, I[Paris, 1954], II [1955] and III [1956]) has revealed that its appearance was rather a surface affair. Perhaps its importance in patristic thought has been overestimated; for after its rather promising beginnings during the time of St. Irenaeus, it did not continue to attract any special attention from either the Fathers or theologians, who in general were to content themselves with repeating the classical formulas without exploring them too deeply. — In the teaching of recent Popes, the theme does not really appear until Pius XII, first in the encyclical *Mystici Corporis*, and a second time in *Munificentissimus:* "We must remember especially that, since the second century, the Virgin Mary has been designated by the holy Fathers as the new Eve, who, although subject to the new Adam, is most intimately associated with Him in that struggle against the infernal foe which, as foretold in the *proto-evangelium*, would finally result in complete victory over sin and death" (Apost. Const. *Munificentissimus Deus*, Nov. 1, 1950; English translation in *Papal Teachings: Our Lady, op. cit.*, p. 317). On this subject see G. Philips, "La Nouvelle Ève dans la théologie contemporaine," *La Nouvelle Ève*, 3 (Paris, 1956), pp. 101–103.

MARY'S SPIRITUAL
MOTHERHOOD

The Exegesis of John 19:26-27 in Tradition

One will have noticed the reserve — some will say the timidity — with which we have entered upon exegesis of the Johannine text: "Mother, behold thy son . . . Son, behold thy Mother." This circumspection is justified by the fact that on this subject tradition itself has maintained considerable reserve. The witnesses that we do possess are very few, and on the place of Mary their contribution is scanty; what is more, they do not all view this mystery in the same light. This amounts to saying that it is quite difficult to determine the exact import of John's text; had it been otherwise, the Fathers would not have been so hesitant in their exegesis. To be sure, we do not have to make our own the hesitations of an interpretation that was still feeling its way and at times even went astray, but it is these very errors that have induced us to proceed only with a great deal of prudence.

A. ORIGEN

Origen is the first witness whom we should call forward, and the text is a universally familiar one in Mariology:

Hence we openly assert that the first fruits of all the Scriptures is the Gospels, and the first fruits of the Gospels is John's. No one can penetrate its meaning unless he has rested on the breast of Jesus and received, from Jesus, Mary for his own mother also. For if Mary

has no son but Jesus, in accordance with sound judgment on this
subject (as far as can be made), and if Jesus says to his Mother:
"Behold thy son," and not "Behold him who is also thy son," this
amounts to saying: "Behold thy son Jesus, to whom thou gavest birth."
For whoever is perfect no longer lives (by himself), but Christ lives
in him; and it is because Christ does live in him that these words
to Mary are spoken of him: "Behold thy Son, Christ" (*Comm. in
Joan.*, I, 6; PG 14, 32AB).

Mary is, therefore, the Mother of those in whom Jesus lives,
for she has but one Son. An assertion that is absolutely prodigious,
and all the more so in that Origen had no special charism for
Mariological utterances, and so much so that even today thirty years
of discussion have not been enough for the reconciliation of the
various ways in which it has been interpreted.[1]

If we place ourselves outside the debate to listen only to Origen
himself — and it is certainly he who is the most qualified to express
his views — it seems that the essence of what is affirmed bears
precisely on the mysterious identification of the individual member
of the faithful with Jesus: he who is perfect is no longer he who
lives; it is Jesus who lives in him. This is so true, Origen continues,
that John, who is perfect, receives her who is the Mother of Jesus
for his mother. When Jesus says to Mary, "Behold thy son," it
is as though he were saying ($\check{\iota}\sigma o\nu$ $\epsilon\check{\iota}\rho\eta\kappa\epsilon$): "Behold thy son Jesus,
to whom thou gavest birth."

If this text were representative of all Origen's Mariology, appraisal
of its content would be an easy matter. Unfortunately it is nothing
of the sort, and any judgment which extends to its over-all context
must be hedged about with reservations and carefully applied shades
of meaning. For Origen feels quite free to say of Mary that there
were occasions when she wavered in her faith (cf. *In Genesim*,
Hom. 1, 14; PG 12, 158B; *In Lucam*, Hom. 14, 17, 19, 20; PG
13, 1833–1838, 1845A–1846A, 1849–1851, 1851B–1852C). He inter-
prets the sword of Simeon's prophecy as a "sword of unbelief,"
infidelitatis gladius (*In Lucam*, Hom. 17; PG 13, 1845B), and this
exegesis is directly reflected in the exegesis of John 19:26-27.

In the homily that we have just cited, he recalls the word that
the Lord had spoken before his Passion: "You will all be scandalized
this night on my account" (Mark 14:27) and adds: "The apostles
were scandalized, would the Lord's Mother have been preserved
from scandal? If she was not scandalized, then Jesus did not die for
her sins! But if all have sinned and are deprived of the glory of God,

if they are justified and redeemed as a free gift (Rom. 3:23-24), then Mary also was scandalized at that moment" (*In Lucam*, Hom. 17; PG 13, 1845B). As we can see this is no random statement, thrown out in a gesture of oratory, but a duly formulated proof; it is based on the universality of the redemption, which presupposes the universality of sin.

In all these positions he assumes, Origen has no intention of putting forward a personal opinion; he seems, rather, only to reflect the ideas of his time. As Msgr. Jouassard remarks, "The point has had to be made so many times that there are absolutely no grounds for us to suppose that he had provoked the reaction of competent authority. Yet Origen used to preach to a full congregation at Caesarea, in an episcopal city, often before the local bishop in person, from time to time in the presence of other bishops, friends and admirers of the master of Alexandria. To these localities in Palestine, in Egypt certainly, if not in Asia Minor (for there is no evidence that there had ever been any reaction in either one or the other of these last two regions), it seems we must admit that these assertions of Origen mentioned above appeared inoffensive, and in no wise in direct contradiction to any official precise and formal teaching of an opposite position that might have been issued" ("Marie à travers la Patristique. Maternité divine, Virginitè, Sainteté," *Maria*, H. du Manoir, 1, [Paris, 1949], p. 79).

We should not be astonished at these statements of Origen's, still less be scandalized; they must be "excused," let us say, by being set in their proper historical context. At a period when Christian devotion was centered entirely on Christ, it seemed to be the accepted thing to oppose the absolutely perfect holiness of the Lord with the sinful condition of all the redeemed; the greatness of Christ was enhanced at the risk of belittling his Mother. Areas of the canvas were placed in shadow, but only to heighten the brilliance of the light.

B. AFTER ORIGEN

Origen's influence was considerable, and his interpretation was substantially to obscure the future appreciation of the Johannine theme. After the master of Alexandria, the interpretation favored by patristic exegesis will follow two paths. The first will see Christ's words as an exhortation to John to uphold Mary in the faith; the second will rather detect in them an outward visible manifestation of the doctrine of the Mystical Body: Mary receives John for a son because John is a part of the Mystical Body of which Jesus, the Son of Mary, is the Head.

— The first of these interpretations, as is only too clear, is completely closed to the idea of Mary's spiritual motherhood. As a rule it takes Simeon's prophecy for its point of departure, interpreting it as a trial of faith, and sees this trial come to pass at the Cross. At times even the Annunciation scene is drawn into this interpretation, and Mary's question: "How shall this happen, since I do not know man?" is presented as evidencing a lack of faith.

This first trend of thought will be represented principally by Amphilocus of Iconium (*Oratio in occursum Domini*, 8; PG 39, 57AB); Basil the Great (*Epist.* 260, 9; PG 32, 965C–968A); the pseudo-Chrysostom (*De occursu Domini*; PG 50, 810–811); the pseudo-Gregory of Nyssa (*De occursu Domini*; PG 46, 1176B); John Chrysostom (on this subject see D. Haugg, *Das erste biblische Marienwort* [Stuttgart, 1938], pp. 19-20); the pseudo-Proclus (*Oratio 5 De laudibus S. Mariae*, 12; PG 65, 741C), Cyril of Alexandria (see the excellent study of Msgr. Jouassard, "L'interpretation par saint Cyrille d'Alexandrie de la scene de Marie au pied de la Croix," *Virgo Immaculata, Acta Congressus Mariologico-Mariani Romae anno 1954 celebrati*, I [Rome, 1954], pp. 28–47); Hesechius of Jerusalem (*Hom. VI, In occursum Domini*, PG 93, 1476B–1478A); Sophronias of Jerusalem (*De Hypapante*, 16; PG 87 [III], 3298C–3299A); John Damascene (*De fide orthodoxa*, lib. 4, c. 14; PG 94, 1161CD).

On the strictly exegetical level, this trend could not come to anything; it starts from an arbitrary and fanciful interpretation of Simeon's prophecy. Luke's text does not in the least say that the sword which was to pierce Mary's soul would be a "sword of unbelief." More than that, this interpretation even goes against the immediate context of Luke, since the Holy Spirit, by the mouth of Elizabeth, proclaims that Mary is blessed because of her faith. But on the practical level, this interpretation blocks the way that would normally lead to a more acccurate understanding of the Marian significance of the scene by the Cross.

— The second trend of interpretation, unaware or pretending to be unaware of the alleged weakness of Mary, will center primarily on the mystery of the Church and the Mystical Body. The scene by the Cross is an action which as it were incorporates a spiritual teaching. In this vein Ambrose, inspired by the notion of the identification of the faithful with Christ and carrying forward Origen's contribution in a positive way, brings to the fore the collective aspect of this reality of belonging to Christ, namely, that of belonging to the Church:

> You will become a "son of thunder" if you are a son of the Church. To you also Christ will say, looking down from the height of that cross on which he was decreed to die: "Behold thy mother." For how truly he could be speaking also to the Church: "Behold thy son." Hence that too is the beginning of your sonship, when you behold Christ in victory on the cross (*In Luc.*, lib. 7, 5; PL 15, 1787CD; cf. *C.S.E.L.* 32, IV, 284).

In conformity with the Johannine theme, Mary represents the Church. The individual member of the faithful, a son of the Church, therefore shares the status of John, to whom it was said: "Behold thy mother."

Augustine, Ambrose's disciple, will add the finishing touches to the thought of his teacher with his affirmation that Mary is the mother of Christ's members:

> She is mother according to the spirit; not of our Head, who is the Savior himself . . . but of his members; (and his members) we ourselves are — *mater membrorum ejus, quod sumus nos* — for by her love she has cooperated in the birth of the faithful in the Church (*De sancta virginitate*, 6; PL 40, 399).

These texts are all in line with each other; the movement of thought does not go from John to the other disciples; on the contrary, it starts from the dogma of the identification of the faithful with Christ. This identification is in some way an extension of the reality that Mary is the Mother of Jesus; if she is proclaimed to be John's mother, it is because she has given birth to Christ, the Head of his Church. This spiritual motherhood in John's regard is but an instance of the universal reality that Mary is the spiritual mother of all who belong to Christ.

As devotion becomes increasingly centered upon the sacred humanity of Christ and contemplation of the mystery of Mary, bolder and bolder statements will be made. Ambrose Autpert (†784) will call Mary the mother of the elect, *mater electorum*, the mother of believers, *mater credentium* (*In Purif.*, VII; PL 89, 1297C), the mother of the nations, *mater gentium* (*De Assumptione* [=Ps. Augustine]; PL 39, 2131); his reasoning is both neat and at the same time evocative of rich theological insights:

> If Christ, I say, is the brother of believers, why would not she

who has given birth to Christ be the mother of believers? (*In Purif.*, VII, PL 89, 1297C).

Fulbert of Chartres († 1029) will give her the name of mother of the whole world, *mater omnium* (*Sermo VI: In Ortu Almae Virginis Mariae Inviolatae*, PL 141, 329D). By the thirteenth century, the faithful will be addressing Mary no longer simply as their Lady (Domina) but as their heavenly mother: "The Mother of God is our Mother, *Mater Dei est Mater nostra*" (*Oratio 52*; PL 158 957A); the Commentary of Berengeaud on Apocalypse XII will say:

> In this Woman we can see the blessed Mary, for she is the Mother of the Church — *eo quod ipsa mater sit Ecclesiae* (In Apoc., XII, 1: PL 17, 876CD).

Rupert of Deutz will bring these reflections to their full-flowering in his application of them to Mary at the foot of the Cross:

> The Mother was standing by near the Cross of her Son, and it is most certain that she was filled with sorrow as she passed through this trial of pain, pain like that a mother suffers in her agony of bringing forth her child. As Simeon had foretold, "And thy own soul a sword shall pierce," she was crucified by the Cross of her Son. Hence Jesus, seeing his mother and the disciple whom he loved, said to his mother: "Woman, behold thy son." To the disciple he said: "Behold thy mother." By what right is the disciple whom Jesus loved the son of the Mother of the Lord, or (by what right is) she his mother? It is because without suffering pain she brought forth the cause of the world's salvation when she brought forth, of her own flesh, God made man; and now her time of bringing forth in great sorrow was to come to pass, as she stood by the Cross as had been foretold of her. . . . Therefore, since the blessed Virgin did bring forth the salvation of us all amid the birth-pangs of a mother at the time of the Passion of her Only (Son), she is truly the mother of us all — *plane omnium nostrum mater est* (In Joan., 13; PL 169, 789CD–790AB).

These texts are to the Johannine theme what the conclusion is to its premises, the fruit to the flower. By comparison with what John has given us, they may seem disproportionate, but only as a fruit to its seed. What John tells us of the Mother of Jesus is the seed; the faith of the Church in her spiritual motherhood is the fruit.[2]

C. CONCLUSION

What are the findings that we have made, on this short expedition into patristic exegesis? It seems to us that there are two:

1) The first current in exegesis, which attributes certain occasions of a wavering in faith to Mary, were starting out from a false interpretation of what is given in the Gospels. This very interpretation is governed, we think, by the principles of the transcendent holiness of Jesus Christ and the universality of the redemption: the Lord alone possesses perfect and absolute holiness, and he has redeemed all men. Hence all men, Mary included, are sinners. Origen is saying that if Mary was not scandalized, then Jesus did not die for her sins. Viewing things from this angle, the Fathers would be in no hurry — and the fact is understandable — to give, or even think of giving, to the Mystical Body a sinful Mother who had wavered in her faith.

The principles of the transcendent holiness of Christ and the universality of the redemption are excellent in themselves, but the conclusions that were deduced from them in Mary's regard were, as we know today, of little worth. The holiness of Christ is so perfect that it has redeemed Mary by preserving her from original sin, and by keeping her from all actual sin. Let us hold on to these principles. At a time when Mary is spoken of almost to the point that Christ is forgotten, when her incomparable dignity is set in relief without always being related to the infinite dignity of our Lord, it is well to keep in mind that all praise, all love directed toward Mary must first of all be praise and love directed toward Christ Jesus who has done marvels for her (cf. Luke 1:49). Mary exists on a supernatural plane only in reference to Christ, and it is precisely this very reference to Christ that must be the hallmark of all true devotion to Mary.

2) The second current in exegesis was centered on the doctrine of the Mystical Body and on the divine maternity. Here we should recall that Mary's spiritual motherhood is the logical conclusion flowing from two fundamental truths. It would not be the best theology to interpret the words of Jesus on the Cross as decreeing, at that moment, Mary to be the Mother of the faithful. From this title we can deduce only an adoptive motherhood, which does not go beyond the juridical character of adoption.

It seems to us that these words must rather be seen as the promulgation of a true spiritual motherhood, that which had been inaugurated on the day of the Incarnation. It is thus a motherhood that is rooted in her divine maternity in regard to Jesus, and presupposes the doctrine of the Mystical Body. Viewed in this light, her spiritual motherhood will not appear as a new motherhood added to the divine maternity, but rather as the unfolding in space and time of the mystery of the Incarnation, of the single reality that Mary is the Mother of Jesus. Again, the mystery of Mary, the Mother of Jesus, is part of the greater mystery of Jesus, the Son of Mary.

[1] Vagaggini ("Maria nelle opere di Origene," *Orientalia christiana analecta*, 131 [Rome, 1942], p. 118) thinks that here the author is rather resorting to hyperbole to make his point (questa maternita, piuttosto che qualcosa di realmente asserito, non sarebbe altro che una espressione iperpolica); to which Müller (*Ecclesia-Maria, op. cit.*, p. 116) answers: This amounts to asserting that Origen's text has no literal meaning.

[2] Mary's spiritual motherhood has been included in the actual teaching of the magisterium: ". . . to her who loved Him more than did Peter, Jesus entrusted in the person of John beneath his saving cross all men as sons" (Pius XII, Allocution of April 21, 1940, *Papal Teachings, op. cit.*, p. 245). [At the foot of the Cross] "she who corporally was the mother of our Head, through the added title of pain and glory became spiritually the mother of all His members" (*Mystici Corporis*, June 29, 1943, English translation of the N.C.W.C., p. 67). "Jesus Himself from His Cross on high ratified by means of a symbolic and efficacious gift the spiritual motherhood of Mary toward men when He pronounced the memorable words: 'Woman, behold thy son.' He thus entrusted all Christians, in the person of the beloved disciple, to the most Blessed Virgin" (Allocution of July 17, 1954, *Papal Teachings, op. cit.*, p. 370)

INDEX